PATH OF THE PLANESWALKER II

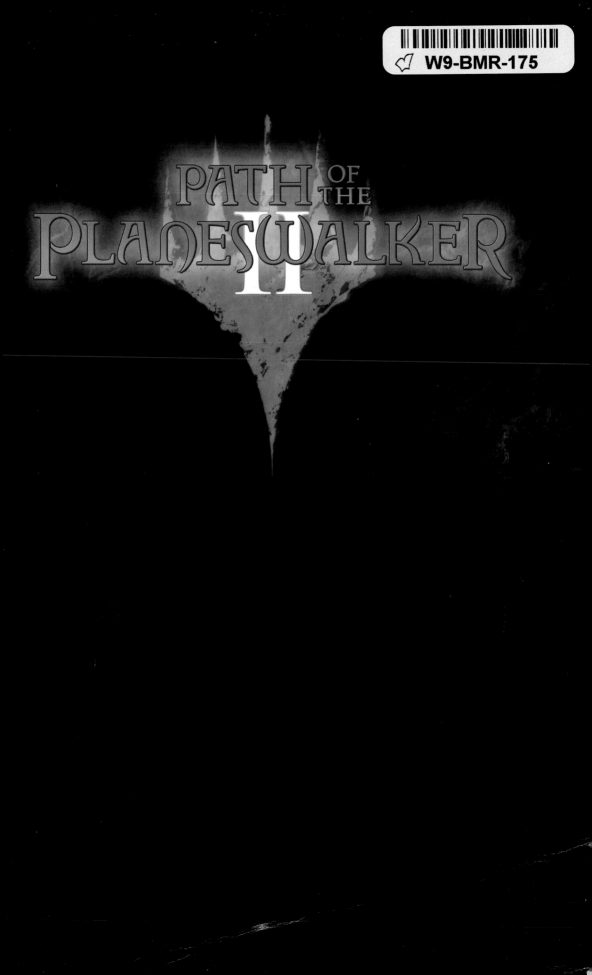

Awakenings

Illustrated by Karl Kopinski, Arthur Suydam,
and various contributing artists
Written by Doug Beyer

Enter the Eldrazi

Illustrated by Dan Scott, Dave Kendall, and Karl Kopinski
Written by Brady Dommermuth

The Wild Son

Illustrated by Alex Horley-Orlandelli, Steve Prescott,
Christopher Moeller, and Kev Walker
Written by Doug Beyer

The Raven's Eye

Illustrated by Dan Brereton, Nic Klein, and Paul Lee
Written by Jenna Helland

Gathering Forces

Illustrated by Dave Dorman, Brian Haberlin
with Doug Sirois, and Christopher Moeller
Written by Jenna Helland

Scarred

Illustrated by Mark Texeira, Paul Davidson, and Steve Prescott
Written by Doug Beyer

Dark Discoveries

Illustrated by Paul Lee, Alex Horley-Orlandelli
with Lucio Parrillo, and Izzy
Written by Jenna Helland and Doug Beyer

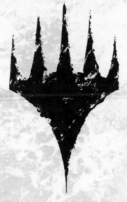

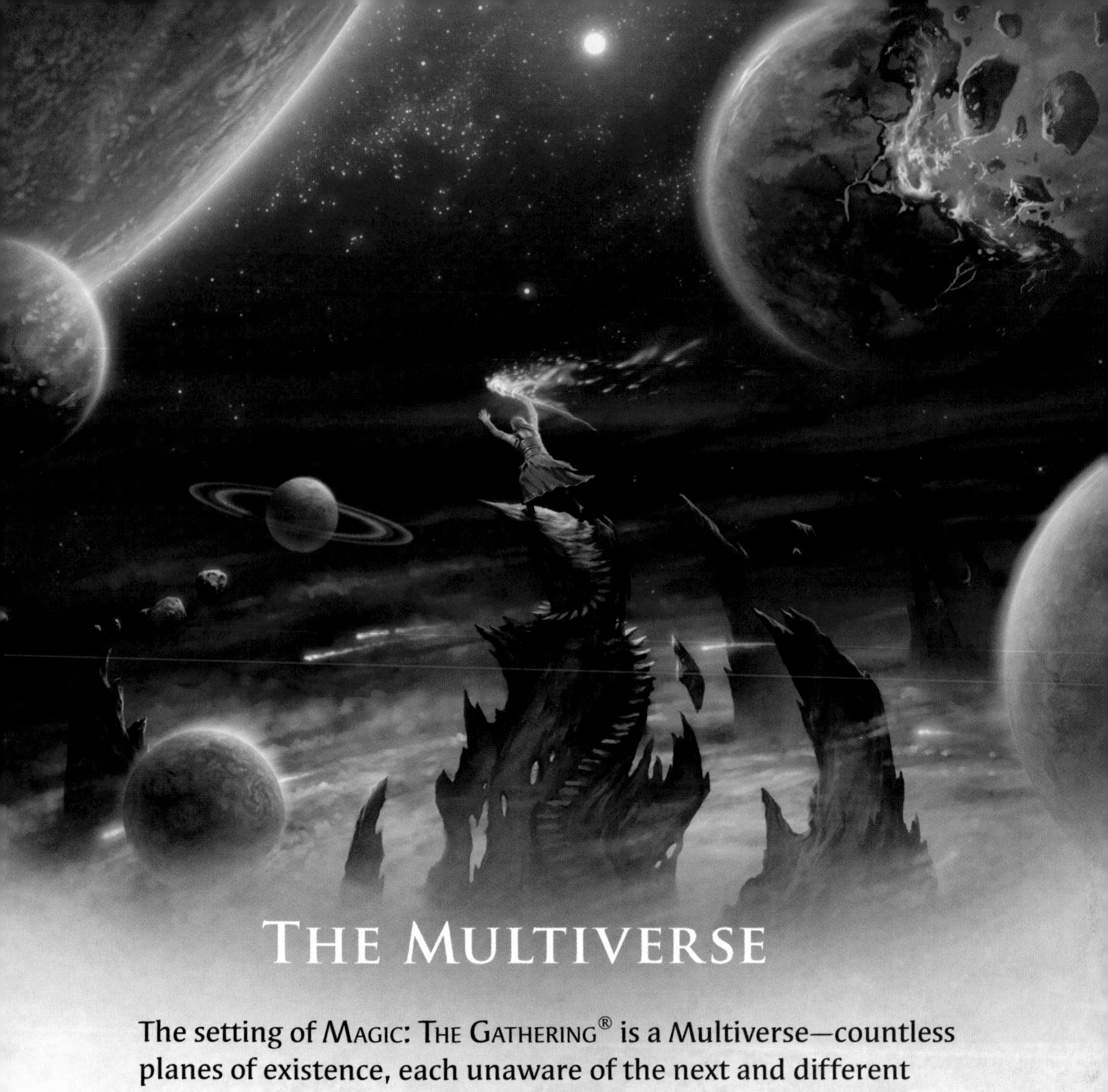

The Multiverse

The setting of Magic: The Gathering® is a Multiverse—countless planes of existence, each unaware of the next and different from the last. One plane might be entombed in snow while another swelters in jungle and a third is covered by city. Only one kind of being can traverse the planes of the Multiverse: the Planeswalker.

Being a Planeswalker elevates and isolates you from your peers. Planeswalkers are blessed with the ability to travel between worlds but cursed with the knowledge that any world is only a tiny corner of the Multiverse. Because of this, Planeswalkers know that only others of their kind can truly understand them. They are iconoclasts, each driven by their own desires and fears.

All Planeswalkers can wield magic, and almost all go forth into the Multiverse in pursuit of further mastery of magic. Destiny determines who is a Planeswalker, but no Planeswalker's fate is preordained. Ultimately, all must make their own path.

Planeswalkers (in order of appearance)

Chandra Nalaar

When Chandra stole a precious scroll from the plane of Kephalai, she expected to gain the knowledge of a powerful fire spell, but also discovered a hidden map that pointed to the plane of Zendikar. The Planeswalker who recovered the scroll, Jace Beleren, found the map as well, putting the two on a collision course to the mysterious chamber known as the Eye of Ugin.

Sarkhan Vol

Sarkhan revered dragons as the expression of ferocity and hunger, but that became a weakness when he encountered the ancient, evil dragon Planeswalker Nicol Bolas. As Sarkhan came to serve the dragon, his sanity unraveled. Nicol Bolas sent him to the plane of Zendikar to watch over the Eye of Ugin, convinced that other Planeswalkers would soon arrive there.

Jace Beleren

A mind magic prodigy, Jace is the *de facto* ruler of the Infinite Consortium, an interplanar cabal he wrested away from the Planeswalker Tezzeret. Jace travels to the plane of Zendikar after discovering a hidden map on a scroll, and there runs into the scroll's thief, Chandra Nalaar, who has made the same discovery. Together they face a third Planeswalker, Sarkhan Vol, who guards the map's destination.

Nicol Bolas

The dragon Planeswalker Nicol Bolas spent millennia as a demigod, a conqueror of countless worlds. But when the Multiverse itself began to crack under the strain of many cataclysms, a group of heroic Planeswalkers intervened to mend it. In doing so, they changed the very nature of the Planeswalker Spark. Now Bolas plots to regain his omnipotence, and his plans require the fealty of many others of his kind.

Tezzeret

The ambitious and ruthless artificer Tezzeret became a servant of Nicol Bolas while on his native plane of Alara. Tezzeret came to control a small piece of Bolas's network—the Infinite Consortium—until the Planeswalker Jace Beleren defeated him and left him for dead.

Garruk Wildspeaker

Garruk is an apex predator who wanders the Multiverse hunting its greatest creatures. His path was altered when the Planeswalker Liliana Vess used the dark magic of an artifact called the Chain Veil, cursing Garruk and corrupting his magic. Now Garruk hunts Liliana across the Multiverse, seeking to free himself of the Veil's curse by whatever means necessary.

Liliana Vess

When Liliana Vess's power began to wane, she struck a dark deal with demons to maintain her youth, beauty, and necromantic power. When she gained a powerful, ancient relic called the Chain Veil, she decided to settle her debt by using it to slay her demon masters. But as she hunts her demons, she is in turn hunted by Garruk Wildspeaker, who now bears the Veil's curse.

Elspeth Tirel

Elspeth fled her home as a child when her community was enslaved by Phyrexians. She eventually found Bant, a utopian shard of the plane of Alara. But when the undead hordes of Grixis invaded, Elspeth had to reveal her true nature to defend her fellow knights. Once they were safe, she left, despondent about her ruined adoptive home. She made her way to Dominaria, a plane where the Phyrexians were defeated long ago.

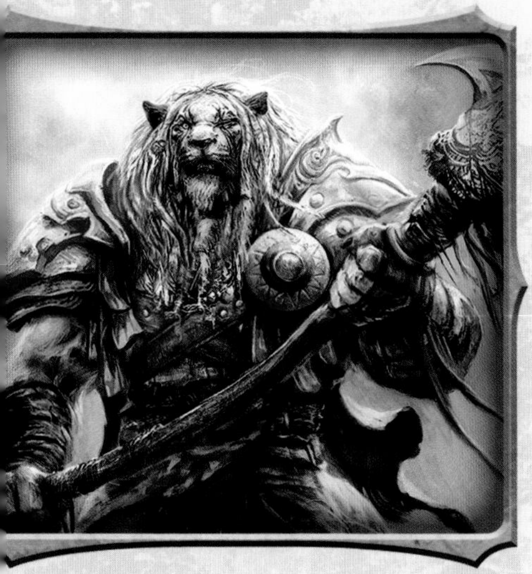

Ajani Goldmane

Ajani is a leonin mage with a strong sense of empathy—he sees the light within others and can call on it. When Elspeth left Alara, Ajani followed her, sensing her grief and hoping to convince her to return to Bant and help it regain stability.

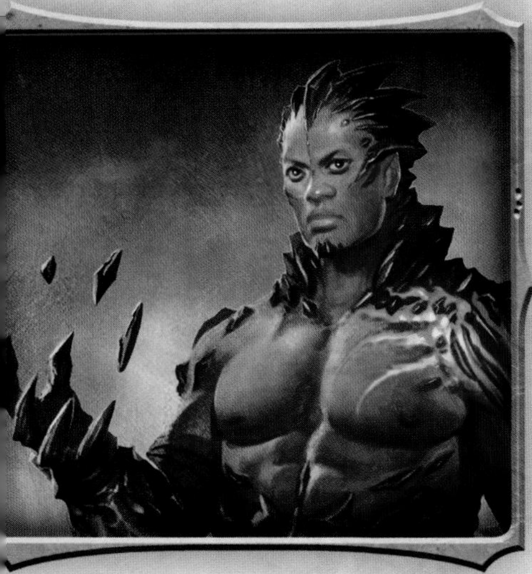

Koth of the Hammer

The geomancer Koth is a Vulshok, a human from the ferrous mountains of Mirrodin. Mirrodin is a plane made entirely of metal, and when the metal starts to blacken and corrode under the influence of a sinister force, Koth searches the Multiverse for Planeswalker allies who might know the how to reverse the corruption.

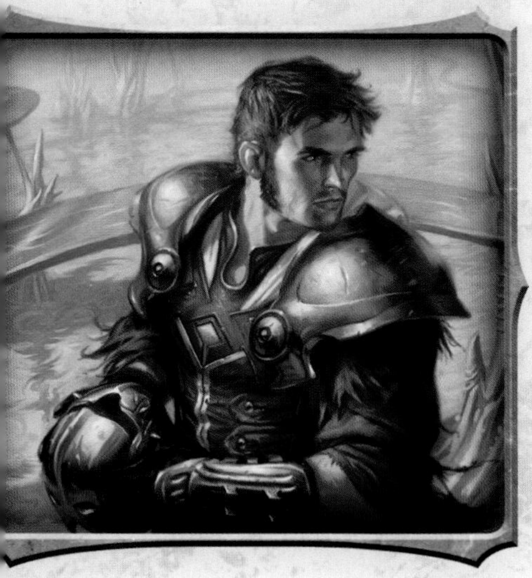

Venser of Urborg

Venser, from the dark isle of Urborg on Dominaria, is a talented artificer who witnessed the repair of the Multiverse itself at the hands of powerful, millennia-old Planeswalkers such as Teferi, Windgrace, and the silver golem Karn. Because he grew up amid the wreckage of the Phyrexian Invasion of Dominaria, Koth seeks him out to help save Mirrodin, the metal plane created by his friend Karn.

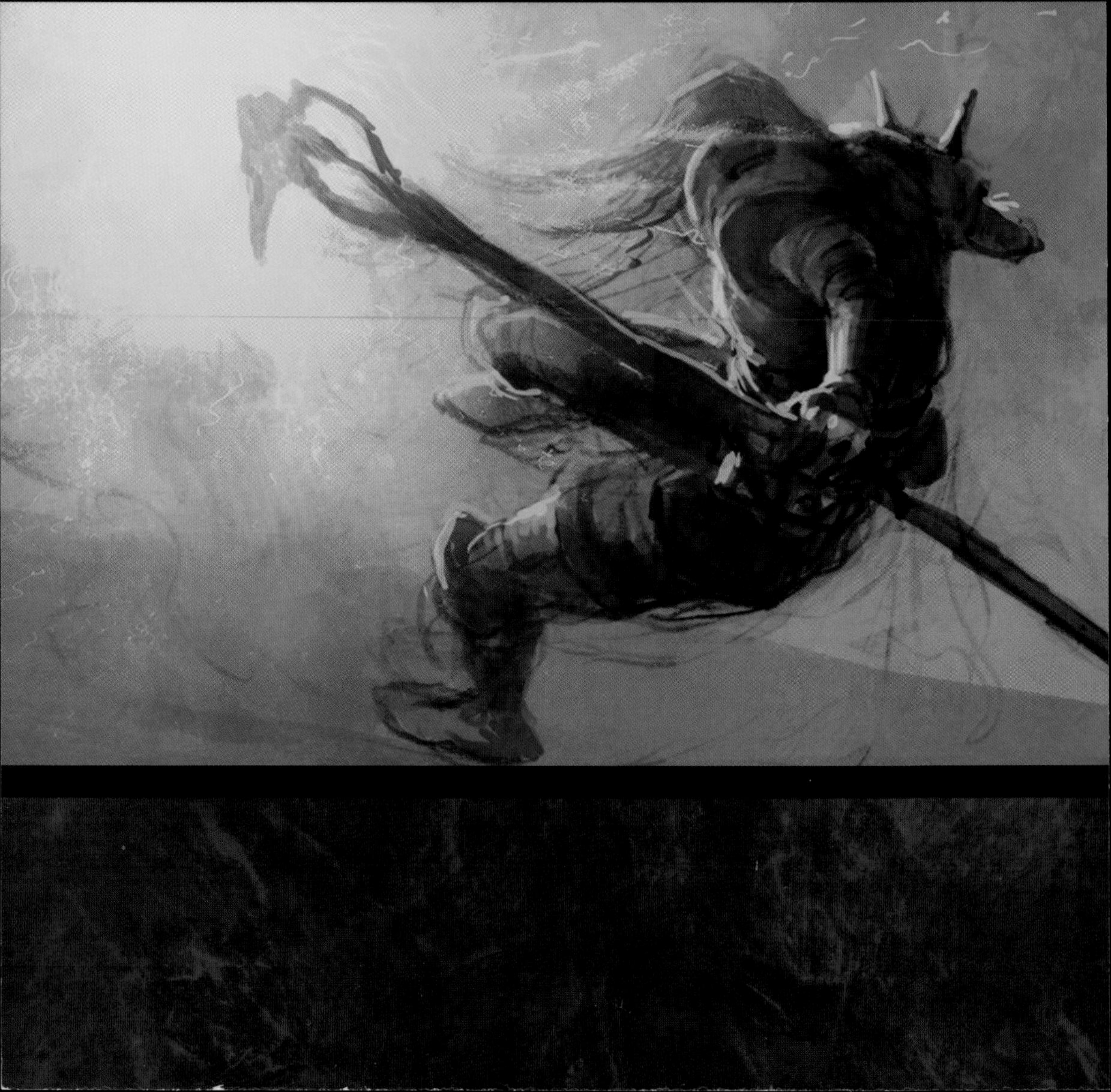

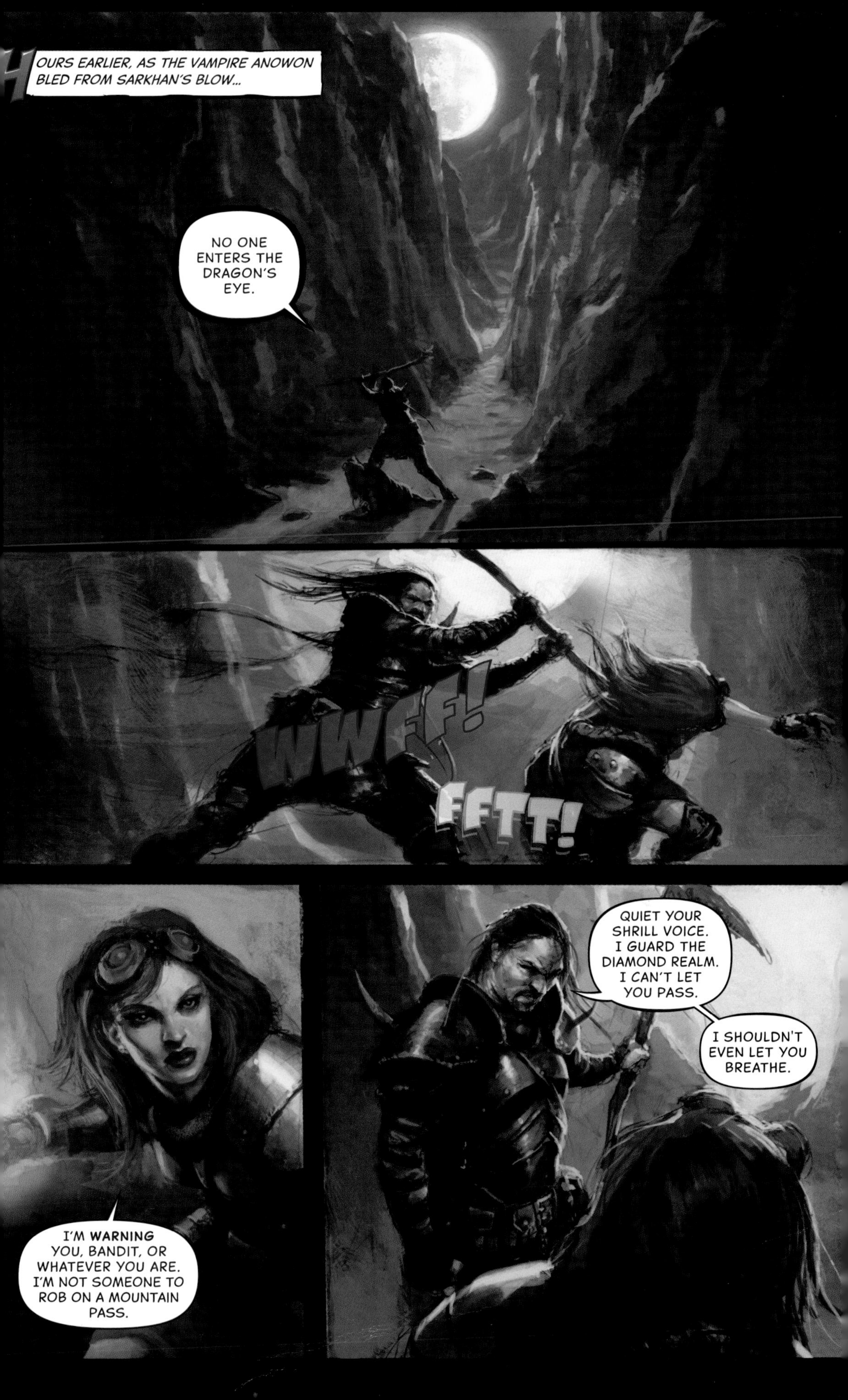
HOURS EARLIER, AS THE VAMPIRE ANOWON BLED FROM SARKHAN'S BLOW...
NO ONE ENTERS THE DRAGON'S EYE.
WWFF!
FFTT!
I'M WARNING YOU, BANDIT, OR WHATEVER YOU ARE. I'M NOT SOMEONE TO ROB ON A MOUNTAIN PASS.
QUIET YOUR SHRILL VOICE. I GUARD THE DIAMOND REALM. I CAN'T LET YOU PASS.
I SHOULDN'T EVEN LET YOU BREATHE.

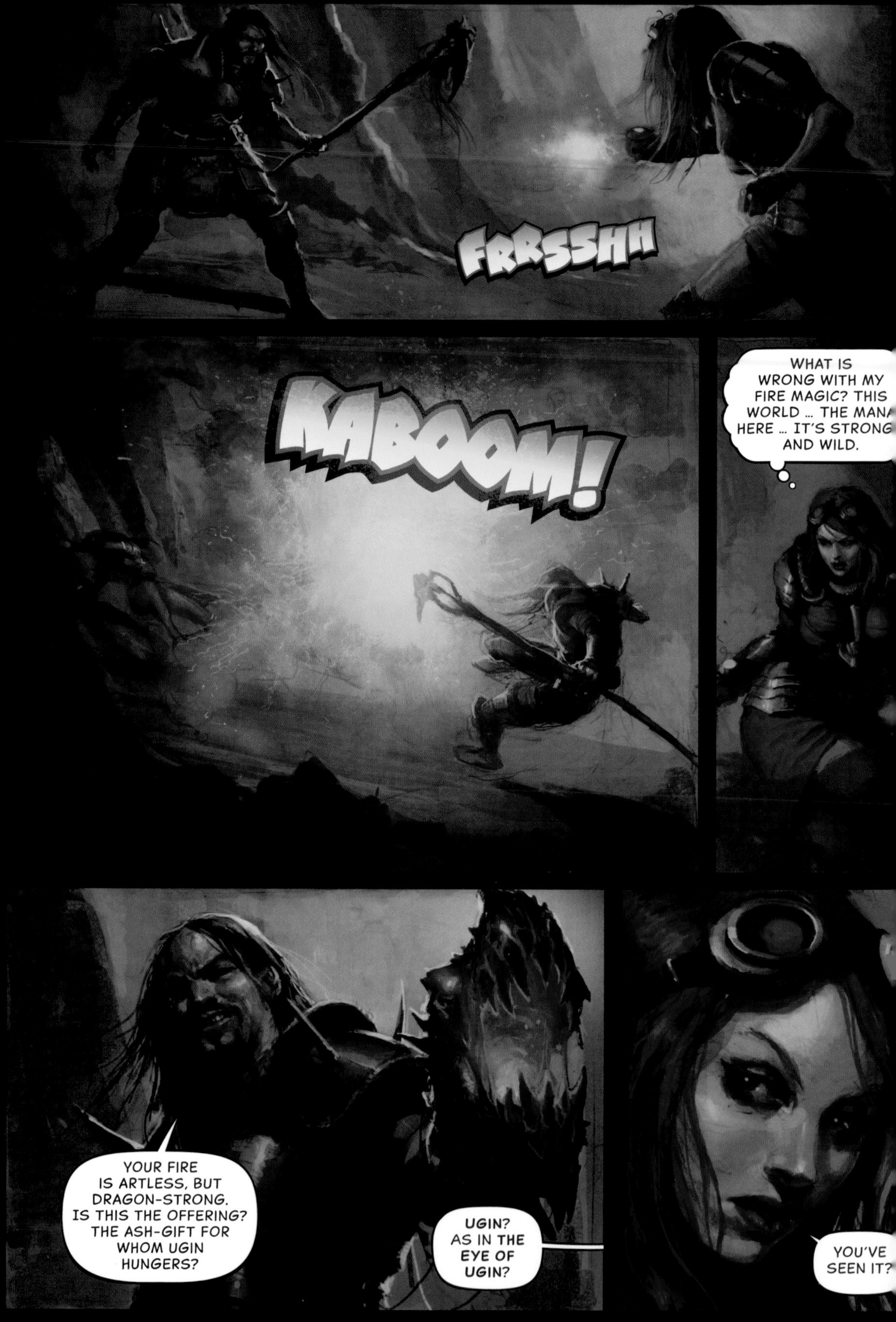
FRRSSHH
KABOOM!
WHAT IS WRONG WITH MY FIRE MAGIC? THIS WORLD ... THE MANA HERE ... IT'S STRONG AND WILD.
YOUR FIRE IS ARTLESS, BUT DRAGON-STRONG. IS THIS THE OFFERING? THE ASH-GIFT FOR WHOM UGIN HUNGERS?
UGIN? AS IN THE EYE OF UGIN?
YOU'VE SEEN IT?

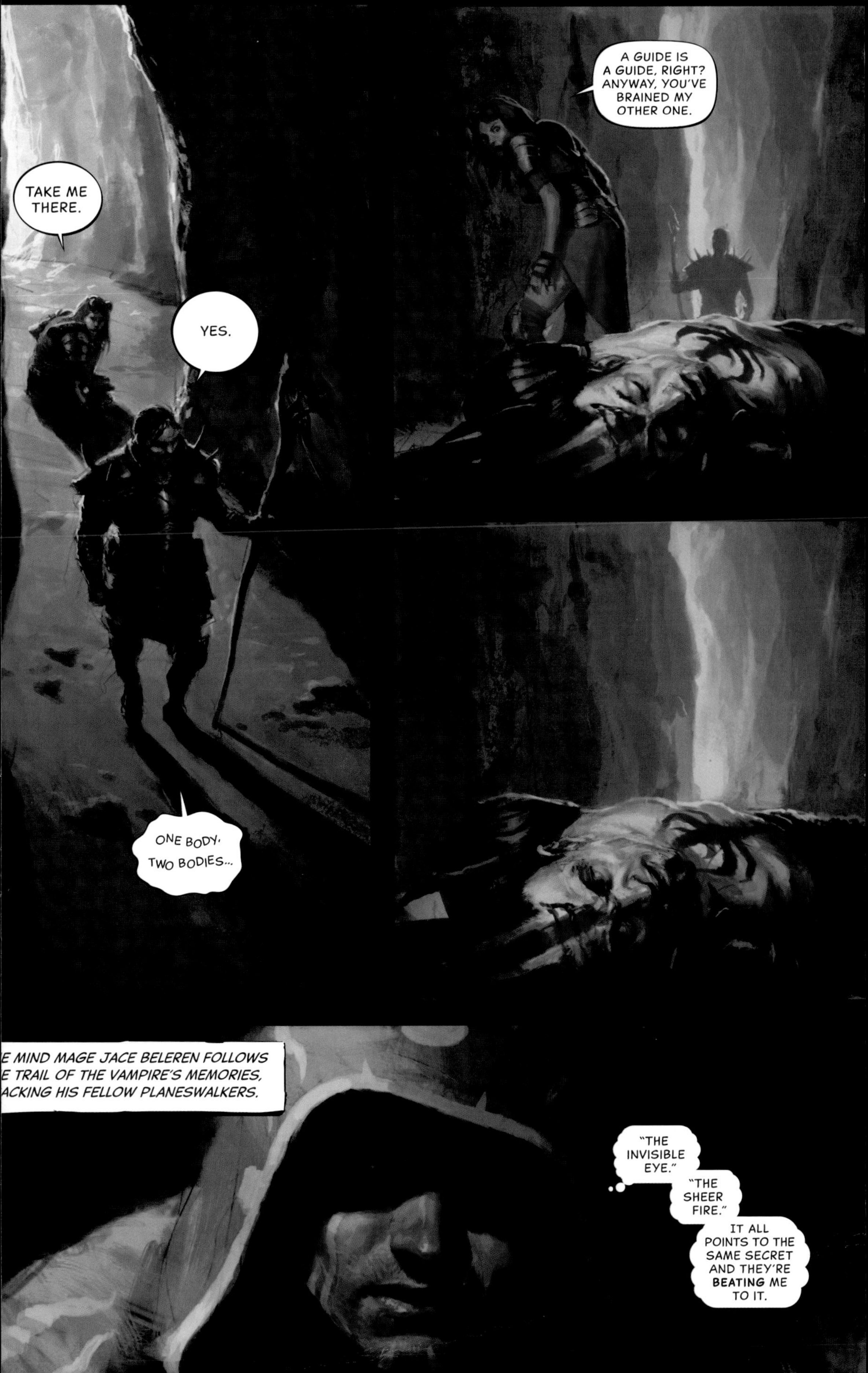
TAKE ME THERE.
YES.
ONE BODY, TWO BODIES...
A GUIDE IS A GUIDE, RIGHT? ANYWAY, YOU'VE BRAINED MY OTHER ONE.
E MIND MAGE JACE BELEREN FOLLOWS E TRAIL OF THE VAMPIRE'S MEMORIES, ACKING HIS FELLOW PLANESWALKERS.
"THE INVISIBLE EYE."
"THE SHEER FIRE."
IT ALL POINTS TO THE SAME SECRET AND THEY'RE BEATING ME TO IT.

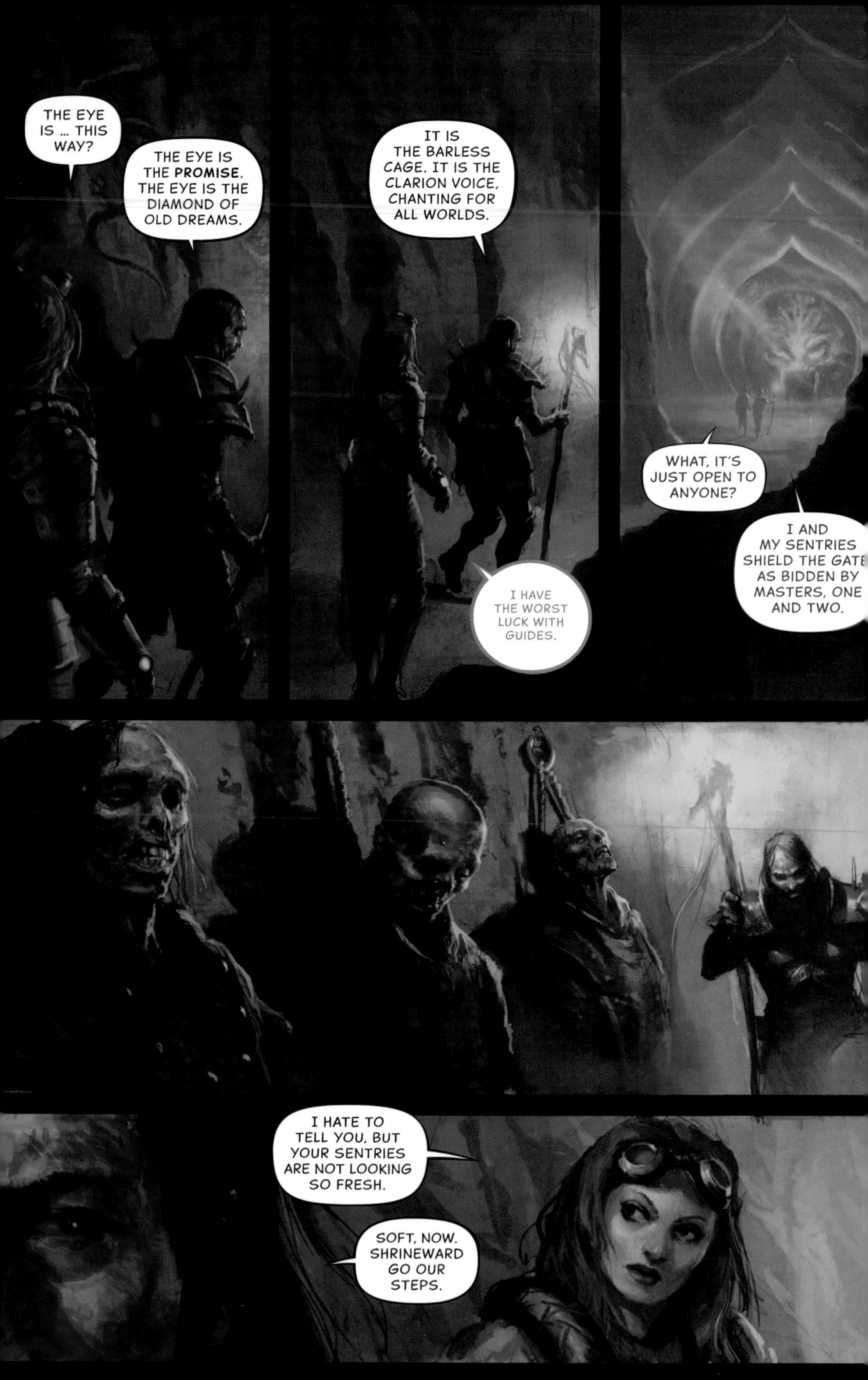
THE EYE IS ... THIS WAY?
THE EYE IS THE **PROMISE**. THE EYE IS THE DIAMOND OF OLD DREAMS.
IT IS THE BARLESS CAGE. IT IS THE CLARION VOICE, CHANTING FOR ALL WORLDS.
I HAVE THE WORST LUCK WITH GUIDES.
WHAT, IT'S JUST OPEN TO ANYONE?
I AND MY SENTRIES SHIELD THE GATE AS BIDDEN BY MASTERS, ONE AND TWO.
I HATE TO TELL YOU, BUT YOUR SENTRIES ARE NOT LOOKING SO FRESH.
SOFT, NOW. SHRINEWARD GO OUR STEPS.

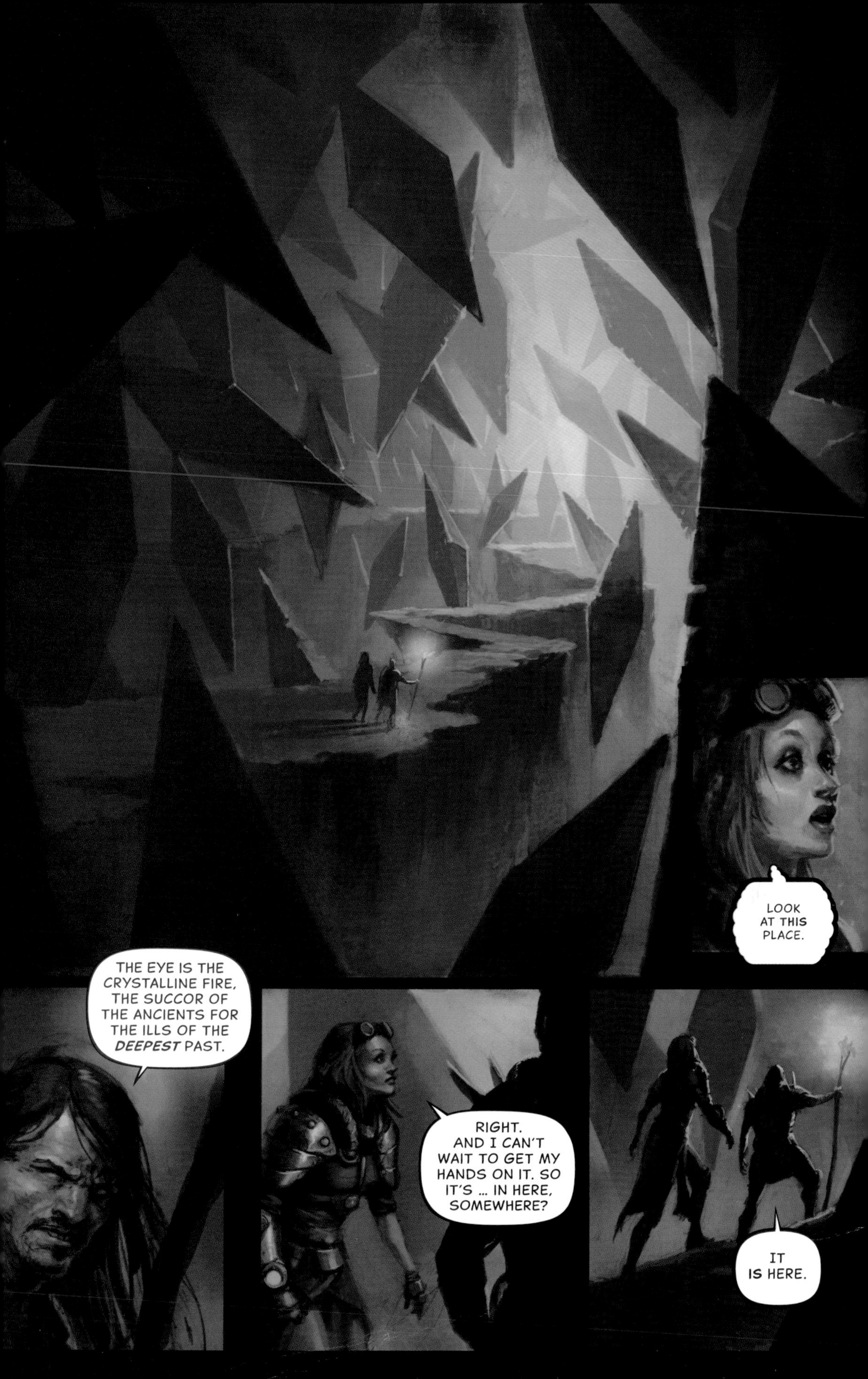
LOOK AT THIS PLACE.
THE EYE IS THE CRYSTALLINE FIRE, THE SUCCOR OF THE ANCIENTS FOR THE ILLS OF THE *DEEPEST* PAST.
RIGHT. AND I CAN'T WAIT TO GET MY HANDS ON IT. SO IT'S ... IN HERE, SOMEWHERE?
IT IS HERE.

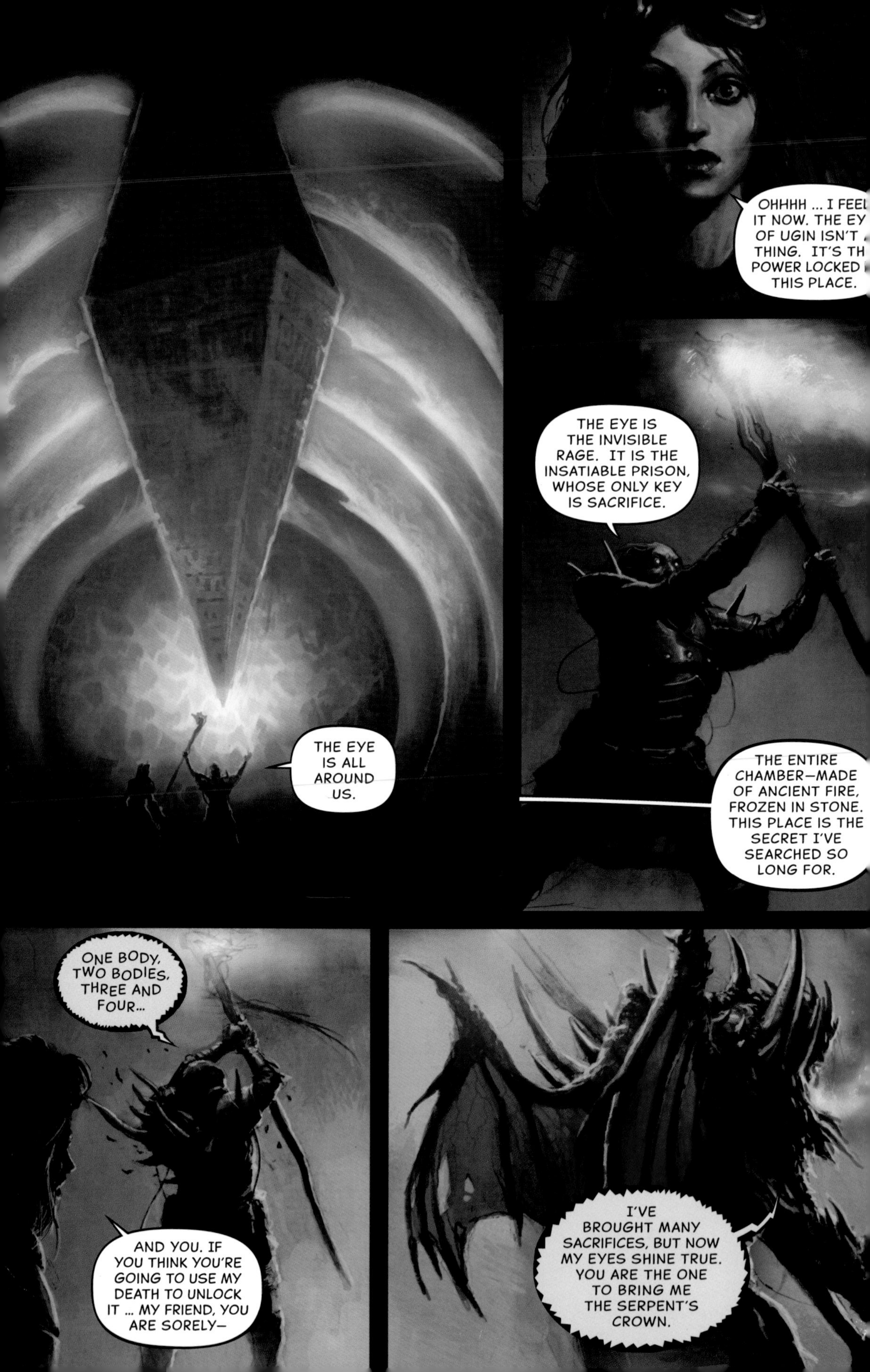

THE EYE IS ALL AROUND US.
OHHHH ... I FEEL IT NOW. THE EY OF UGIN ISN'T THING. IT'S TH POWER LOCKED THIS PLACE.
THE EYE IS THE INVISIBLE RAGE. IT IS THE INSATIABLE PRISON, WHOSE ONLY KEY IS SACRIFICE.
THE ENTIRE CHAMBER—MADE OF ANCIENT FIRE, FROZEN IN STONE. THIS PLACE IS THE SECRET I'VE SEARCHED SO LONG FOR.
ONE BODY, TWO BODIES, THREE AND FOUR...
AND YOU. IF YOU THINK YOU'RE GOING TO USE MY DEATH TO UNLOCK IT ... MY FRIEND, YOU ARE SORELY—
I'VE BROUGHT MANY SACRIFICES, BUT NOW MY EYES SHINE TRUE. YOU ARE THE ONE TO BRING ME THE SERPENT'S CROWN.

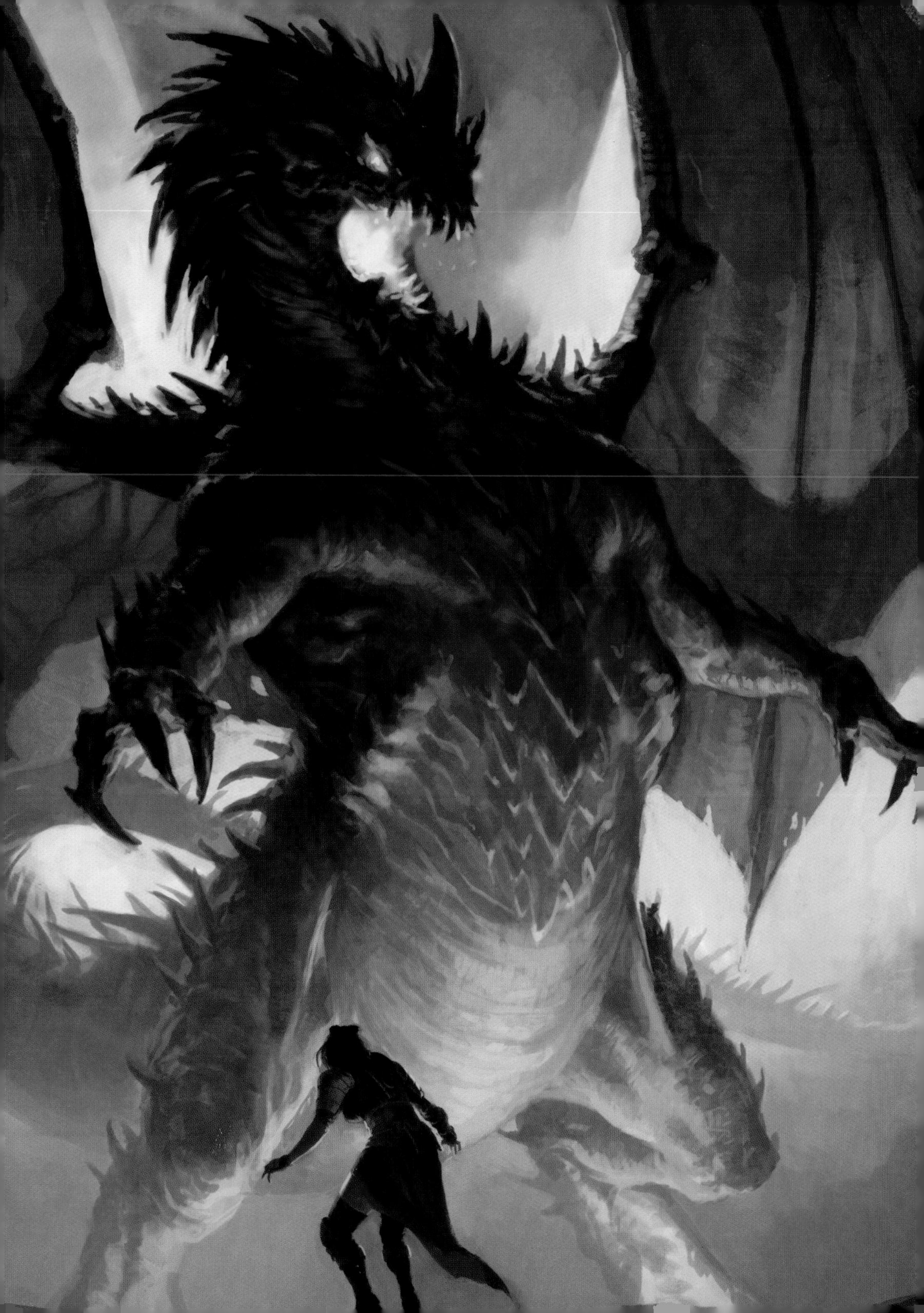

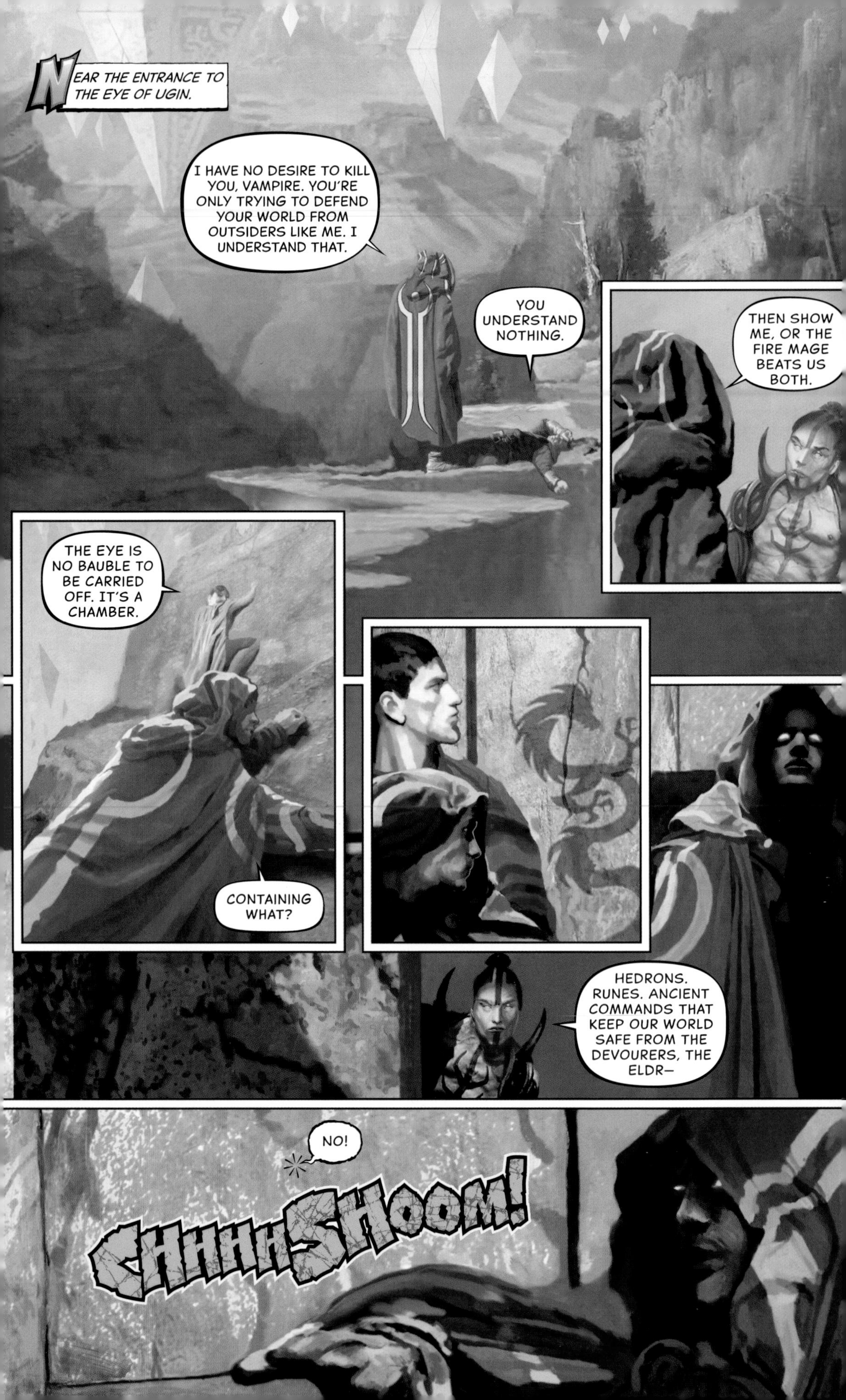
NEAR THE ENTRANCE TO THE EYE OF UGIN.
I HAVE NO DESIRE TO KILL YOU, VAMPIRE. YOU'RE ONLY TRYING TO DEFEND YOUR WORLD FROM OUTSIDERS LIKE ME. I UNDERSTAND THAT.
YOU UNDERSTAND NOTHING.
THEN SHOW ME, OR THE FIRE MAGE BEATS US BOTH.
THE EYE IS NO BAUBLE TO BE CARRIED OFF. IT'S A CHAMBER.
CONTAINING WHAT?
HEDRONS. RUNES. ANCIENT COMMANDS THAT KEEP OUR WORLD SAFE FROM THE DEVOURERS, THE ELDR–
NO!
CHHHHSHOOM!

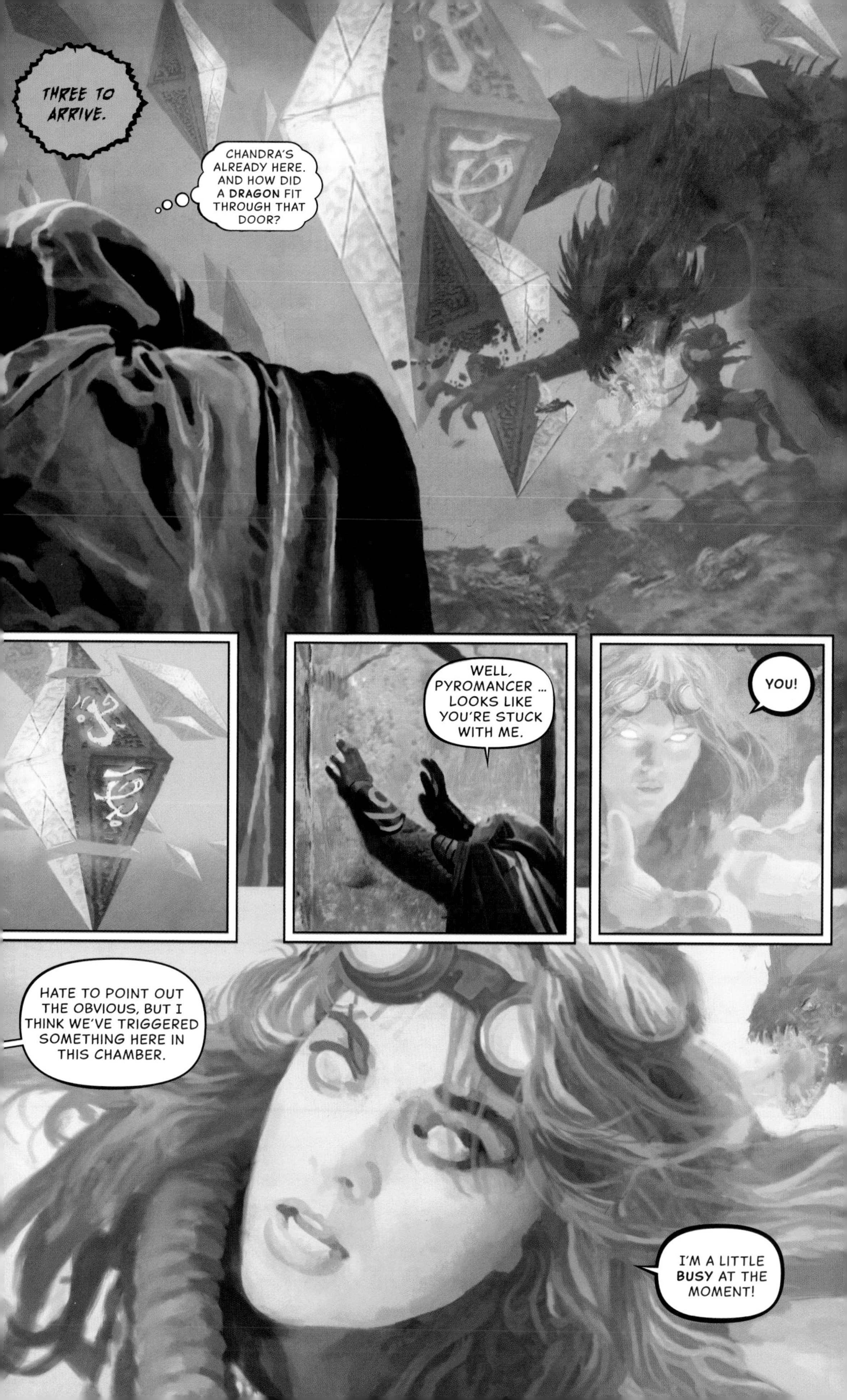
THREE TO ARRIVE.
CHANDRA'S ALREADY HERE. AND HOW DID A DRAGON FIT THROUGH THAT DOOR?
WELL, PYROMANCER ... LOOKS LIKE YOU'RE STUCK WITH ME.
YOU!
HATE TO POINT OUT THE OBVIOUS, BUT I THINK WE'VE TRIGGERED SOMETHING HERE IN THIS CHAMBER.
I'M A LITTLE BUSY AT THE MOMENT!

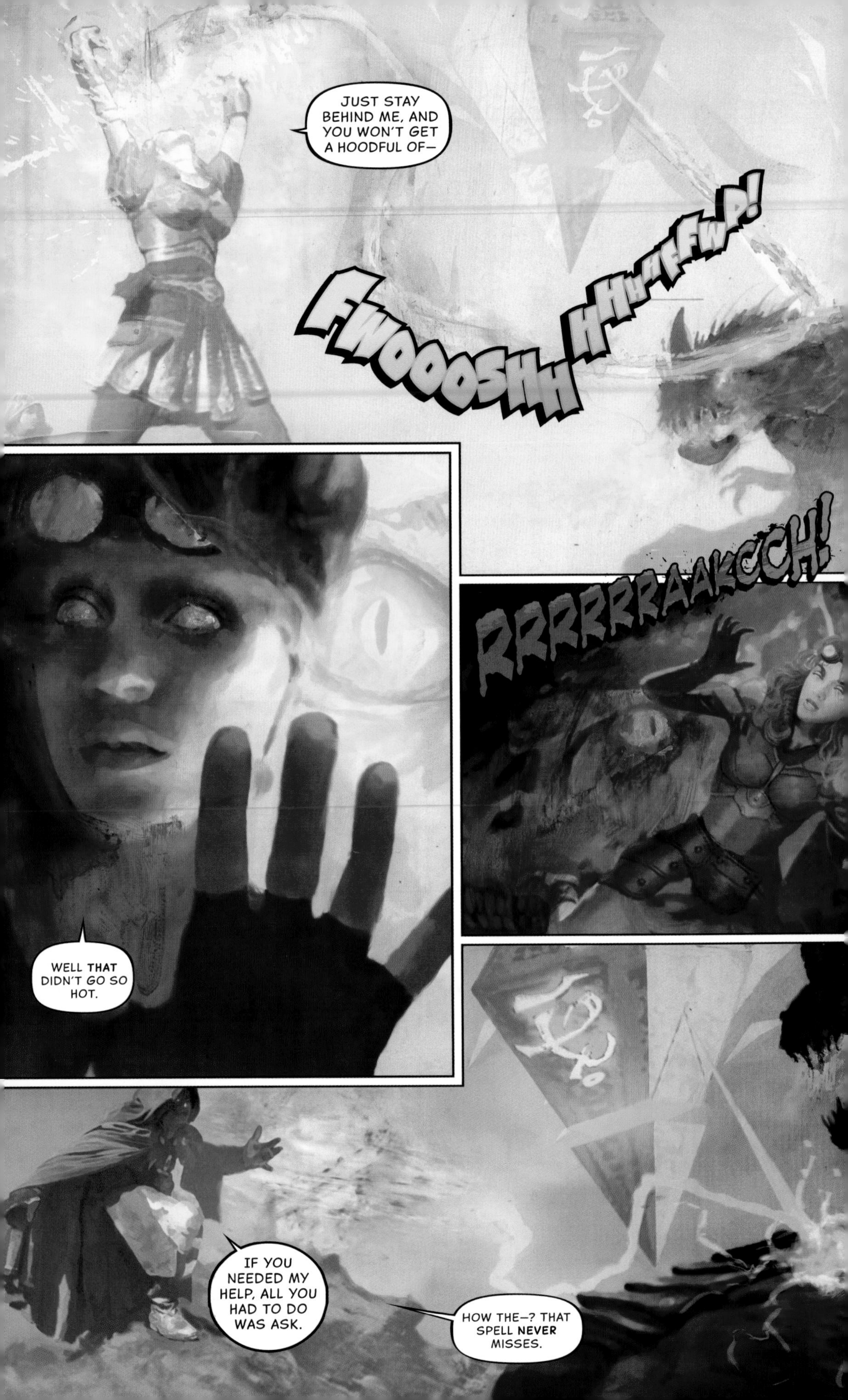
JUST STAY BEHIND ME, AND YOU WON'T GET A HOODFUL OF—
FWOOOOSHHHHHHFFWP!
WELL THAT DIDN'T GO SO HOT.
RRRRRRAAKCCH!
IF YOU NEEDED MY HELP, ALL YOU HAD TO DO WAS ASK.
HOW THE—? THAT SPELL NEVER MISSES.

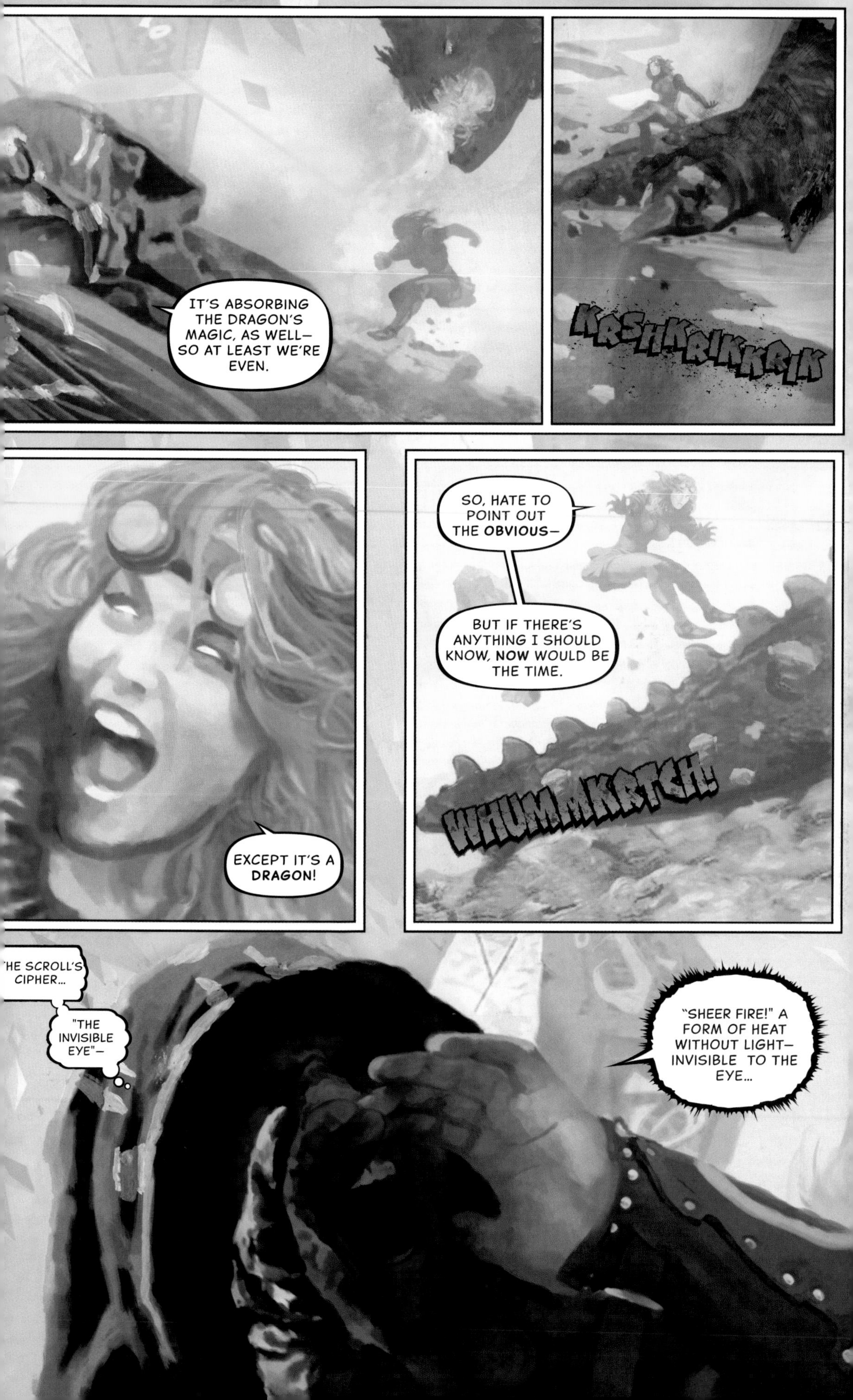

IT'S ABSORBING THE DRAGON'S MAGIC, AS WELL—SO AT LEAST WE'RE EVEN.
KRSHKRIKKRIK
EXCEPT IT'S A **DRAGON**!
SO, HATE TO POINT OUT THE **OBVIOUS**—
BUT IF THERE'S ANYTHING I SHOULD KNOW, **NOW** WOULD BE THE TIME.
WHUMMKRTCH!
THE SCROLL'S CIPHER...
"THE INVISIBLE EYE"—
"SHEER FIRE!" A FORM OF HEAT WITHOUT LIGHT—INVISIBLE TO THE EYE...

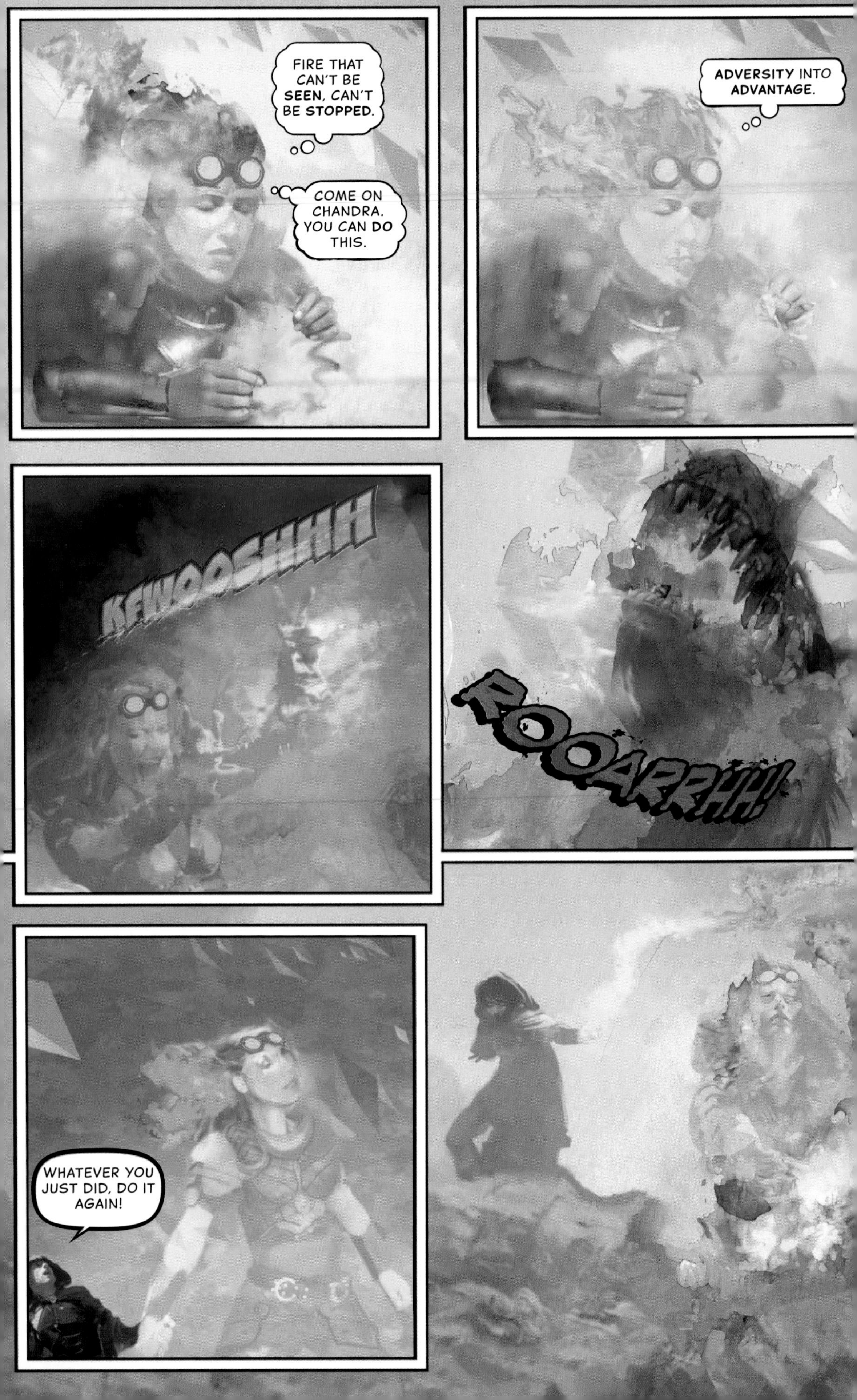
FIRE THAT CAN'T BE SEEN, CAN'T BE STOPPED.
COME ON CHANDRA. YOU CAN DO THIS.
ADVERSITY INTO ADVANTAGE.
KFWOOSHHH
ROOARRHH!
WHATEVER YOU JUST DID, DO IT AGAIN!

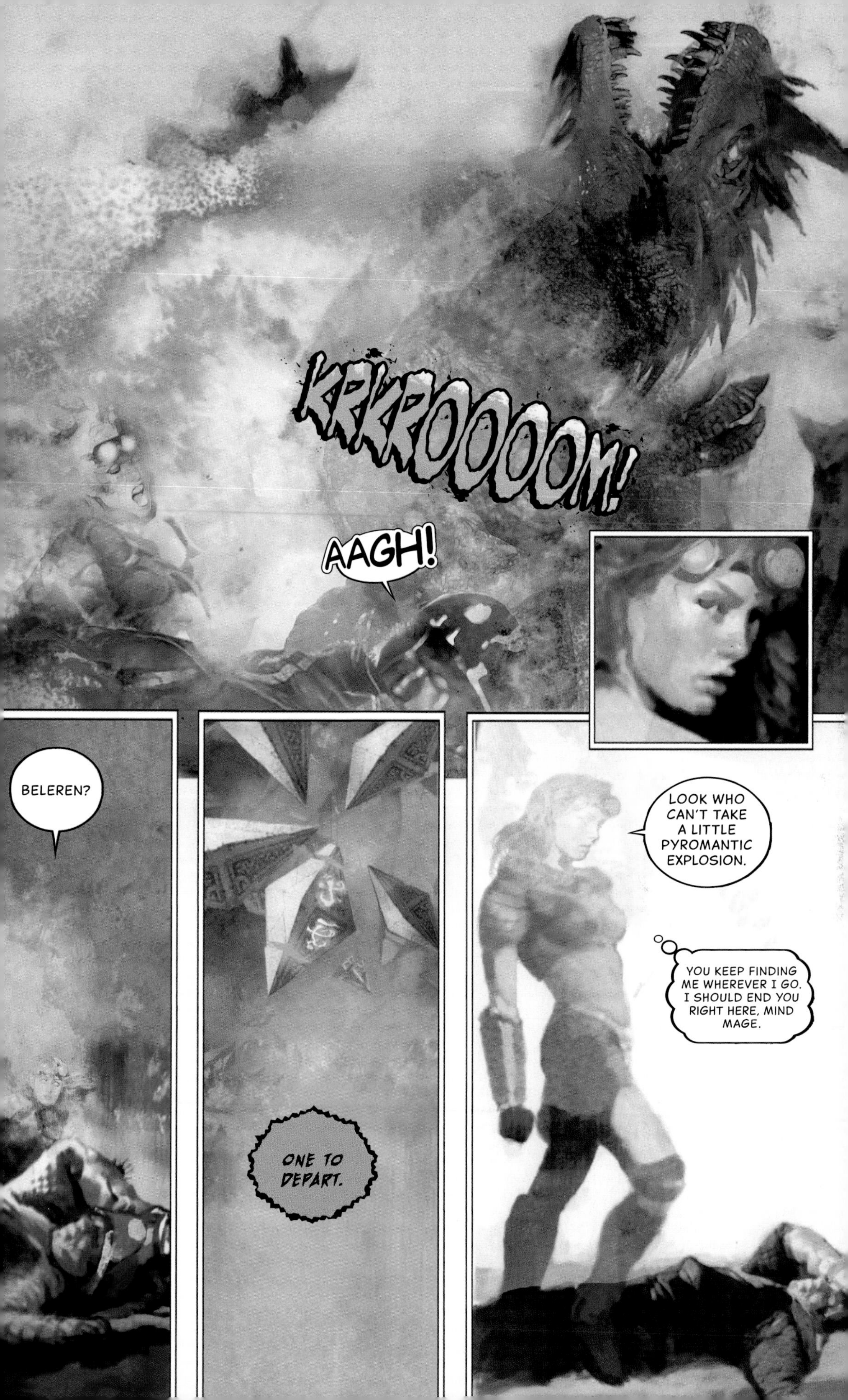
KRKROOOOOM!
AAGH!
BELEREN?
ONE TO DEPART.
LOOK WHO CAN'T TAKE A LITTLE PYROMANTIC EXPLOSION.
YOU KEEP FINDING ME WHEREVER I GO. I SHOULD END YOU RIGHT HERE, MIND MAGE.

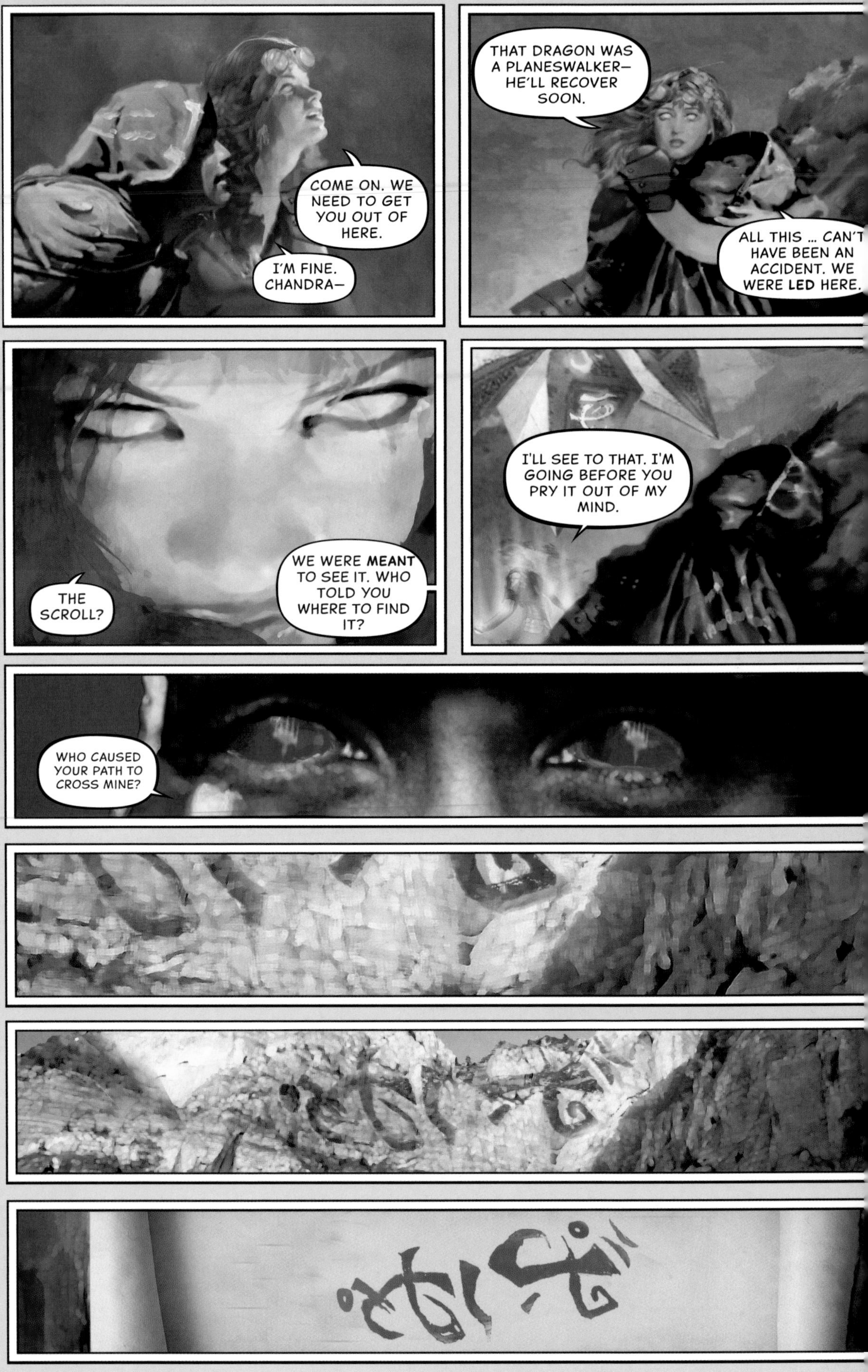
COME ON. WE NEED TO GET YOU OUT OF HERE.
I'M FINE. CHANDRA—
THAT DRAGON WAS A PLANESWALKER— HE'LL RECOVER SOON.
ALL THIS ... CAN'T HAVE BEEN AN ACCIDENT. WE WERE **LED** HERE.
THE SCROLL?
WE WERE **MEANT** TO SEE IT. WHO TOLD YOU WHERE TO FIND IT?
I'LL SEE TO THAT. I'M GOING BEFORE YOU PRY IT OUT OF MY MIND.
WHO CAUSED YOUR PATH TO CROSS MINE?

ENTER THE ELDRAZI

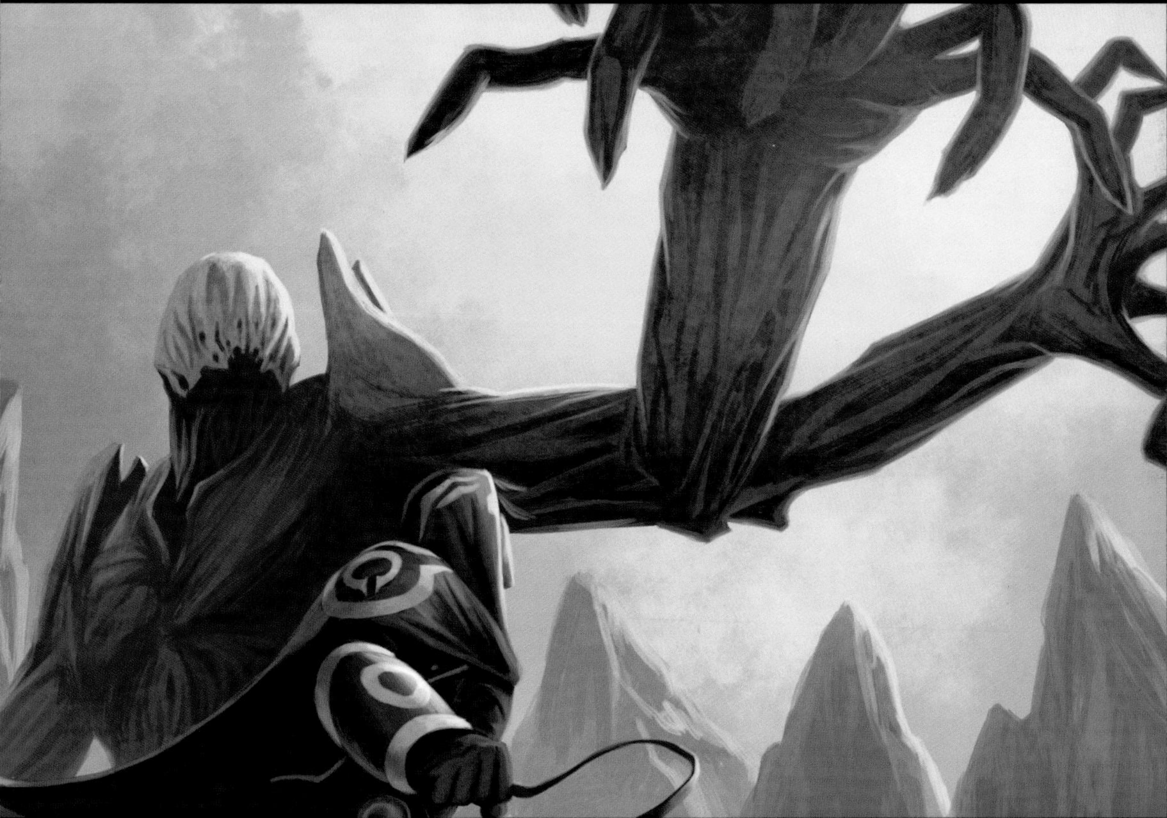

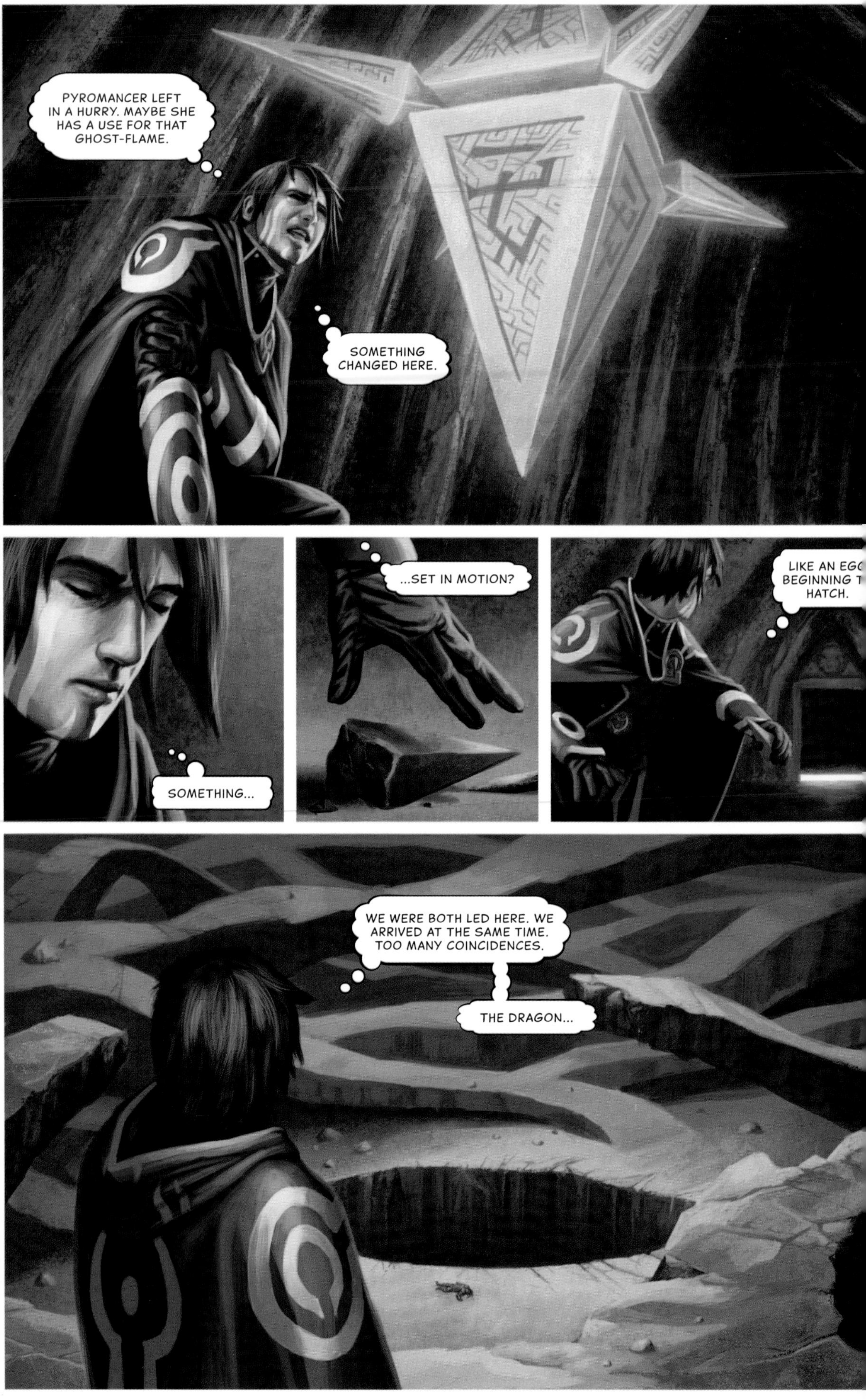
PYROMANCER LEFT IN A HURRY. MAYBE SHE HAS A USE FOR THAT GHOST-FLAME.
SOMETHING CHANGED HERE.
SOMETHING...
...SET IN MOTION?
LIKE AN EG BEGINNING T HATCH.
WE WERE BOTH LED HERE. WE ARRIVED AT THE SAME TIME. TOO MANY COINCIDENCES.
THE DRAGON...

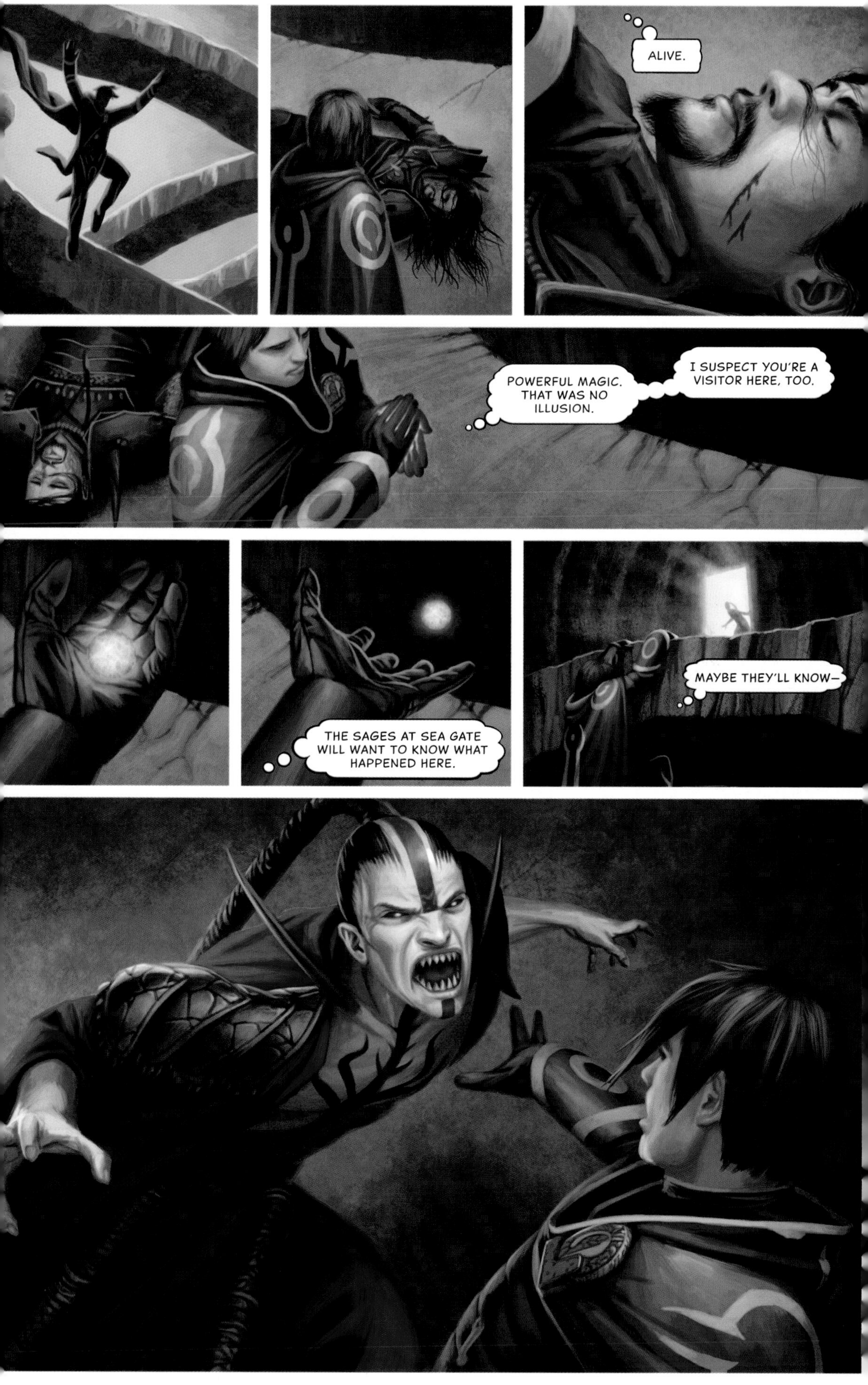
ALIVE.
POWERFUL MAGIC. THAT WAS NO ILLUSION.
I SUSPECT YOU'RE A VISITOR HERE, TOO.
THE SAGES AT SEA GATE WILL WANT TO KNOW WHAT HAPPENED HERE.
MAYBE THEY'LL KNOW—

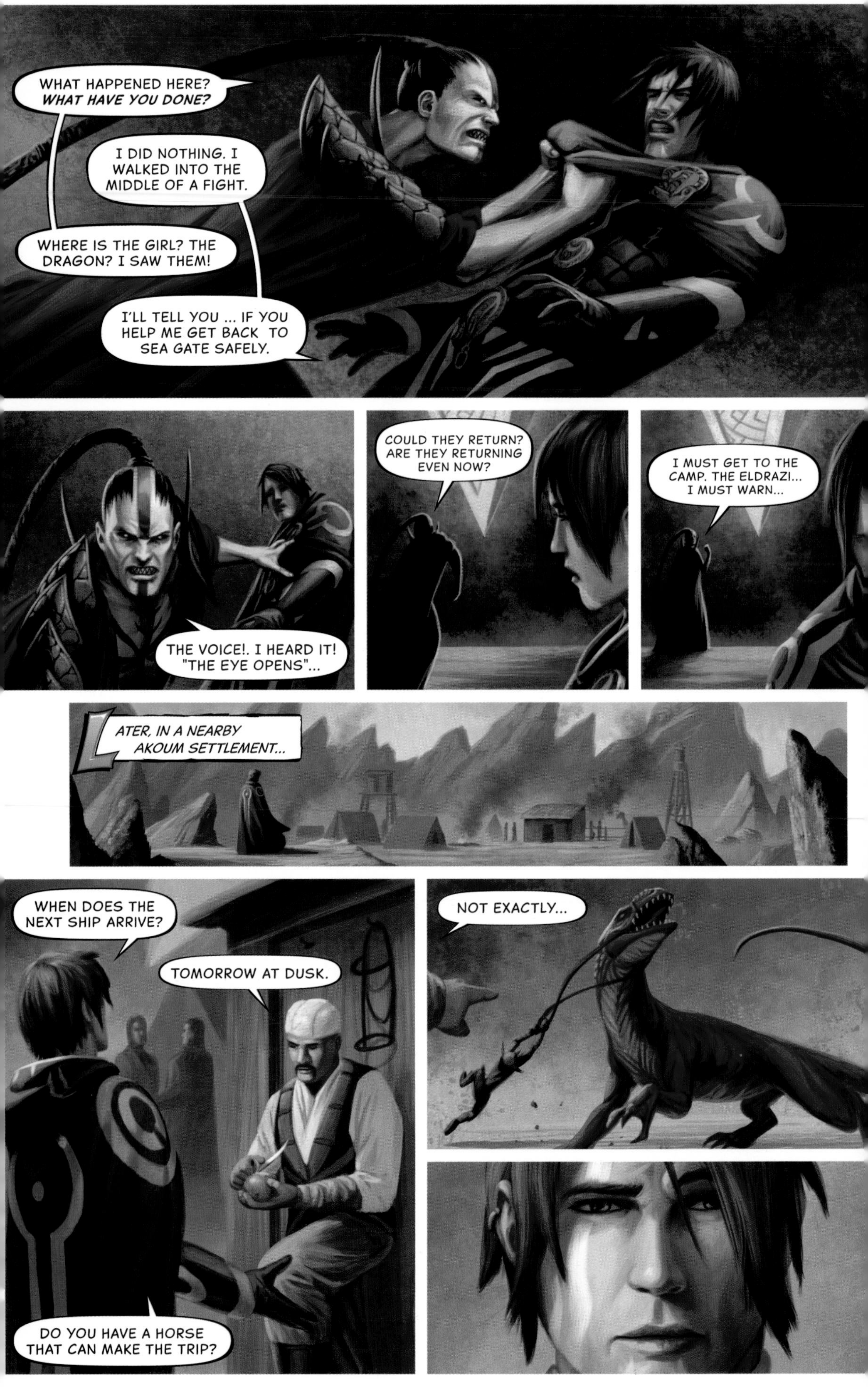
WHAT HAPPENED HERE? *WHAT HAVE YOU DONE?*
I DID NOTHING. I WALKED INTO THE MIDDLE OF A FIGHT.
WHERE IS THE GIRL? THE DRAGON? I SAW THEM!
I'LL TELL YOU ... IF YOU HELP ME GET BACK TO SEA GATE SAFELY.
THE VOICE!. I HEARD IT! "THE EYE OPENS"...
COULD THEY RETURN? ARE THEY RETURNING EVEN NOW?
I MUST GET TO THE CAMP. THE ELDRAZI... I MUST WARN...
LATER, IN A NEARBY AKOUM SETTLEMENT...
WHEN DOES THE NEXT SHIP ARRIVE?
TOMORROW AT DUSK.
DO YOU HAVE A HORSE THAT CAN MAKE THE TRIP?
NOT EXACTLY...

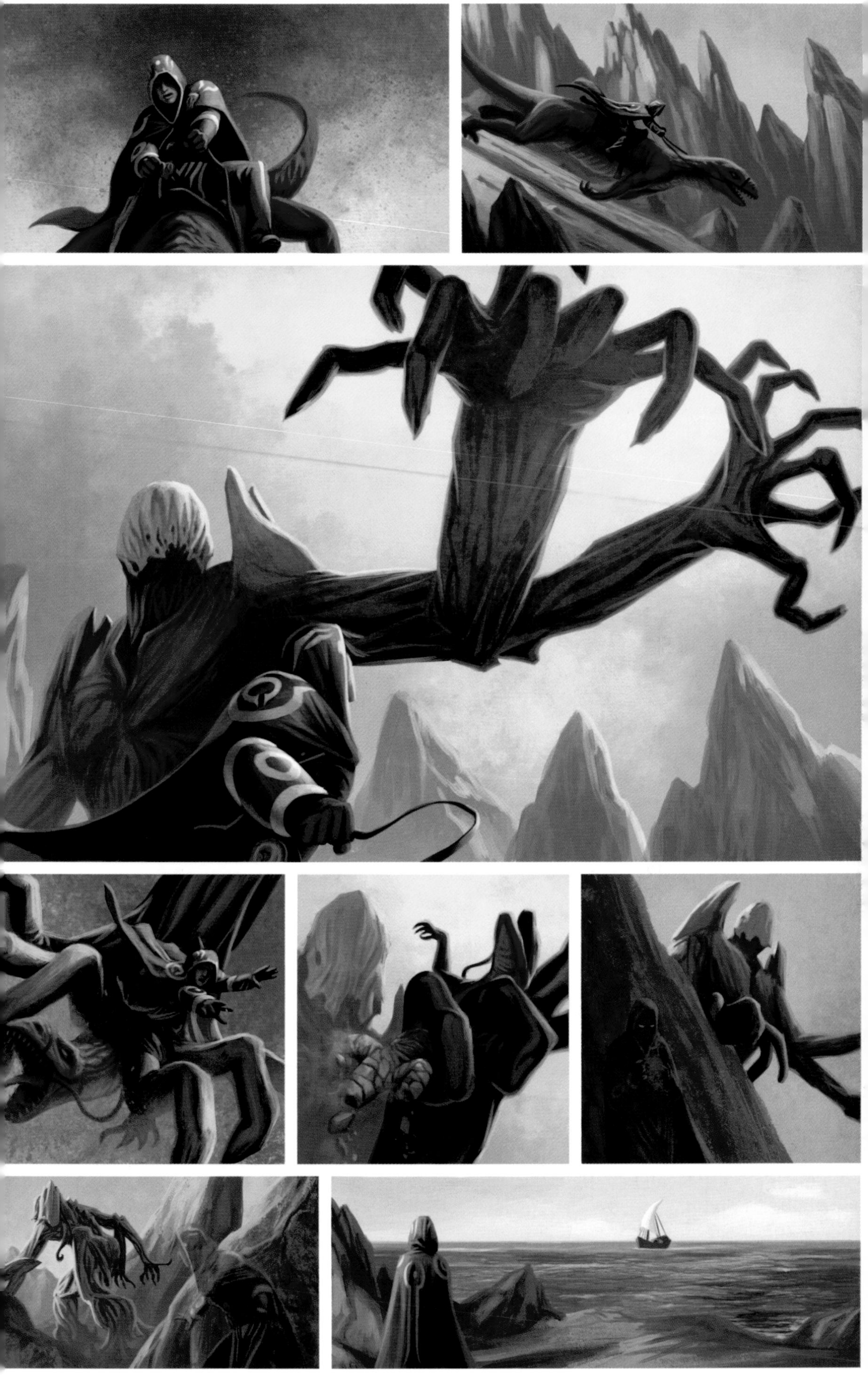

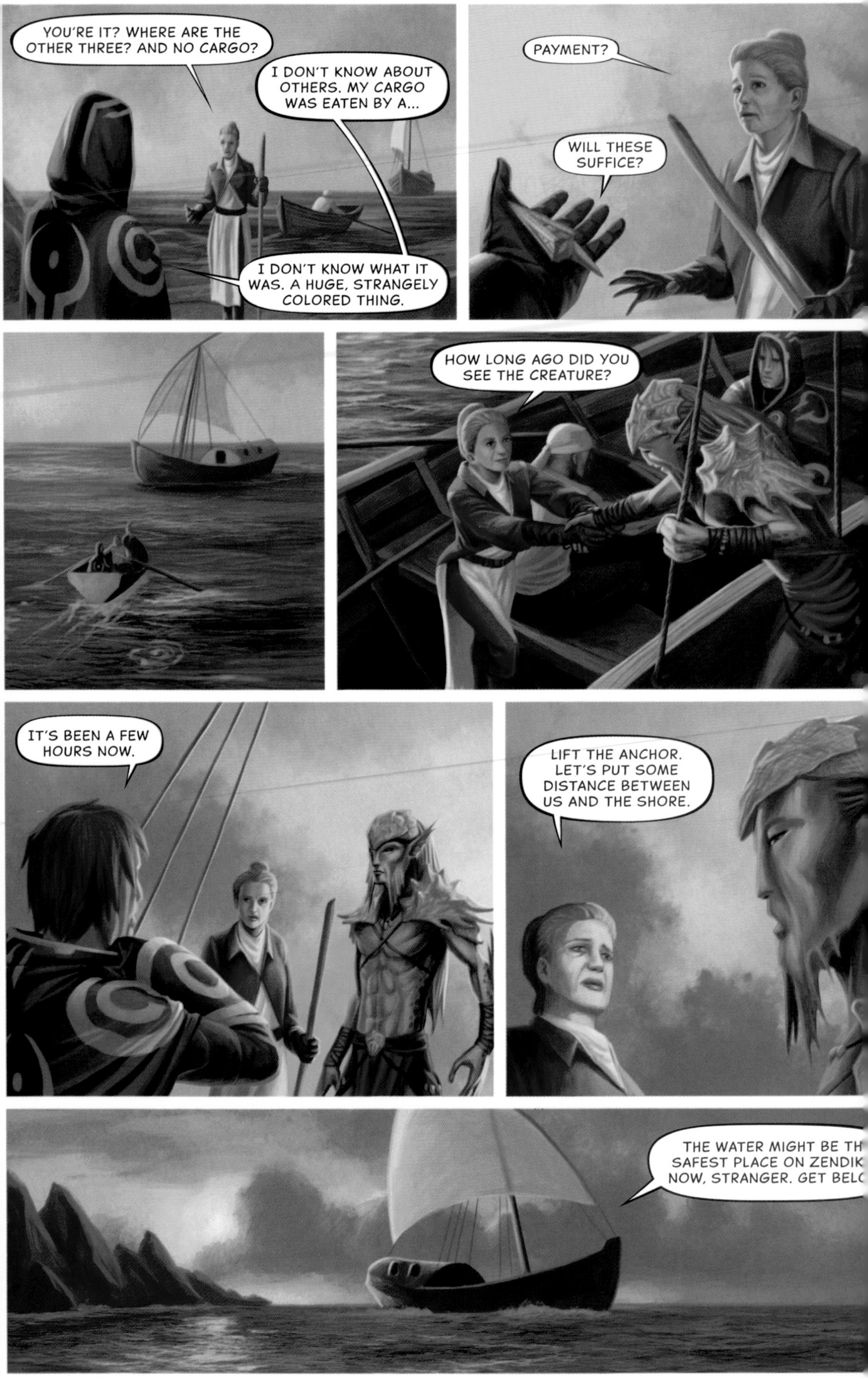
YOU'RE IT? WHERE ARE THE OTHER THREE? AND NO CARGO?
I DON'T KNOW ABOUT OTHERS. MY CARGO WAS EATEN BY A...
I DON'T KNOW WHAT IT WAS. A HUGE, STRANGELY COLORED THING.
PAYMENT?
WILL THESE SUFFICE?
HOW LONG AGO DID YOU SEE THE CREATURE?
IT'S BEEN A FEW HOURS NOW.
LIFT THE ANCHOR. LET'S PUT SOME DISTANCE BETWEEN US AND THE SHORE.
THE WATER MIGHT BE TH
SAFEST PLACE ON ZENDIK
NOW, STRANGER. GET BEL

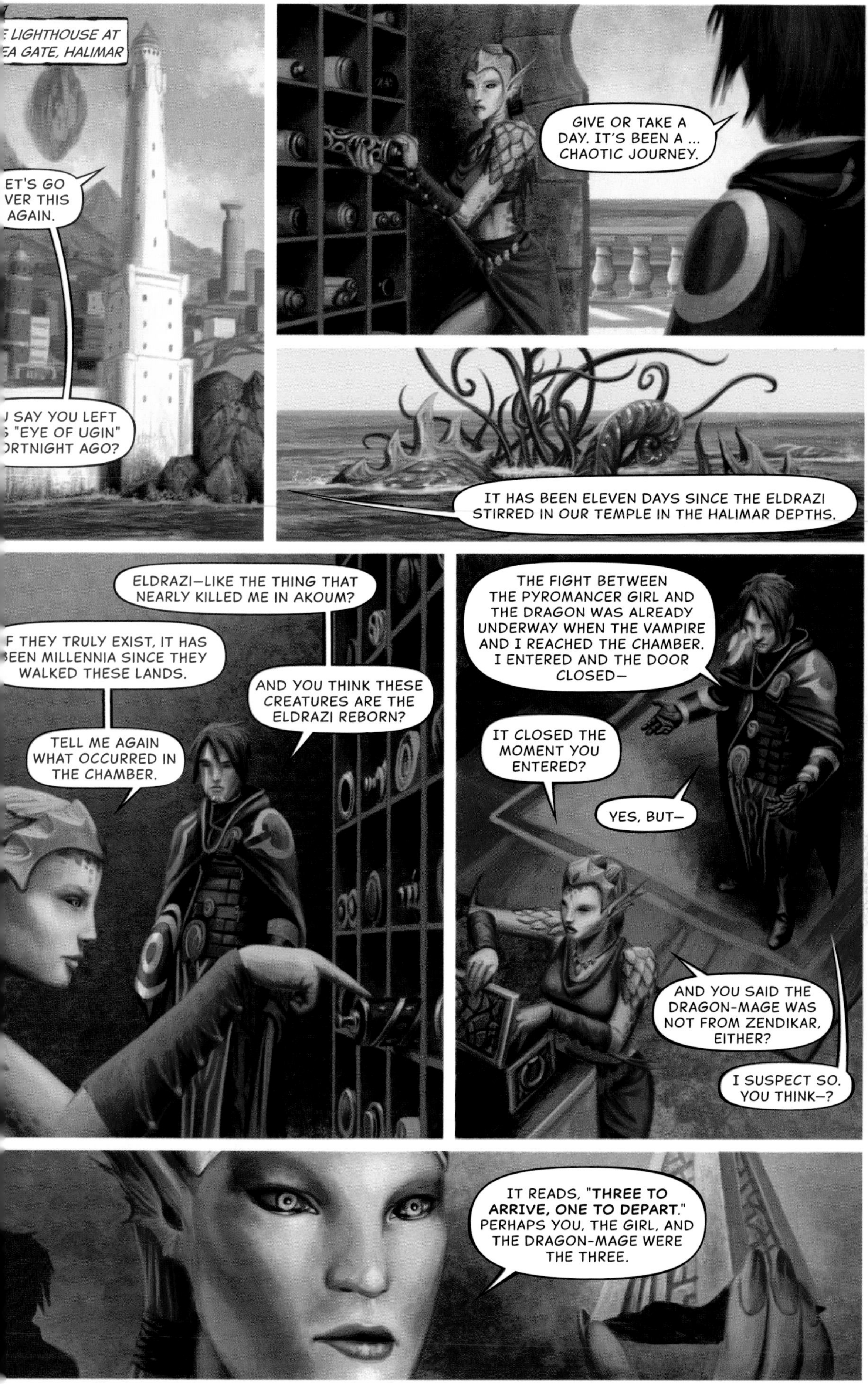

E LIGHTHOUSE AT EA GATE, HALIMAR
ET'S GO VER THIS AGAIN.
U SAY YOU LEFT S "EYE OF UGIN" ORTNIGHT AGO?
GIVE OR TAKE A DAY. IT'S BEEN A ... CHAOTIC JOURNEY.
IT HAS BEEN ELEVEN DAYS SINCE THE ELDRAZI STIRRED IN OUR TEMPLE IN THE HALIMAR DEPTHS.
ELDRAZI—LIKE THE THING THAT NEARLY KILLED ME IN AKOUM?
F THEY TRULY EXIST, IT HAS EEN MILLENNIA SINCE THEY WALKED THESE LANDS.
AND YOU THINK THESE CREATURES ARE THE ELDRAZI REBORN?
TELL ME AGAIN WHAT OCCURRED IN THE CHAMBER.
THE FIGHT BETWEEN THE PYROMANCER GIRL AND THE DRAGON WAS ALREADY UNDERWAY WHEN THE VAMPIRE AND I REACHED THE CHAMBER. I ENTERED AND THE DOOR CLOSED—
IT CLOSED THE MOMENT YOU ENTERED?
YES, BUT—
AND YOU SAID THE DRAGON-MAGE WAS NOT FROM ZENDIKAR, EITHER?
I SUSPECT SO. YOU THINK—?
IT READS, "THREE TO ARRIVE, ONE TO DEPART." PERHAPS YOU, THE GIRL, AND THE DRAGON-MAGE WERE THE THREE.

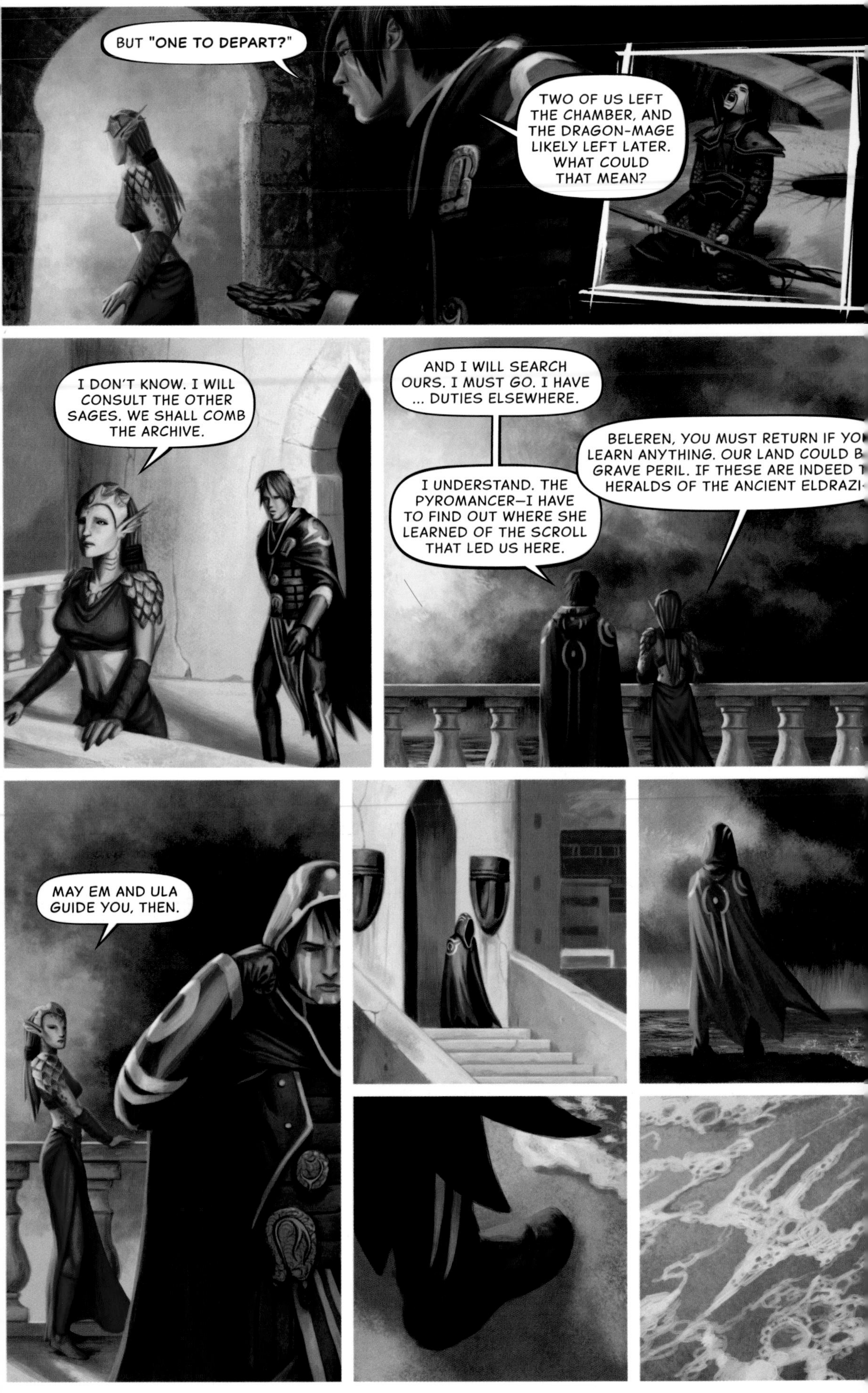

BUT "ONE TO DEPART?"
TWO OF US LEFT THE CHAMBER, AND THE DRAGON-MAGE LIKELY LEFT LATER. WHAT COULD THAT MEAN?
I DON'T KNOW. I WILL CONSULT THE OTHER SAGES. WE SHALL COMB THE ARCHIVE.
AND I WILL SEARCH OURS. I MUST GO. I HAVE ... DUTIES ELSEWHERE.
BELEREN, YOU MUST RETURN IF YO
LEARN ANYTHING. OUR LAND COULD B
GRAVE PERIL. IF THESE ARE INDEED T
HERALDS OF THE ANCIENT ELDRAZI-
I UNDERSTAND. THE PYROMANCER—I HAVE TO FIND OUT WHERE SHE LEARNED OF THE SCROLL THAT LED US HERE.
MAY EM AND ULA GUIDE YOU, THEN.

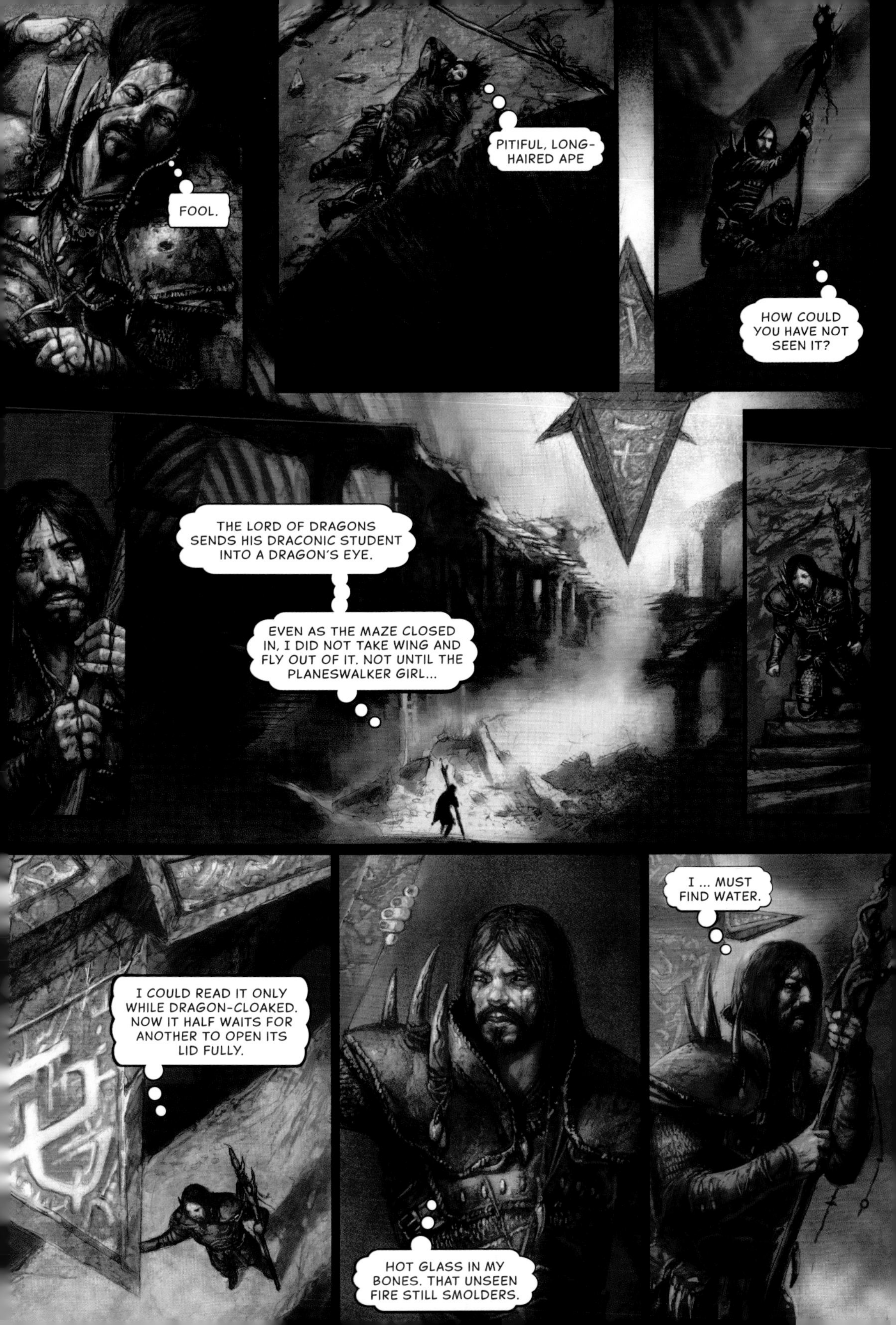
FOOL.
PITIFUL, LONG-HAIRED APE
HOW COULD YOU HAVE NOT SEEN IT?
THE LORD OF DRAGONS SENDS HIS DRACONIC STUDENT INTO A DRAGON'S EYE.
EVEN AS THE MAZE CLOSED IN, I DID NOT TAKE WING AND FLY OUT OF IT. NOT UNTIL THE PLANESWALKER GIRL...
I COULD READ IT ONLY WHILE DRAGON-CLOAKED. NOW IT HALF WAITS FOR ANOTHER TO OPEN ITS LID FULLY.
HOT GLASS IN MY BONES. THAT UNSEEN FIRE STILL SMOLDERS.
I ... MUST FIND WATER.

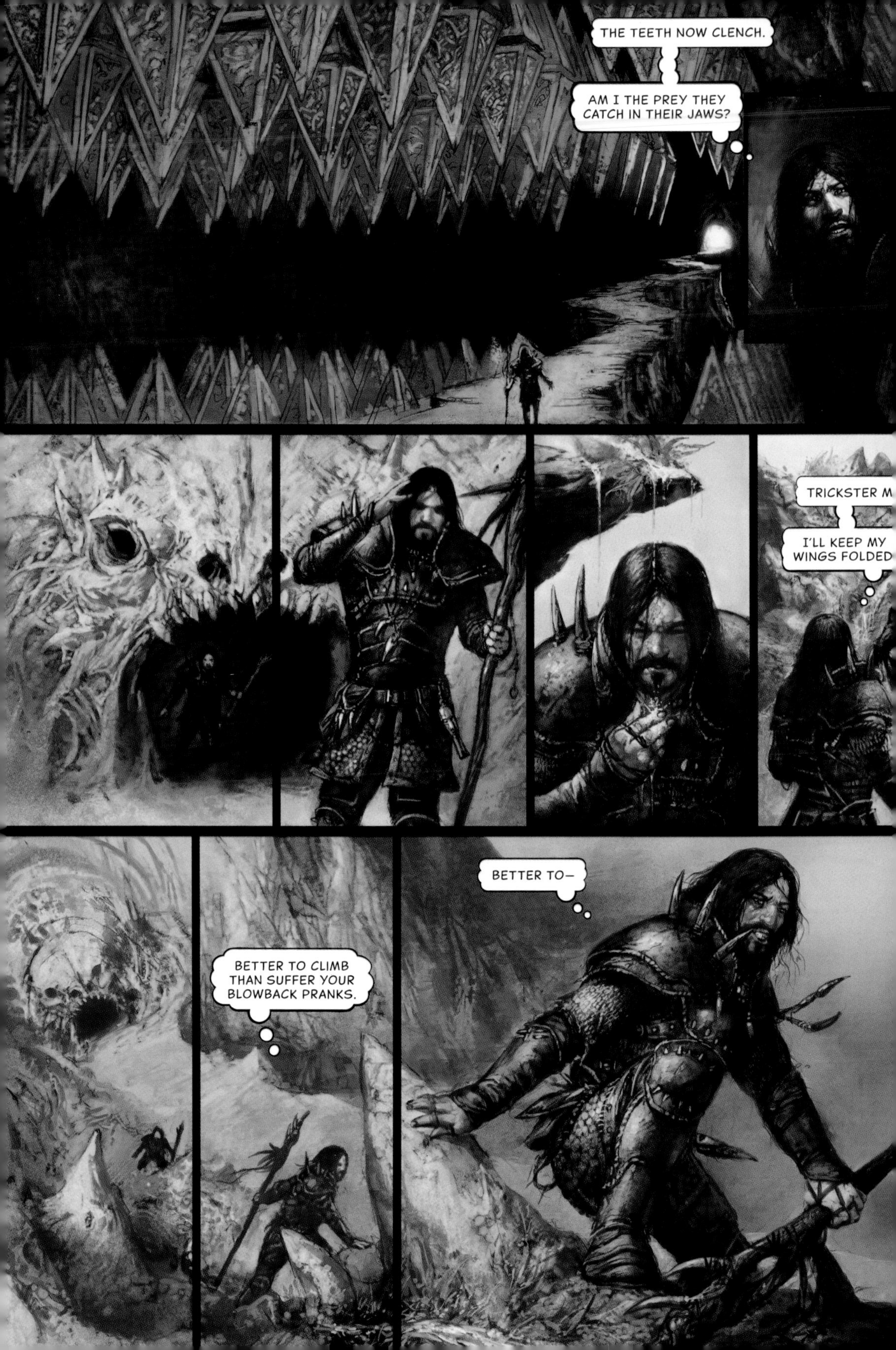
THE TEETH NOW CLENCH.
AM I THE PREY THEY CATCH IN THEIR JAWS?
TRICKSTER M
I'LL KEEP MY WINGS FOLDED
BETTER TO CLIMB THAN SUFFER YOUR BLOWBACK PRANKS.
BETTER TO—

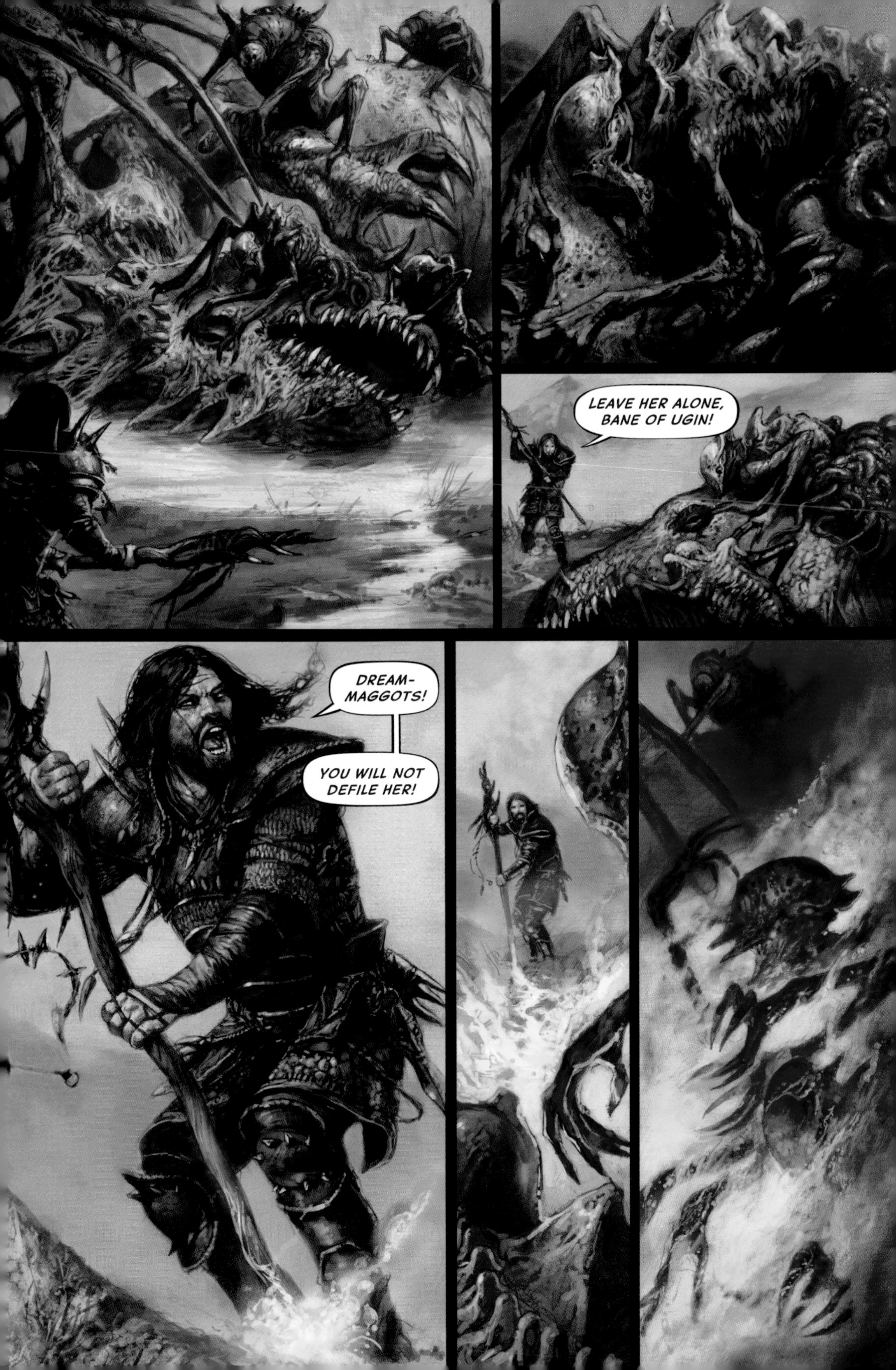
LEAVE HER ALONE, BANE OF UGIN!
DREAM-MAGGOTS!
YOU WILL NOT DEFILE HER!

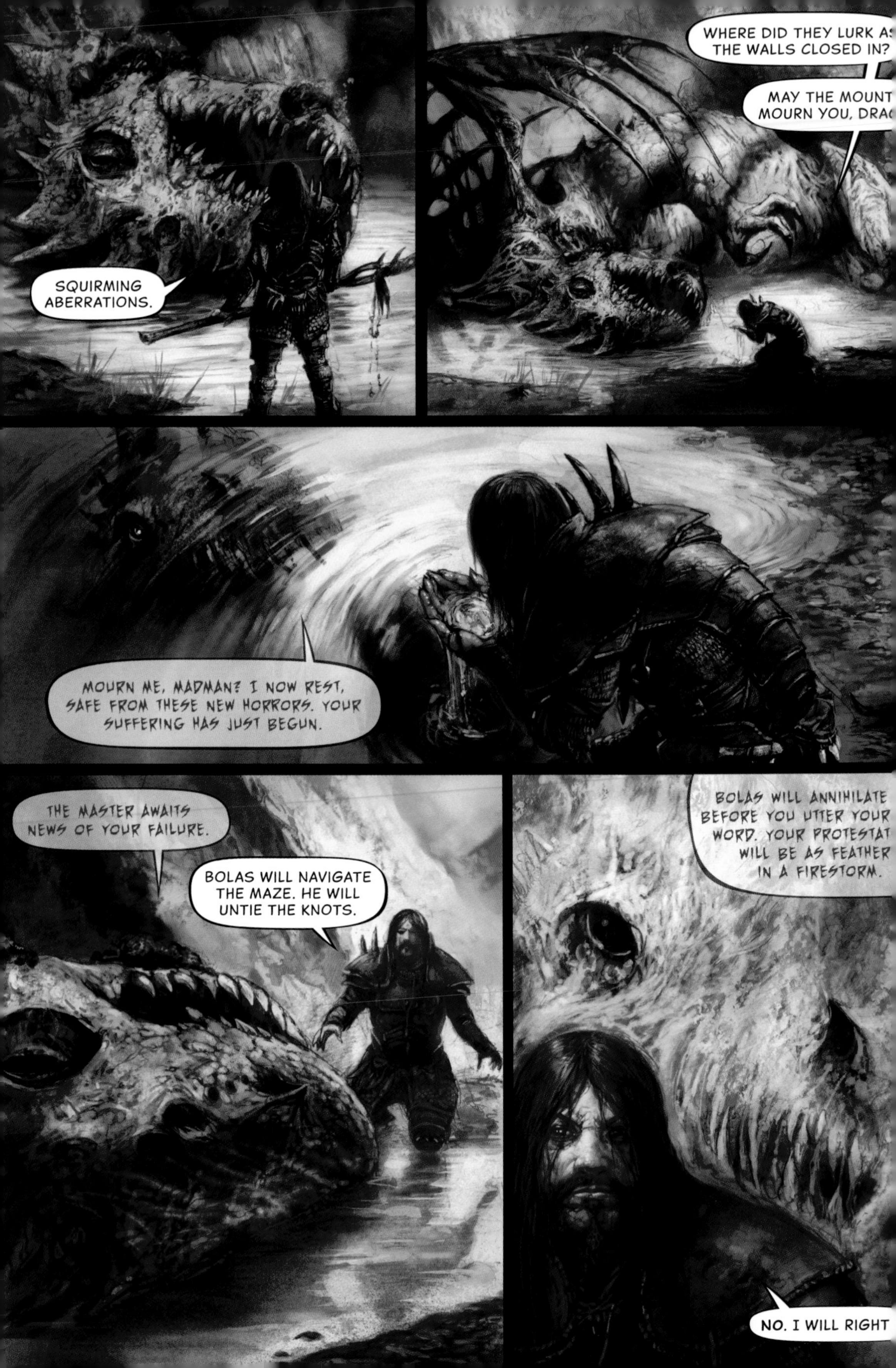
SQUIRMING ABERRATIONS.
WHERE DID THEY LURK A THE WALLS CLOSED IN?
MAY THE MOUNT MOURN YOU, DRA
MOURN ME, MADMAN? I NOW REST, SAFE FROM THESE NEW HORRORS. YOUR SUFFERING HAS JUST BEGUN.
THE MASTER AWAITS NEWS OF YOUR FAILURE.
BOLAS WILL NAVIGATE THE MAZE. HE WILL UNTIE THE KNOTS.
BOLAS WILL ANNIHILATE BEFORE YOU UTTER YOUR WORD. YOUR PROTESTAT WILL BE AS FEATHER IN A FIRESTORM.
NO. I WILL RIGHT

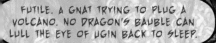

FUTILE. A GNAT TRYING TO PLUG A VOLCANO. NO DRAGON'S BAUBLE CAN LULL THE EYE OF UGIN BACK TO SLEEP.

YOU WERE SENT TO FAIL.

I WILL RESTORE IT. I WILL MATCH ITS MAJESTY.

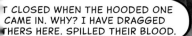

I AM NO DRAGON'S BAUBLE! I WAS SENT FOR A REASON.

IT CLOSED WHEN THE HOODED ONE CAME IN. WHY? I HAVE DRAGGED OTHERS HERE. SPILLED THEIR BLOOD.

THEY WERE NOT WORTHY OTHERS.

WORTHY OF...

HE WAS A PLANESWALKER, TOO.

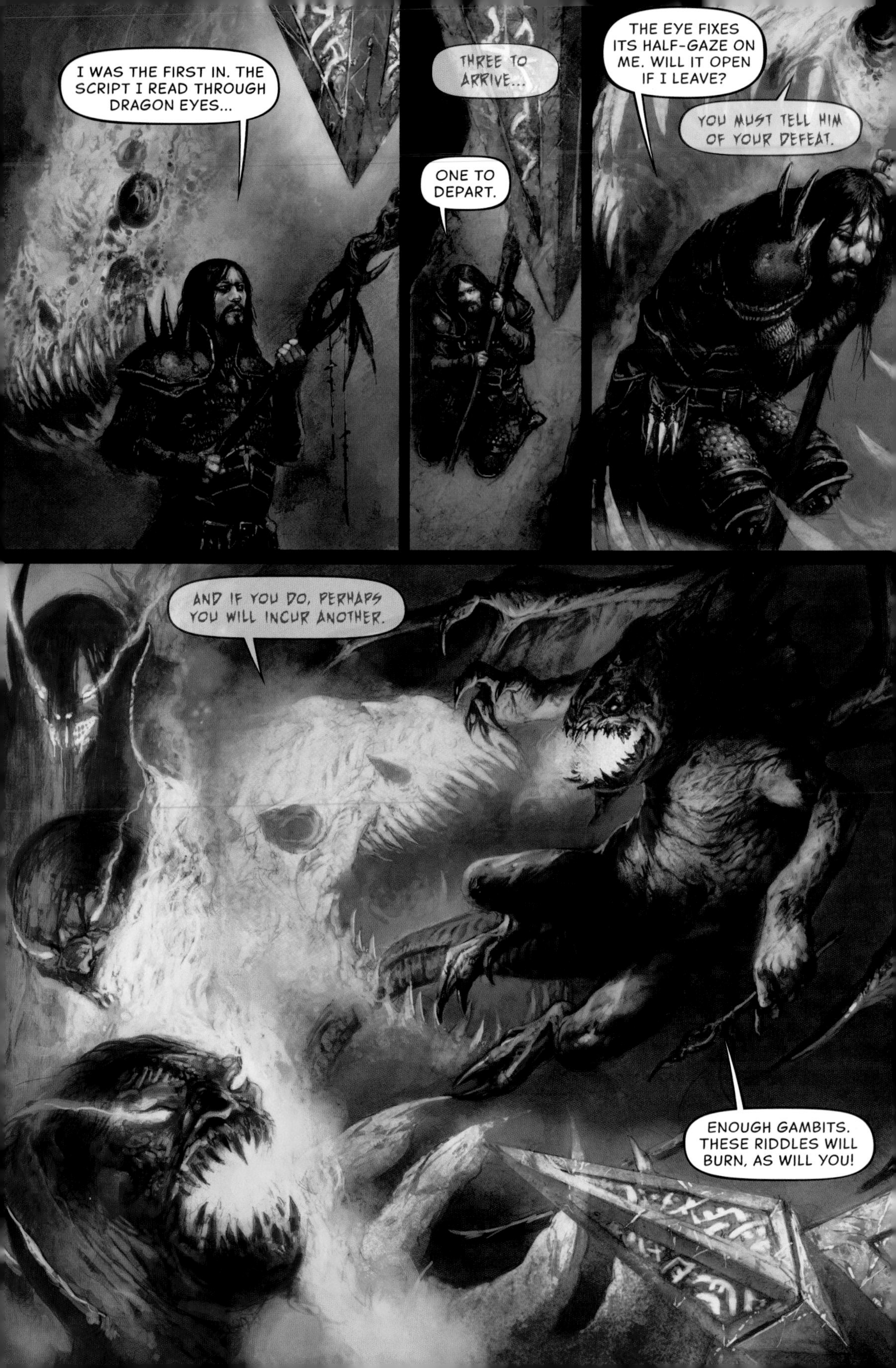

I WAS THE FIRST IN. THE SCRIPT I READ THROUGH DRAGON EYES...
THREE TO ARRIVE...
ONE TO DEPART.
THE EYE FIXES ITS HALF-GAZE ON ME. WILL IT OPEN IF I LEAVE?
YOU MUST TELL HIM OF YOUR DEFEAT.
AND IF YOU DO, PERHAPS YOU WILL INCUR ANOTHER.
ENOUGH GAMBITS. THESE RIDDLES WILL BURN, AS WILL YOU!

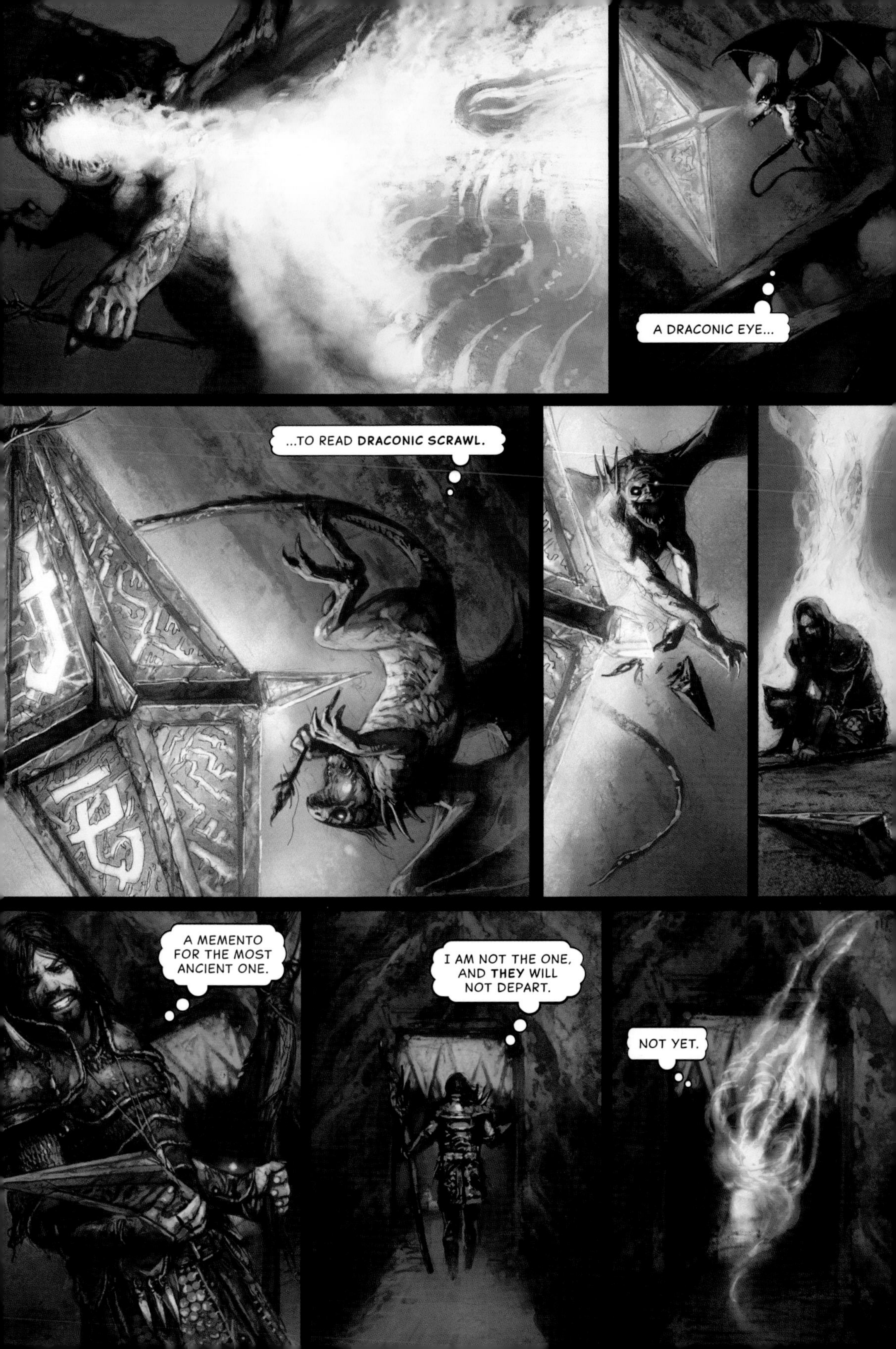
A DRACONIC EYE...
...TO READ DRACONIC SCRAWL.
A MEMENTO FOR THE MOST ANCIENT ONE.
I AM NOT THE ONE, AND THEY WILL NOT DEPART.
NOT YET.

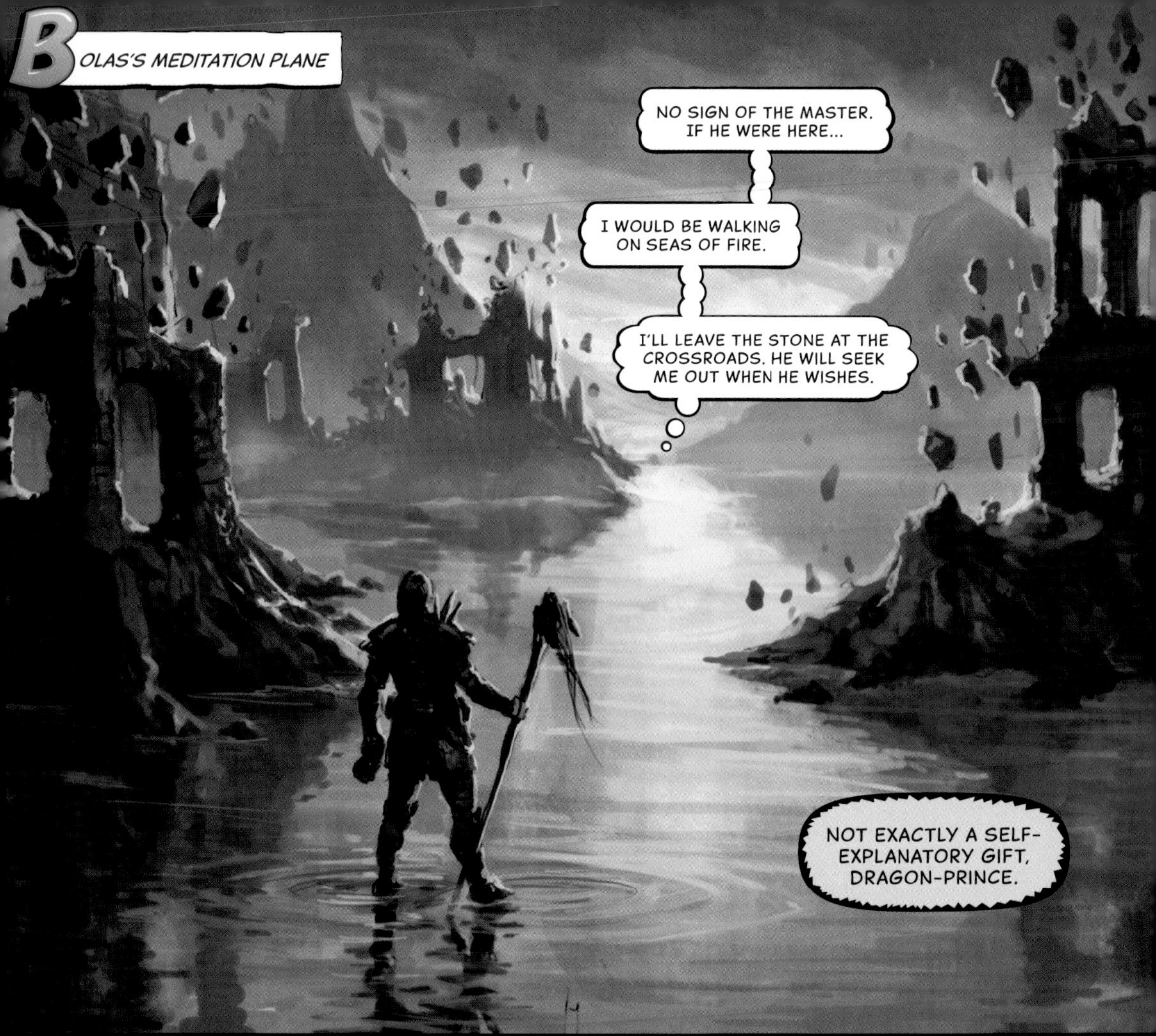
BOLAS'S MEDITATION PLANE
NO SIGN OF THE MASTER. IF HE WERE HERE...
I WOULD BE WALKING ON SEAS OF FIRE.
I'LL LEAVE THE STONE AT THE CROSSROADS. HE WILL SEEK ME OUT WHEN HE WISHES.
NOT EXACTLY A SELF-EXPLANATORY GIFT, DRAGON-PRINCE.

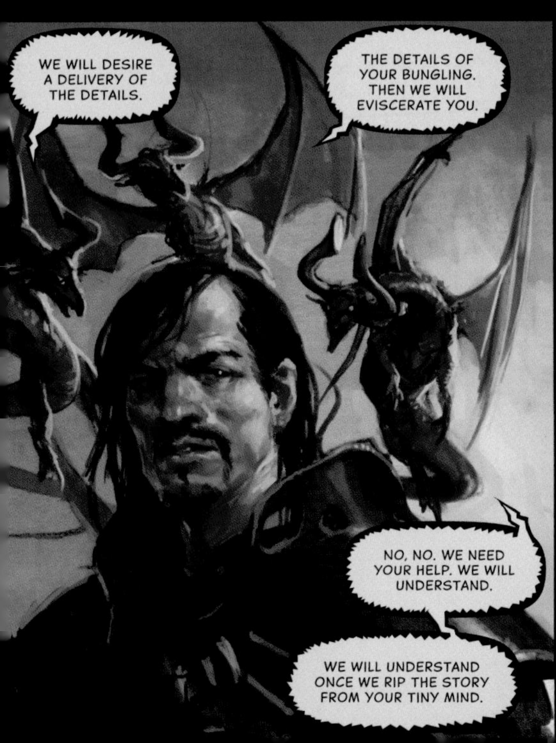
WE WILL DESIRE A DELIVERY OF THE DETAILS.
THE DETAILS OF YOUR BUNGLING. THEN WE WILL EVISCERATE YOU.
NO, NO. WE NEED YOUR HELP. WE WILL UNDERSTAND.
WE WILL UNDERSTAND ONCE WE RIP THE STORY FROM YOUR TINY MIND.

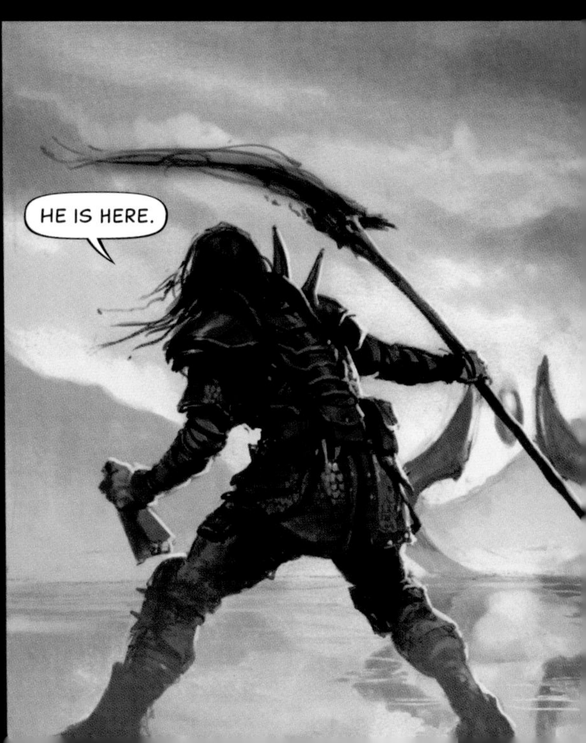
HE IS HERE.

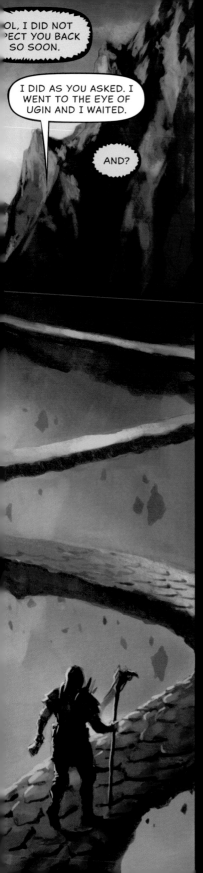

OL, I DID NOT ?ECT YOU BACK SO SOON.

I DID AS YOU ASKED. I WENT TO THE EYE OF UGIN AND I WAITED.

AND?

WEEKS, I LANGUISHED THERE. THE STONE HUMMED AND SHOOK AS THOUGH ALIVE. THERE WAS A VOICE, OR SPIRIT...

I SUBSISTED ON VERMIN.

MOCKED BY THE VERY WALLS.

MIND PULLED TAUT BY THE MUFFLED WHISPERS.

AND WHAT DO YOU HEAR NOW?

NOTHING. I THINK I HEAR NOTHING. NOTHING LIKE WHAT WAS THERE.

MAKE YOUR WAY TO THE DONJON.

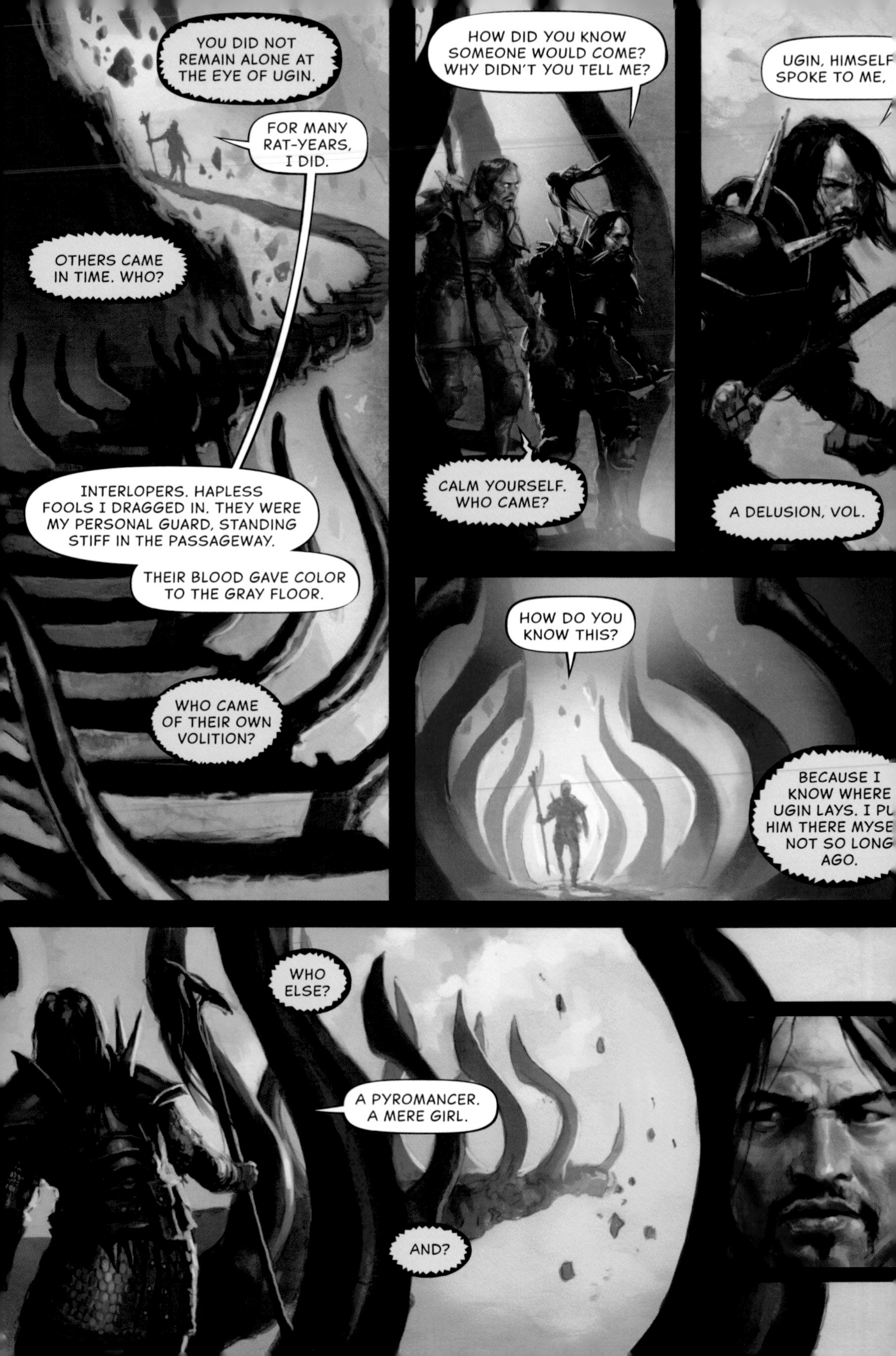
YOU DID NOT REMAIN ALONE AT THE EYE OF UGIN.
FOR MANY RAT-YEARS, I DID.
OTHERS CAME IN TIME. WHO?
INTERLOPERS. HAPLESS FOOLS I DRAGGED IN. THEY WERE MY PERSONAL GUARD, STANDING STIFF IN THE PASSAGEWAY.
THEIR BLOOD GAVE COLOR TO THE GRAY FLOOR.
WHO CAME OF THEIR OWN VOLITION?
HOW DID YOU KNOW SOMEONE WOULD COME? WHY DIDN'T YOU TELL ME?
CALM YOURSELF. WHO CAME?
UGIN, HIMSELF SPOKE TO ME,
A DELUSION, VOL.
HOW DO YOU KNOW THIS?
BECAUSE I KNOW WHERE UGIN LAYS. I PU HIM THERE MYSE NOT SO LONG AGO.
WHO ELSE?
A PYROMANCER. A MERE GIRL.
AND?

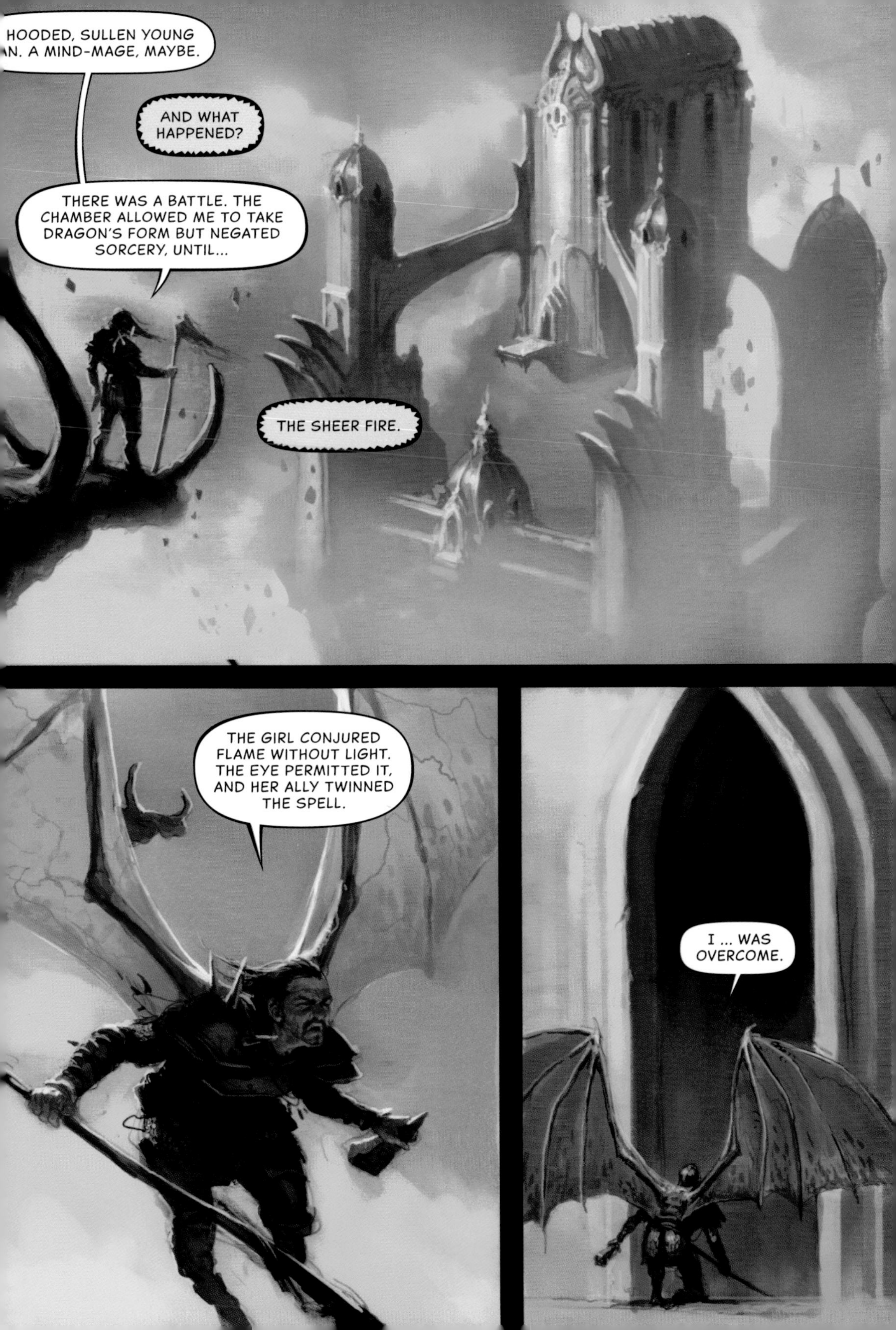
HOODED, SULLEN YOUNG N. A MIND-MAGE, MAYBE.
AND WHAT HAPPENED?
THERE WAS A BATTLE. THE CHAMBER ALLOWED ME TO TAKE DRAGON'S FORM BUT NEGATED SORCERY, UNTIL...
THE SHEER FIRE.
THE GIRL CONJURED FLAME WITHOUT LIGHT. THE EYE PERMITTED IT, AND HER ALLY TWINNED THE SPELL.
I ... WAS OVERCOME.

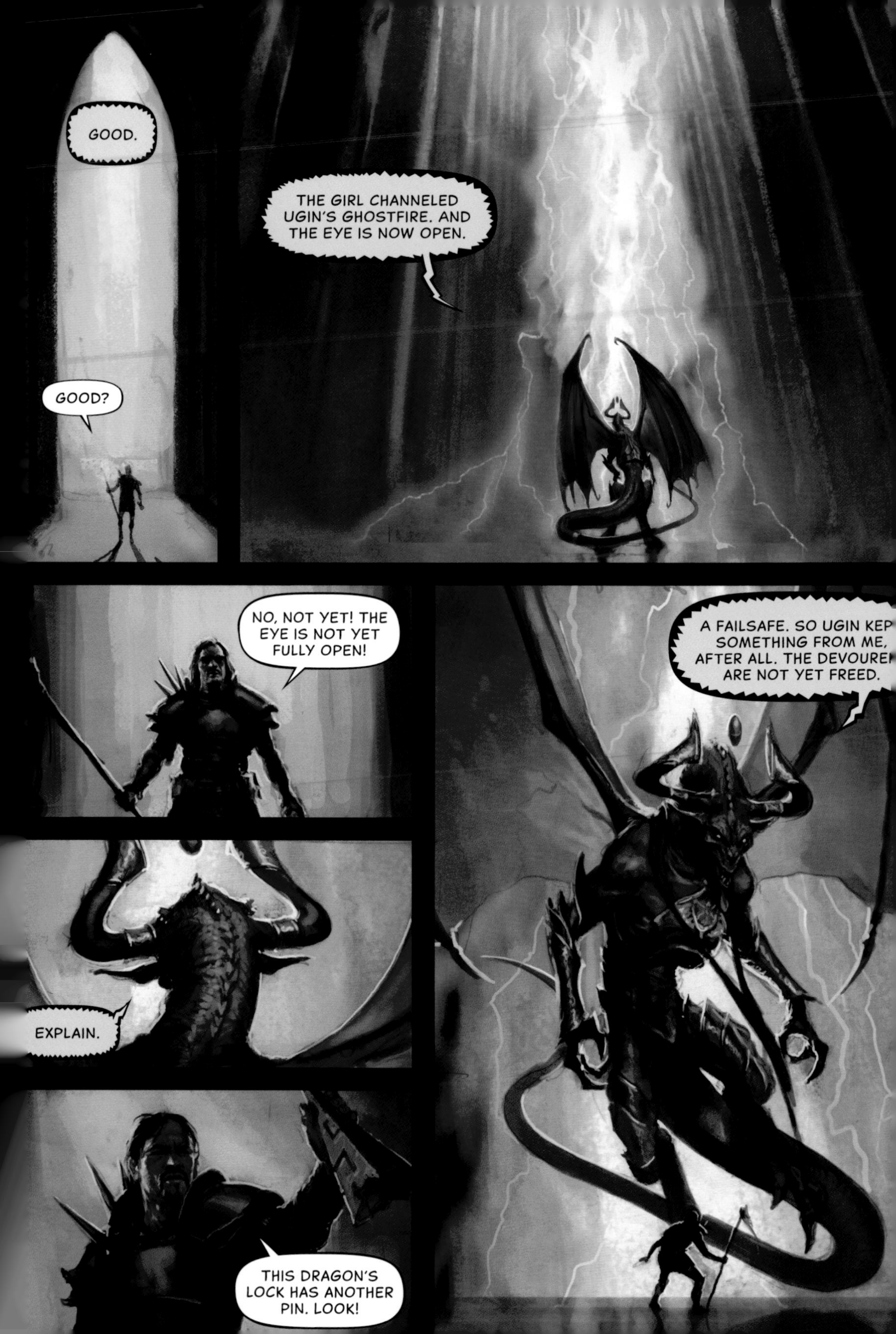
GOOD.
GOOD?
THE GIRL CHANNELED UGIN'S GHOSTFIRE. AND THE EYE IS NOW OPEN.
NO, NOT YET! THE EYE IS NOT YET FULLY OPEN!
EXPLAIN.
THIS DRAGON'S LOCK HAS ANOTHER PIN. LOOK!
A FAILSAFE. SO UGIN KEP SOMETHING FROM ME, AFTER ALL. THE DEVOURE ARE NOT YET FREED.

THANK YOU, VOL.
YOU MAY LEAVE.

?? YOU SENT ME TO
GUARD THE EYE OF
GIN AND I FAILED. IS
HIS FORGIVENESS?

NO, THIS IS DISMISSAL. I
DIDN'T SEND YOU TO ENSURE
NO ONE ENTERED THE EYE. I SENT
YOU TO ENSURE THEY DID. DO YOU
THINK IT A COINCIDENCE THAT TWO
PLANESWALKERS ARRIVED THERE
WHEN THEY DID?

YOU SENT ME
TO FESTER?
AS A HELPLESS
PROXY?

YOU KNEW
THEY WOULD
COME?

NEW THE GIRL
ULD COME. THE
HER—I HAD TO
AY THE ODDS.

WHAT OF THE
LOCK? WILL THE
EYE BE FULLY
OPENED?

WE WILL SEE WHICH
OF THE OTHERS ANSWERS
UGIN'S CALL. BE AT EASE,
SARKHAN VOL...

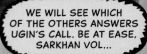

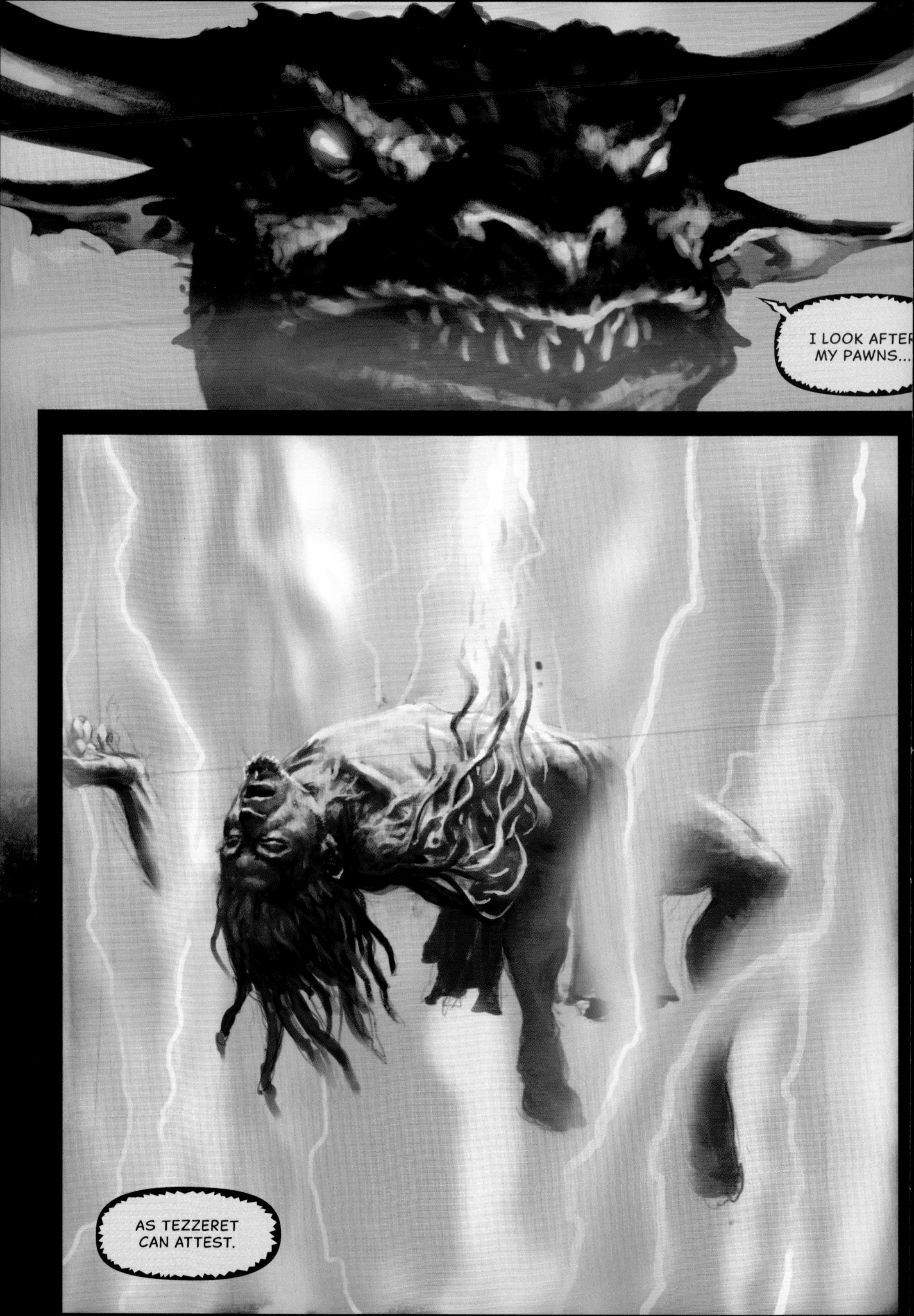
I LOOK AFTER MY PAWNS...
AS TEZZERET CAN ATTEST.

The Wild Son

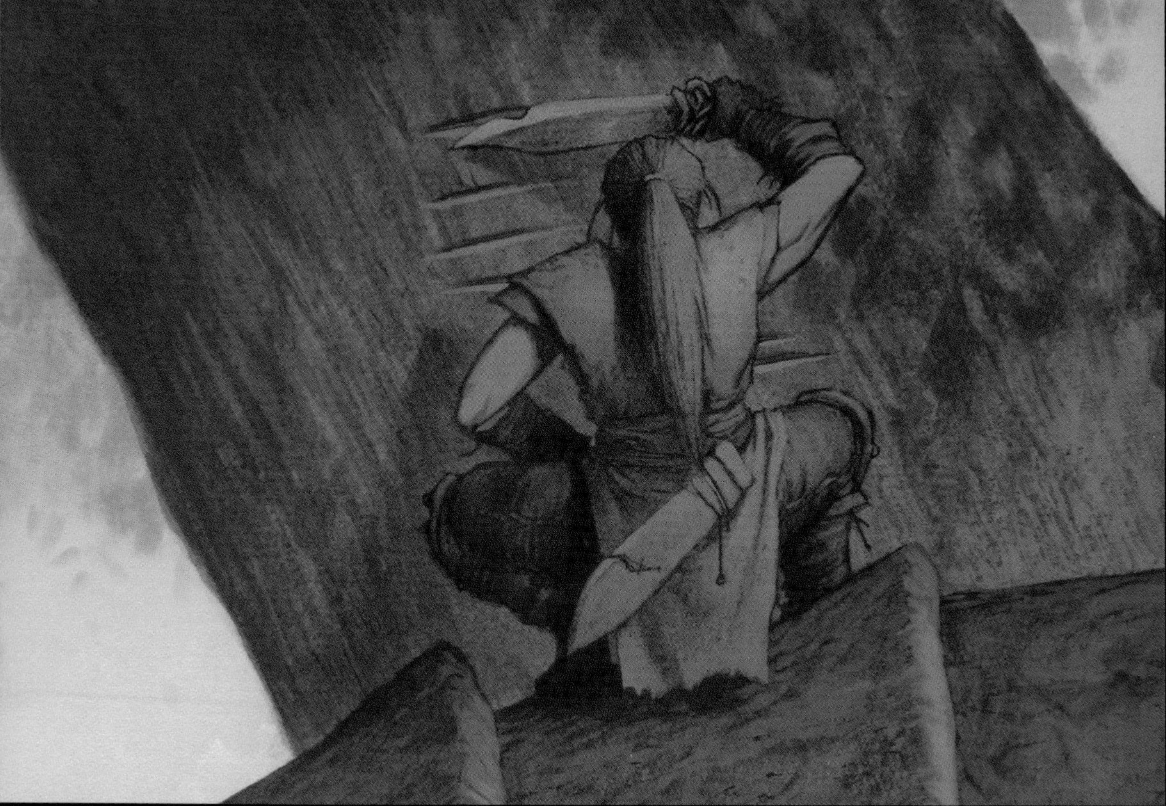

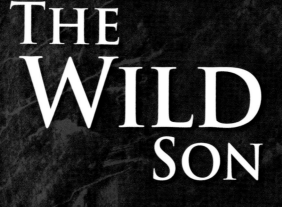

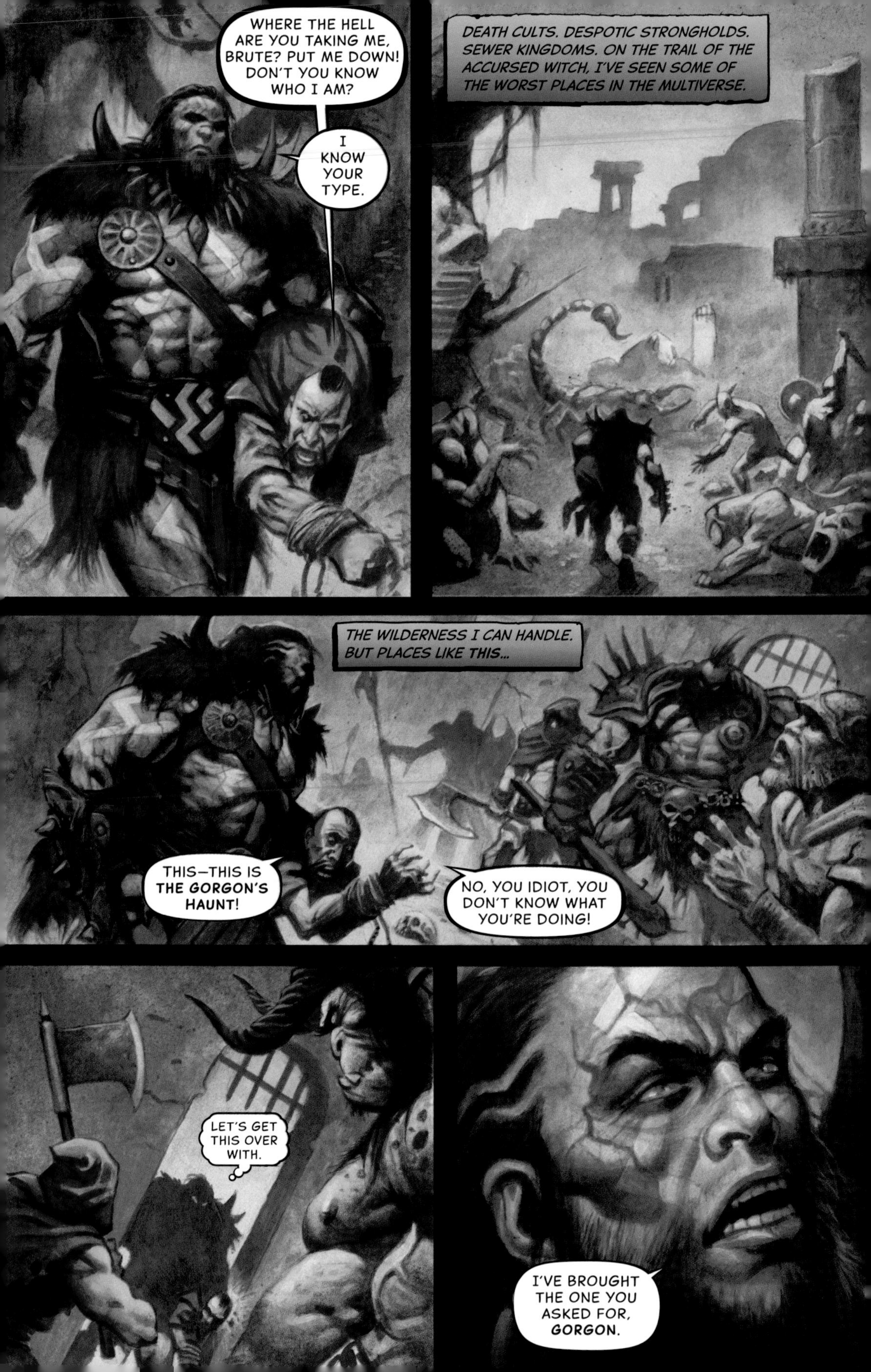
WHERE THE HELL ARE YOU TAKING ME, BRUTE? PUT ME DOWN! DON'T YOU KNOW WHO I AM?
I KNOW YOUR TYPE.
DEATH CULTS. DESPOTIC STRONGHOLDS. SEWER KINGDOMS. ON THE TRAIL OF THE ACCURSED WITCH, I'VE SEEN SOME OF THE WORST PLACES IN THE MULTIVERSE.
THE WILDERNESS I CAN HANDLE. BUT PLACES LIKE THIS...
THIS—THIS IS THE GORGON'S HAUNT!
NO, YOU IDIOT, YOU DON'T KNOW WHAT YOU'RE DOING!
LET'S GET THIS OVER WITH.
I'VE BROUGHT THE ONE YOU ASKED FOR, GORGON.

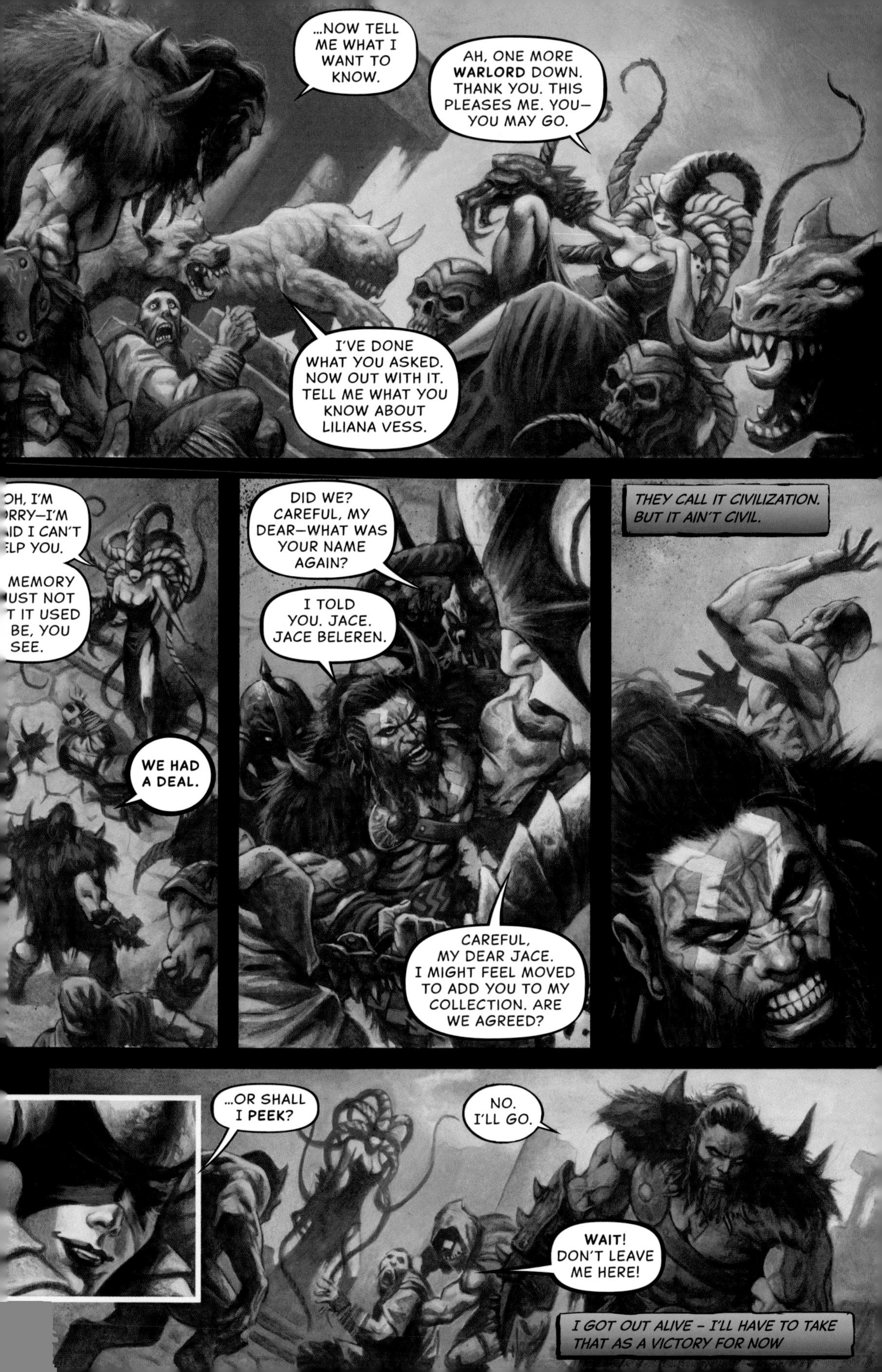

...NOW TELL ME WHAT I WANT TO KNOW.
AH, ONE MORE **WARLORD** DOWN. THANK YOU. THIS PLEASES ME. YOU—YOU MAY GO.
I'VE DONE WHAT YOU ASKED. NOW OUT WITH IT. TELL ME WHAT YOU KNOW ABOUT LILIANA VESS.
OH, I'M RRY—I'M ID I CAN'T ELP YOU.
MEMORY UST NOT T IT USED BE, YOU SEE.
WE HAD A DEAL.
DID WE? CAREFUL, MY DEAR—WHAT WAS YOUR NAME AGAIN?
I TOLD YOU. JACE. JACE BELEREN.
CAREFUL, MY DEAR JACE. I MIGHT FEEL MOVED TO ADD YOU TO MY COLLECTION. ARE WE AGREED?
THEY CALL IT CIVILIZATION. BUT IT AIN'T CIVIL.
...OR SHALL I **PEEK**?
NO. I'LL GO.
WAIT! DON'T LEAVE ME HERE!
I GOT OUT ALIVE – I'LL HAVE TO TAKE THAT AS A VICTORY FOR NOW

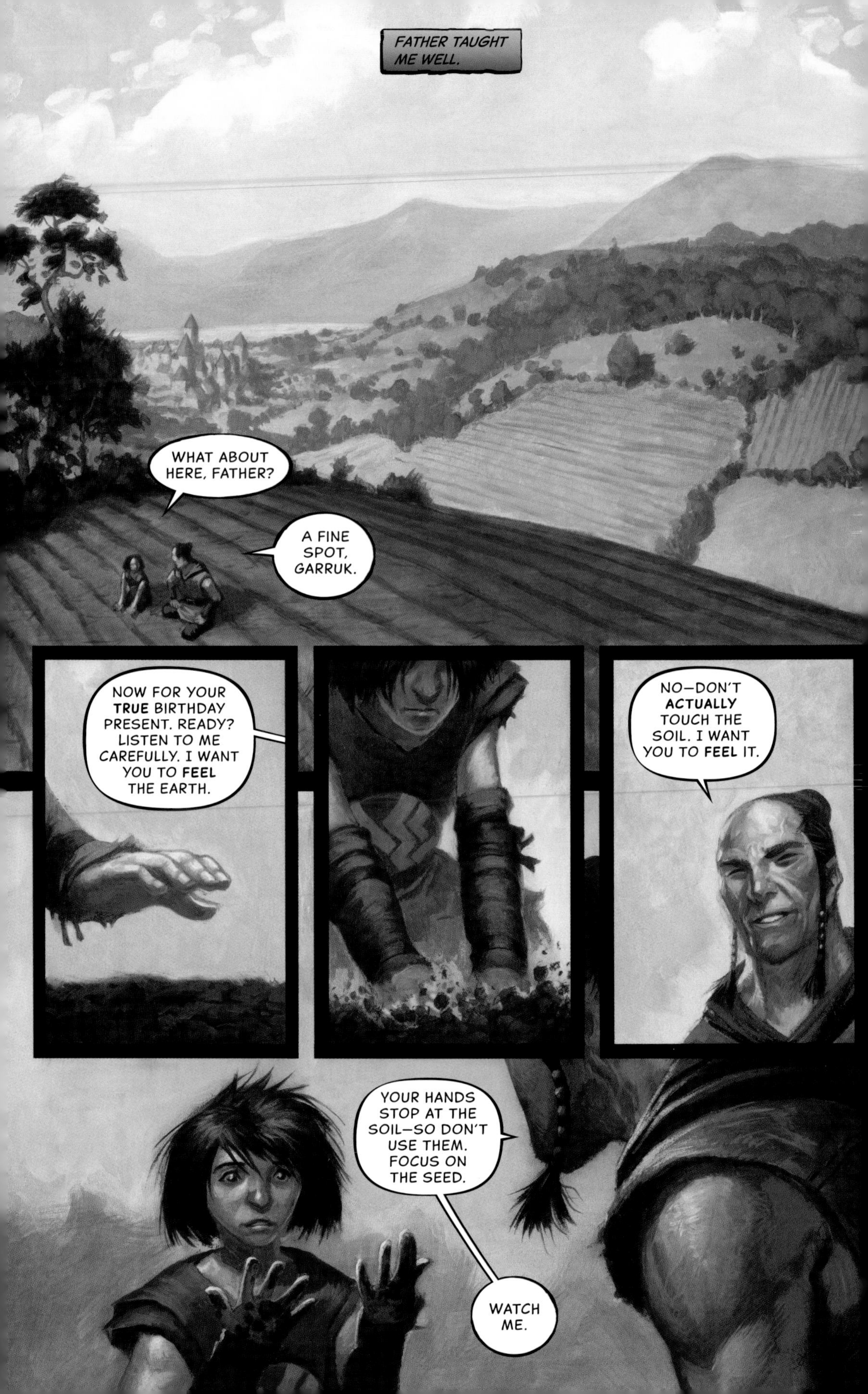
FATHER TAUGHT ME WELL.
WHAT ABOUT HERE, FATHER?
A FINE SPOT, GARRUK.
NOW FOR YOUR **TRUE** BIRTHDAY PRESENT. READY? LISTEN TO ME CAREFULLY. I WANT YOU TO **FEEL** THE EARTH.
NO—DON'T **ACTUALLY** TOUCH THE SOIL. I WANT YOU TO **FEEL** IT.
YOUR HANDS STOP AT THE SOIL—SO DON'T USE THEM. FOCUS ON THE SEED.
WATCH ME.

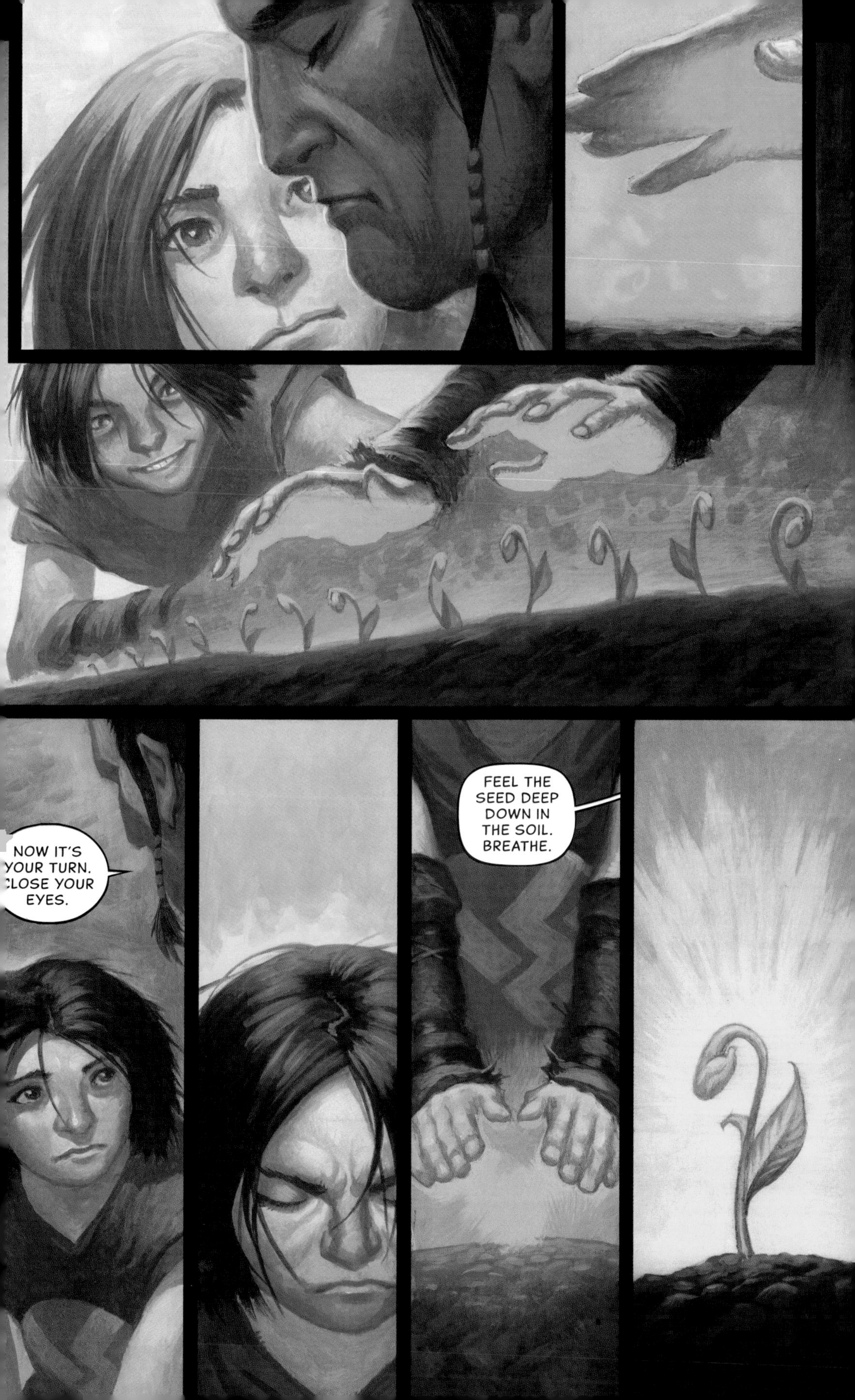
NOW IT'S YOUR TURN. CLOSE YOUR EYES.
FEEL THE SEED DEEP DOWN IN THE SOIL. BREATHE.

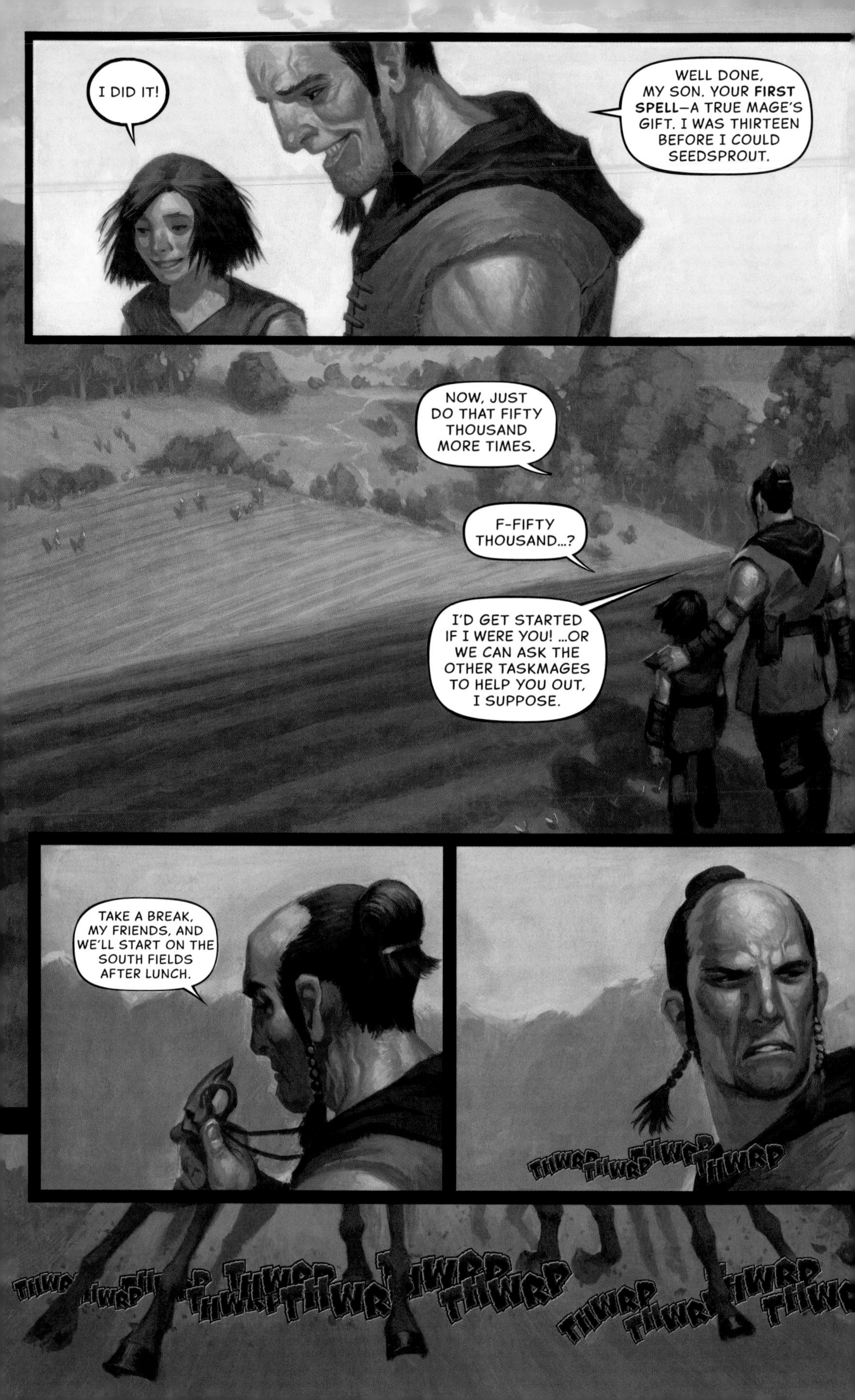
I DID IT!
WELL DONE, MY SON. YOUR **FIRST SPELL**—A TRUE MAGE'S GIFT. I WAS THIRTEEN BEFORE I COULD SEEDSPROUT.
NOW, JUST DO THAT FIFTY THOUSAND MORE TIMES.
F-FIFTY THOUSAND...?
I'D GET STARTED IF I WERE YOU! ...OR WE CAN ASK THE OTHER TASKMAGES TO HELP YOU OUT, I SUPPOSE.
TAKE A BREAK, MY FRIENDS, AND WE'LL START ON THE SOUTH FIELDS AFTER LUNCH.
THWRP THWRP THWRP THWRP
THWRP THWRP THWRP THWRP THWRP THWRP THWRP

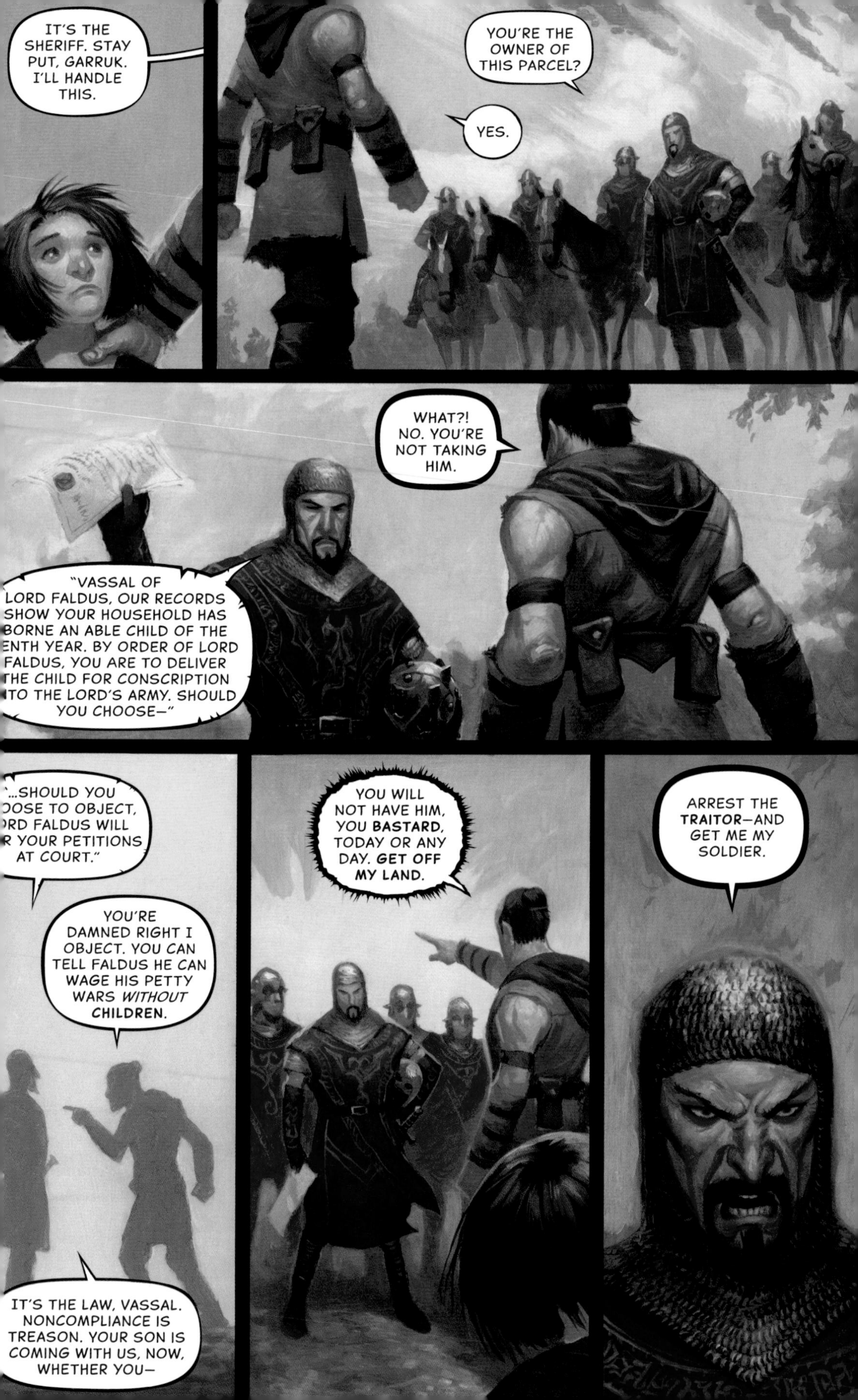
IT'S THE SHERIFF. STAY PUT, GARRUK. I'LL HANDLE THIS.
YOU'RE THE OWNER OF THIS PARCEL?
YES.
WHAT?! NO. YOU'RE NOT TAKING HIM.
"VASSAL OF LORD FALDUS, OUR RECORDS SHOW YOUR HOUSEHOLD HAS BORNE AN ABLE CHILD OF THE ENTH YEAR. BY ORDER OF LORD FALDUS, YOU ARE TO DELIVER THE CHILD FOR CONSCRIPTION TO THE LORD'S ARMY. SHOULD YOU CHOOSE—"
"...SHOULD YOU OOSE TO OBJECT, ORD FALDUS WILL R YOUR PETITIONS AT COURT."
YOU'RE DAMNED RIGHT I OBJECT. YOU CAN TELL FALDUS HE CAN WAGE HIS PETTY WARS WITHOUT CHILDREN.
IT'S THE LAW, VASSAL. NONCOMPLIANCE IS TREASON. YOUR SON IS COMING WITH US, NOW, WHETHER YOU—
YOU WILL NOT HAVE HIM, YOU BASTARD, TODAY OR ANY DAY. GET OFF MY LAND.
ARREST THE TRAITOR—AND GET ME MY SOLDIER.

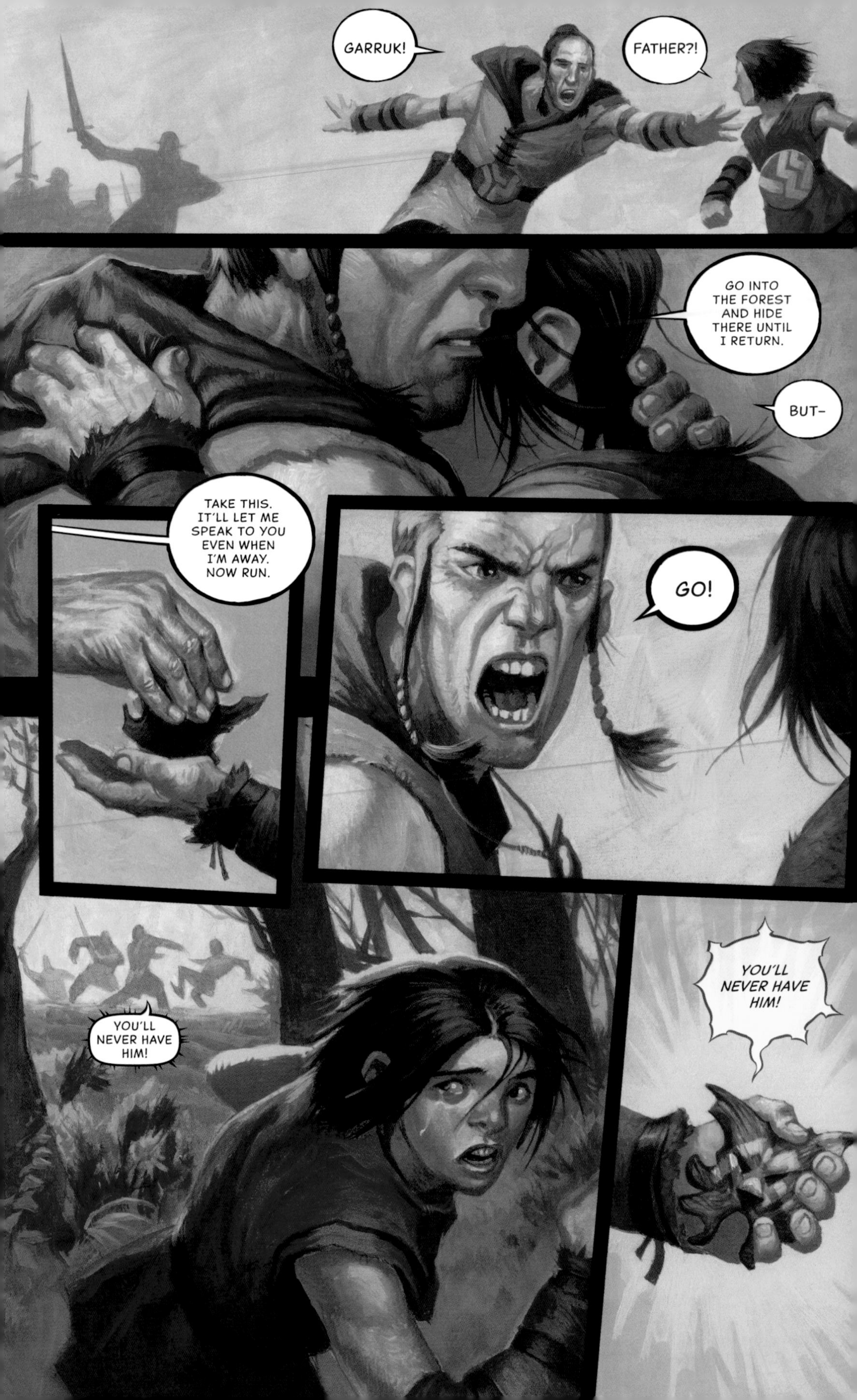
GARRUK!
FATHER?!
GO INTO THE FOREST AND HIDE THERE UNTIL I RETURN.
BUT–
TAKE THIS. IT'LL LET ME SPEAK TO YOU EVEN WHEN I'M AWAY. NOW RUN.
GO!
YOU'LL NEVER HAVE HIM!
YOU'LL NEVER HAVE HIM!

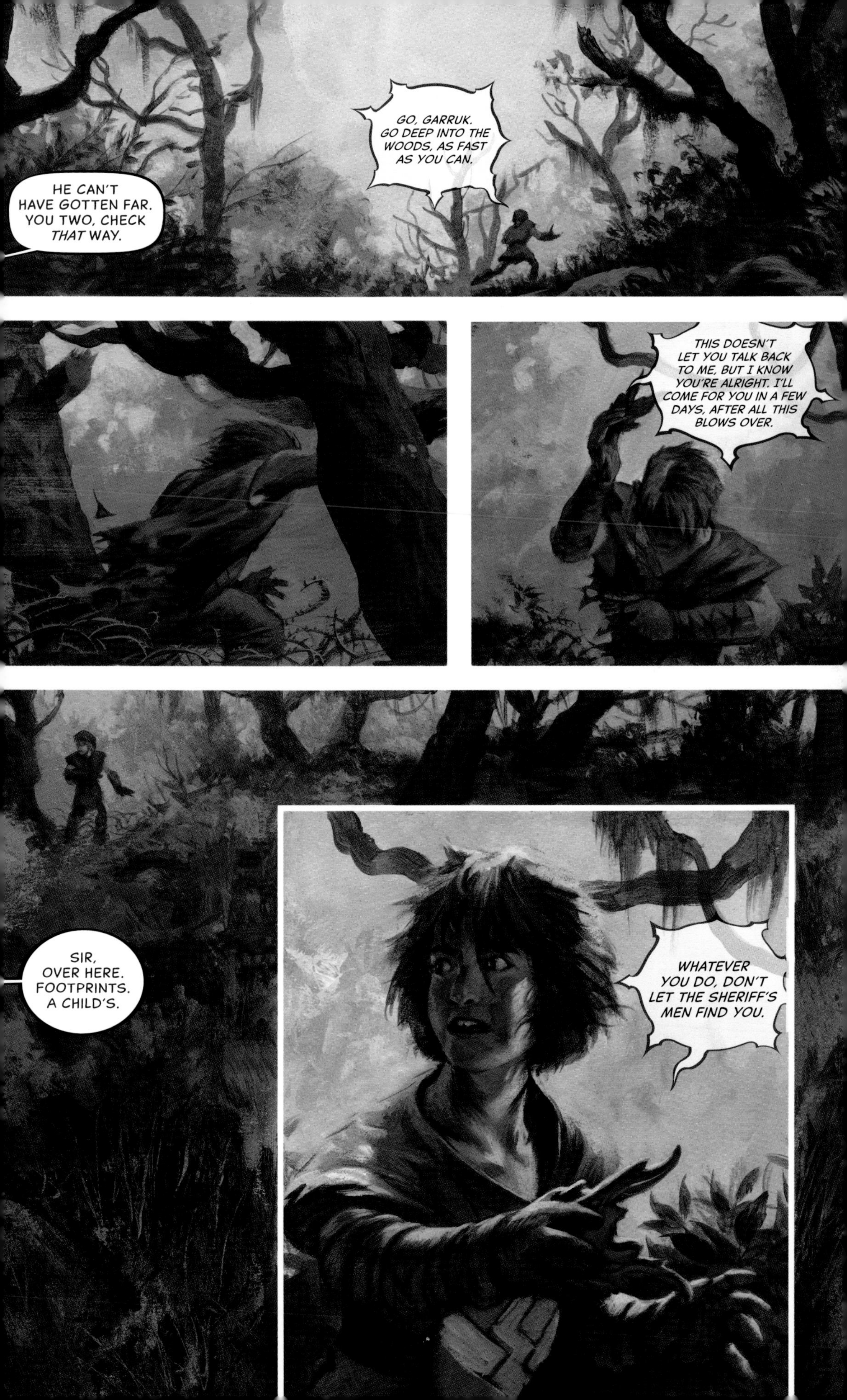
GO, GARRUK. GO DEEP INTO THE WOODS, AS FAST AS YOU CAN.
HE CAN'T HAVE GOTTEN FAR. YOU TWO, CHECK *THAT* WAY.
THIS DOESN'T LET YOU TALK BACK TO ME, BUT I KNOW YOU'RE ALRIGHT. I'LL COME FOR YOU IN A FEW DAYS, AFTER ALL THIS BLOWS OVER.
SIR, OVER HERE. FOOTPRINTS. A CHILD'S.
WHATEVER YOU DO, DON'T LET THE SHERIFF'S MEN FIND YOU.

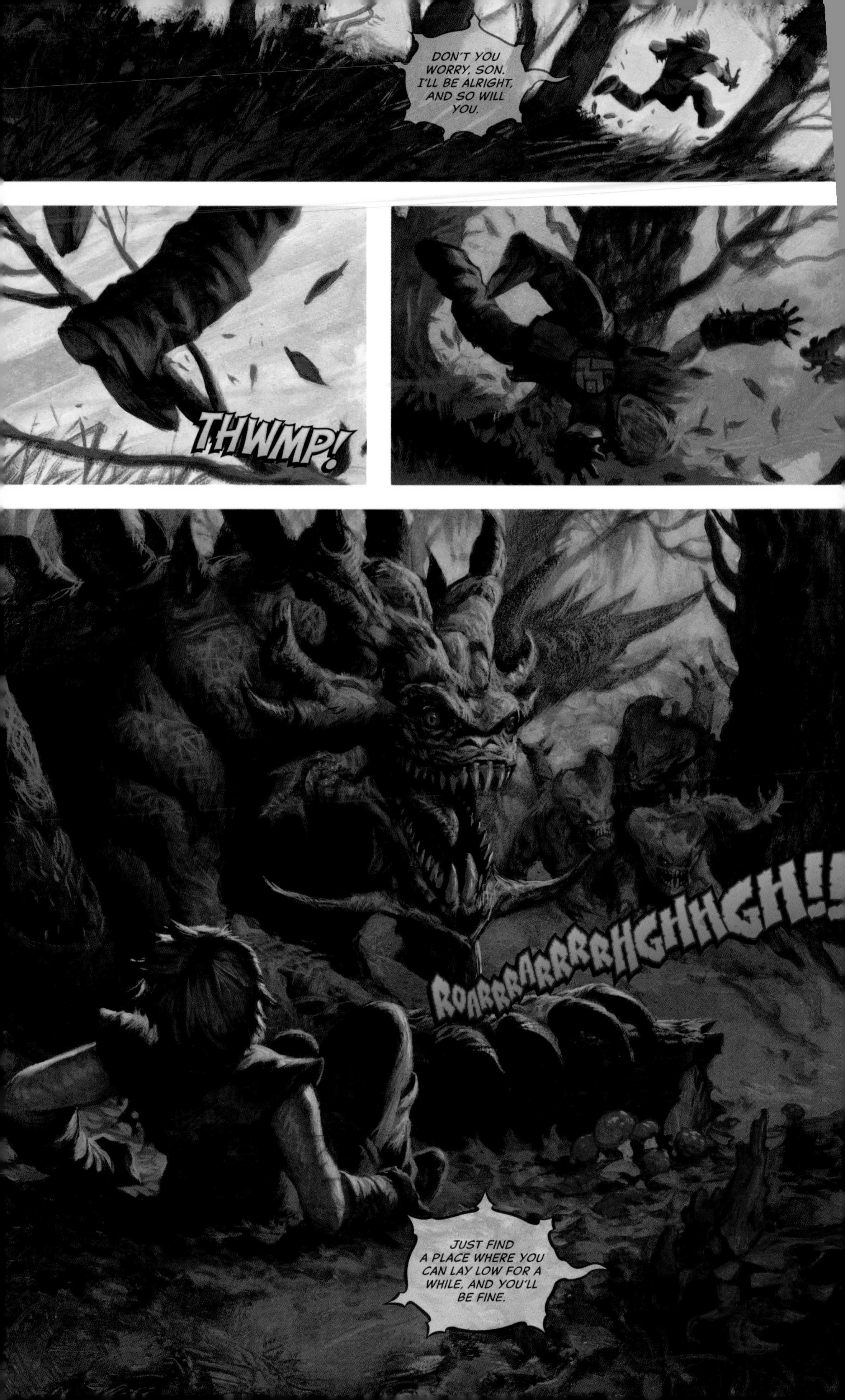
DON'T YOU WORRY, SON. I'LL BE ALRIGHT, AND SO WILL YOU.
THWMP!
ROARRRARRRRHGHHGH!!
JUST FIND A PLACE WHERE YOU CAN LAY LOW FOR A WHILE, AND YOU'LL BE FINE.

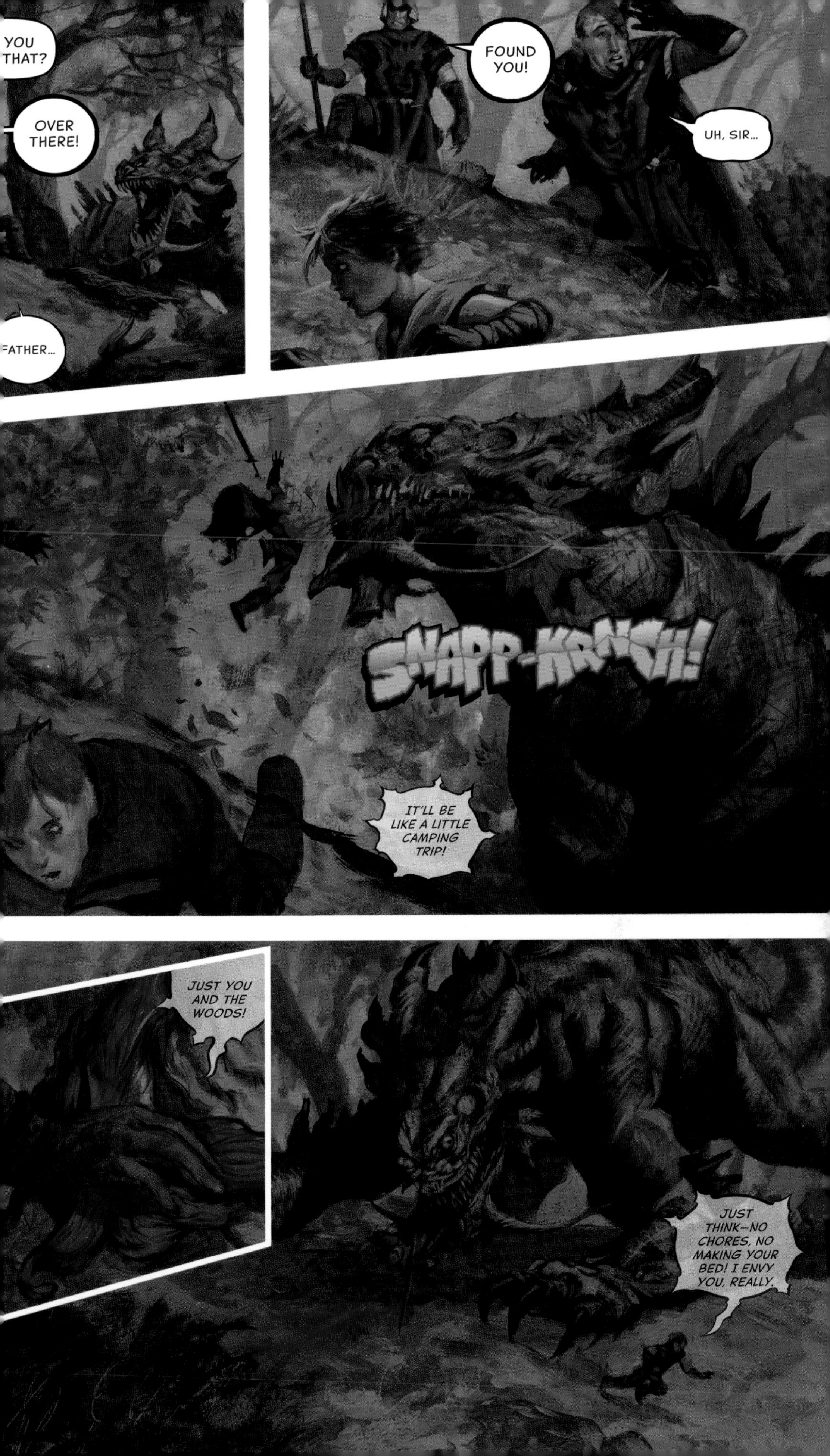
YOU
THAT?
OVER
THERE!
FATHER...
FOUND
YOU!
UH, SIR...
SNAPP-KRNCH!
IT'LL BE
LIKE A LITTLE
CAMPING
TRIP!
JUST YOU
AND THE
WOODS!
JUST
THINK—NO
CHORES, NO
MAKING YOUR
BED! I ENVY
YOU, REALLY.

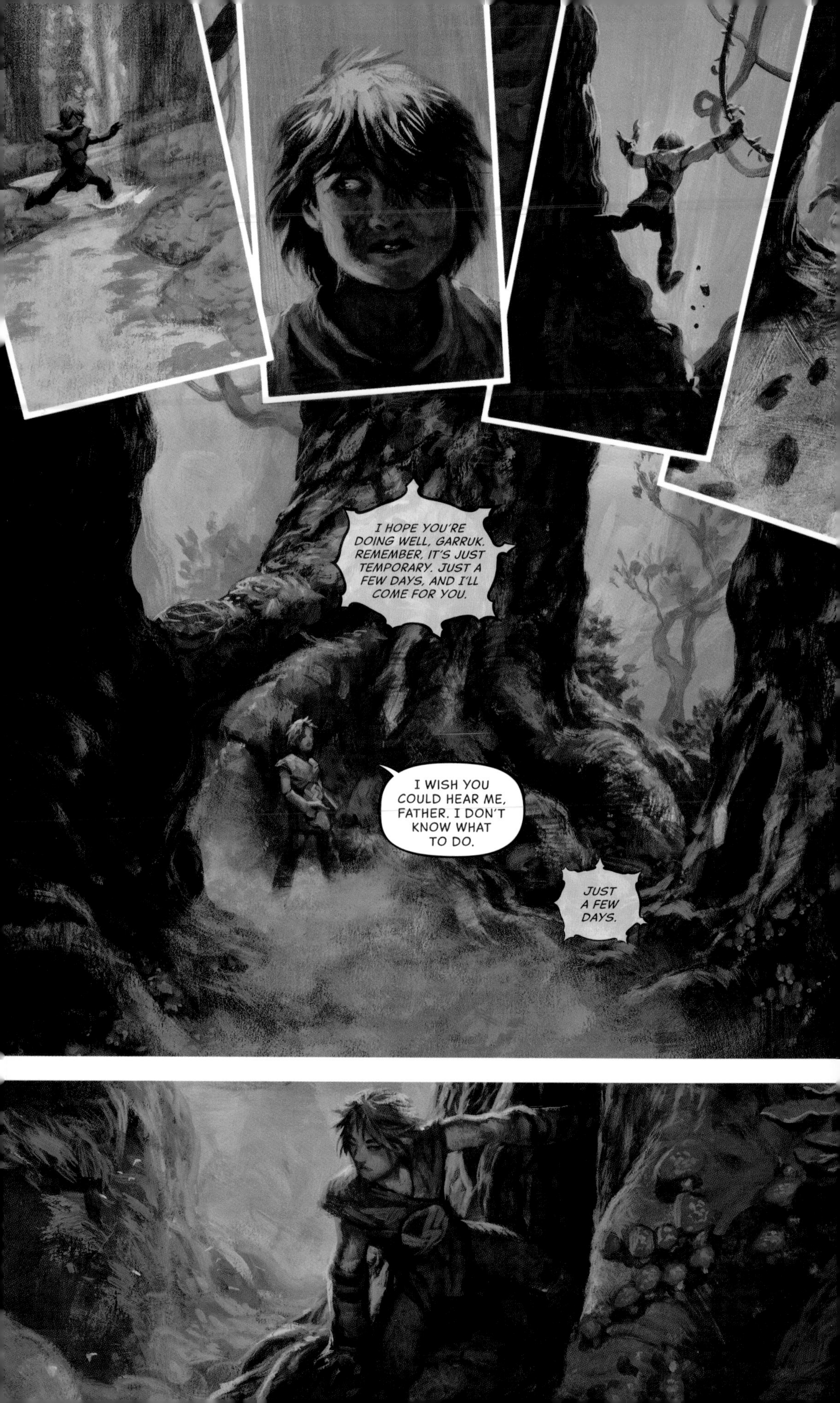
I HOPE YOU'RE DOING WELL, GARRUK. REMEMBER, IT'S JUST TEMPORARY. JUST A FEW DAYS, AND I'LL COME FOR YOU.
I WISH YOU COULD HEAR ME, FATHER. I DON'T KNOW WHAT TO DO.
JUST A FEW DAYS.

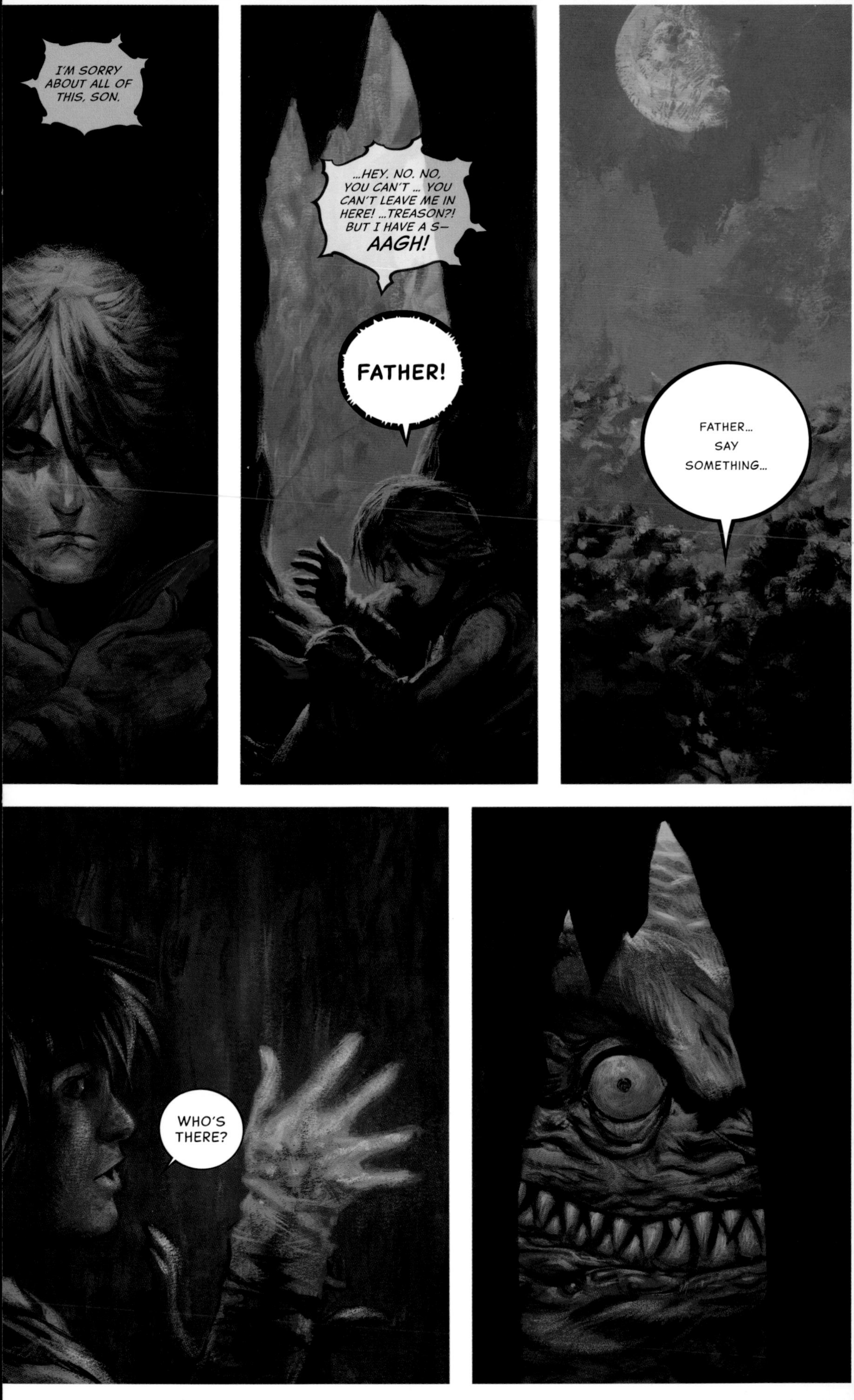
I'M SORRY ABOUT ALL OF THIS, SON.
...HEY. NO. NO, YOU CAN'T ... YOU CAN'T LEAVE ME IN HERE! ...TREASON?! BUT I HAVE A S—
AAGH!
FATHER!
FATHER... SAY SOMETHING...
WHO'S THERE?

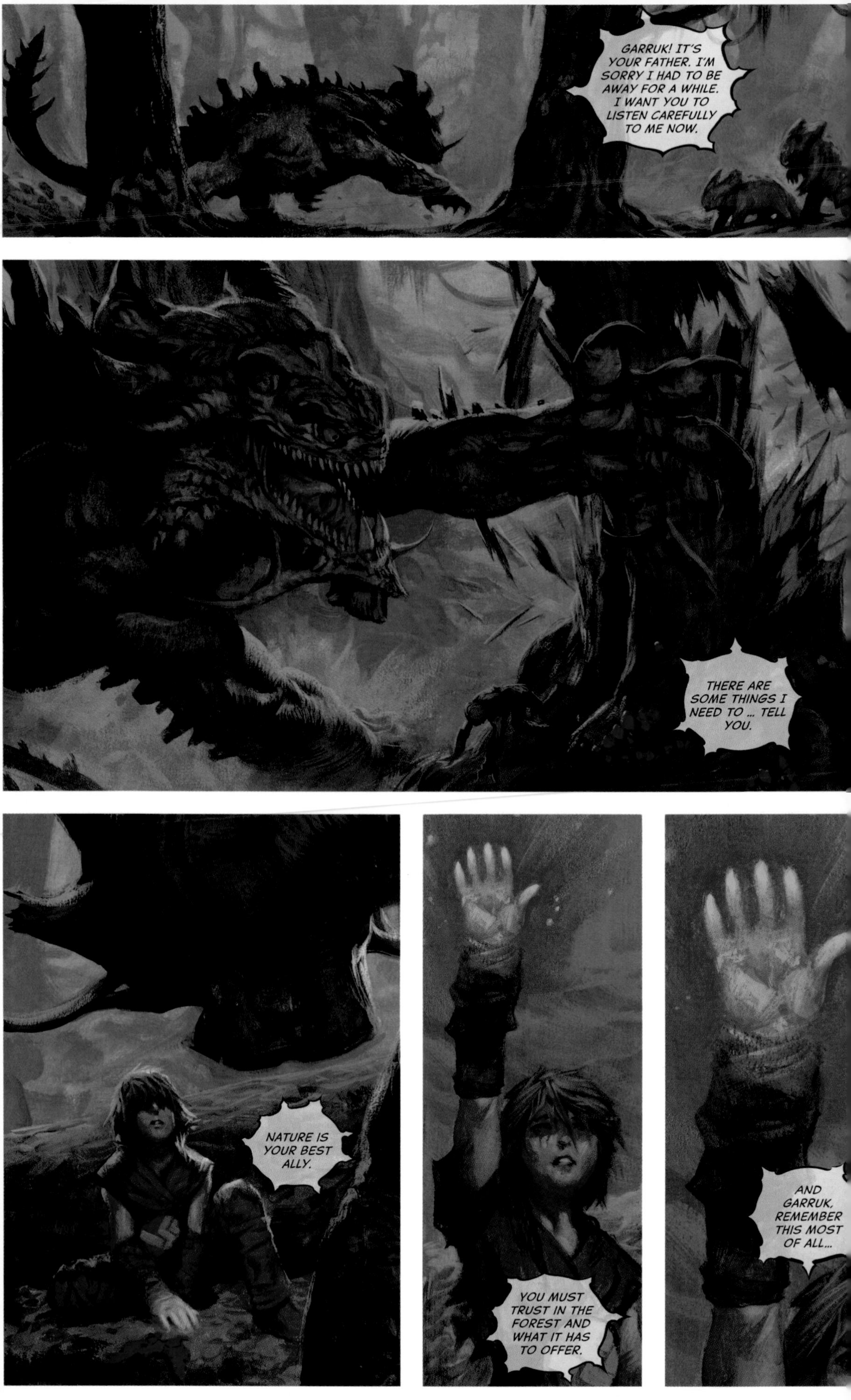
GARRUK! IT'S YOUR FATHER. I'M SORRY I HAD TO BE AWAY FOR A WHILE. I WANT YOU TO LISTEN CAREFULLY TO ME NOW.
THERE ARE SOME THINGS I NEED TO ... TELL YOU.
NATURE IS YOUR BEST ALLY.
YOU MUST TRUST IN THE FOREST AND WHAT IT HAS TO OFFER.
AND GARRUK, REMEMBER THIS MOST OF ALL...

ANYONE WHO CAN SPEAK CAN LIE.

EXPECT DECEIT.

I LOVE YOU, SON.

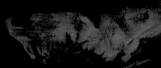

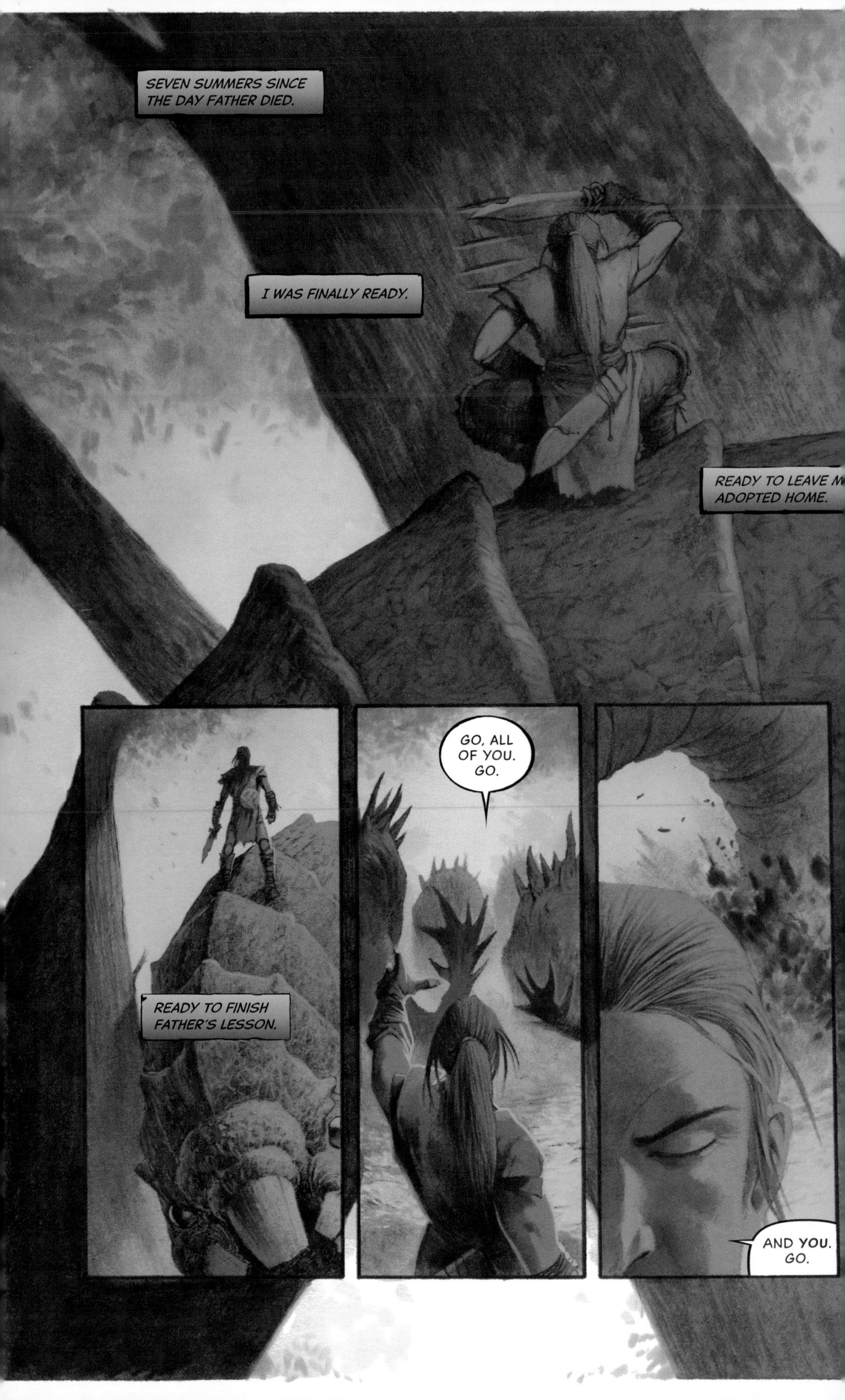
SEVEN SUMMERS SINCE THE DAY FATHER DIED.
I WAS FINALLY READY.
READY TO LEAVE M
ADOPTED HOME.
READY TO FINISH FATHER'S LESSON.
GO, ALL OF YOU. GO.
AND YOU. GO.

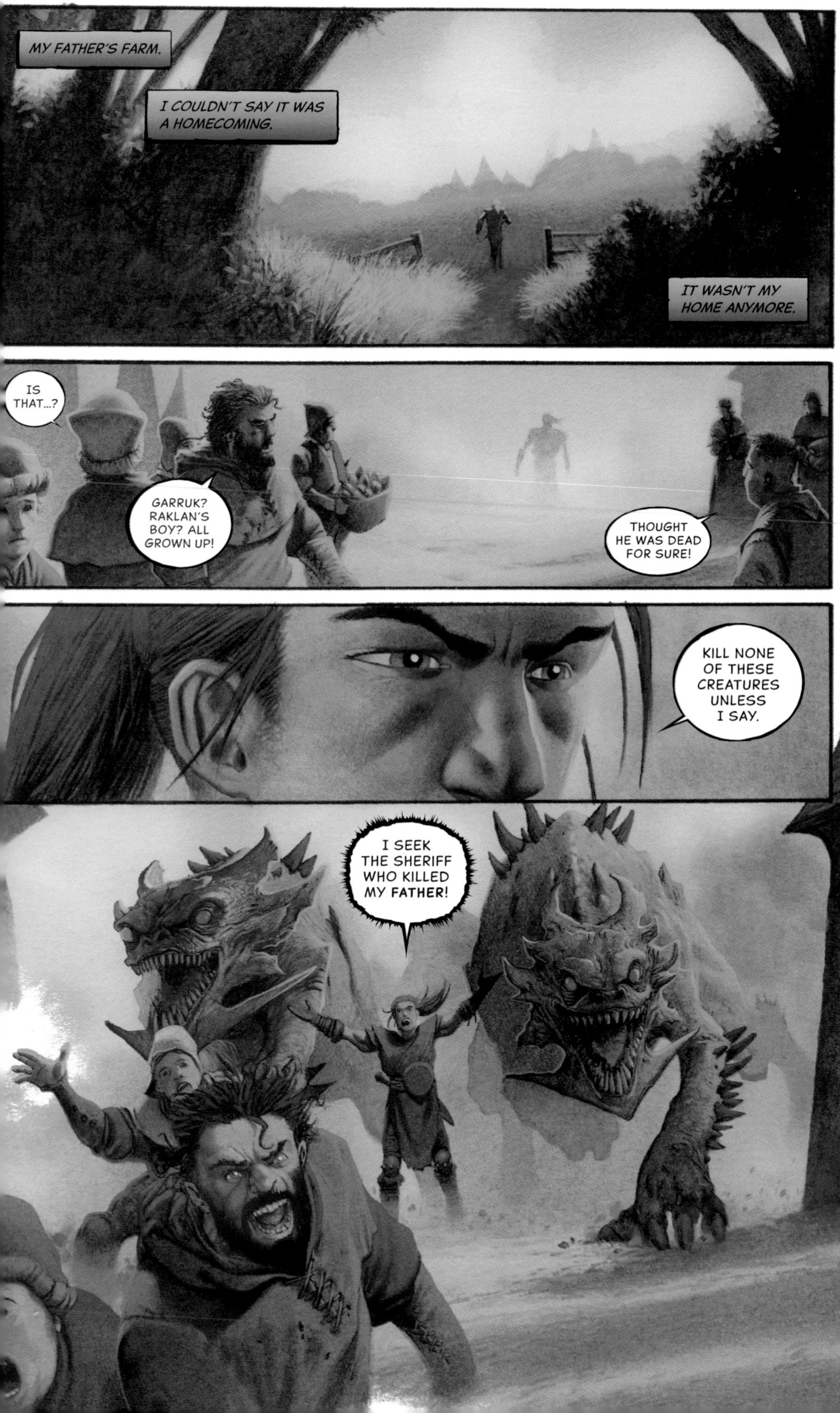
MY FATHER'S FARM.
I COULDN'T SAY IT WAS A HOMECOMING.
IT WASN'T MY HOME ANYMORE.
IS THAT...?
GARRUK? RAKLAN'S BOY? ALL GROWN UP!
THOUGHT HE WAS DEAD FOR SURE!
KILL NONE OF THESE CREATURES UNLESS I SAY.
I SEEK THE SHERIFF WHO KILLED MY **FATHER**!

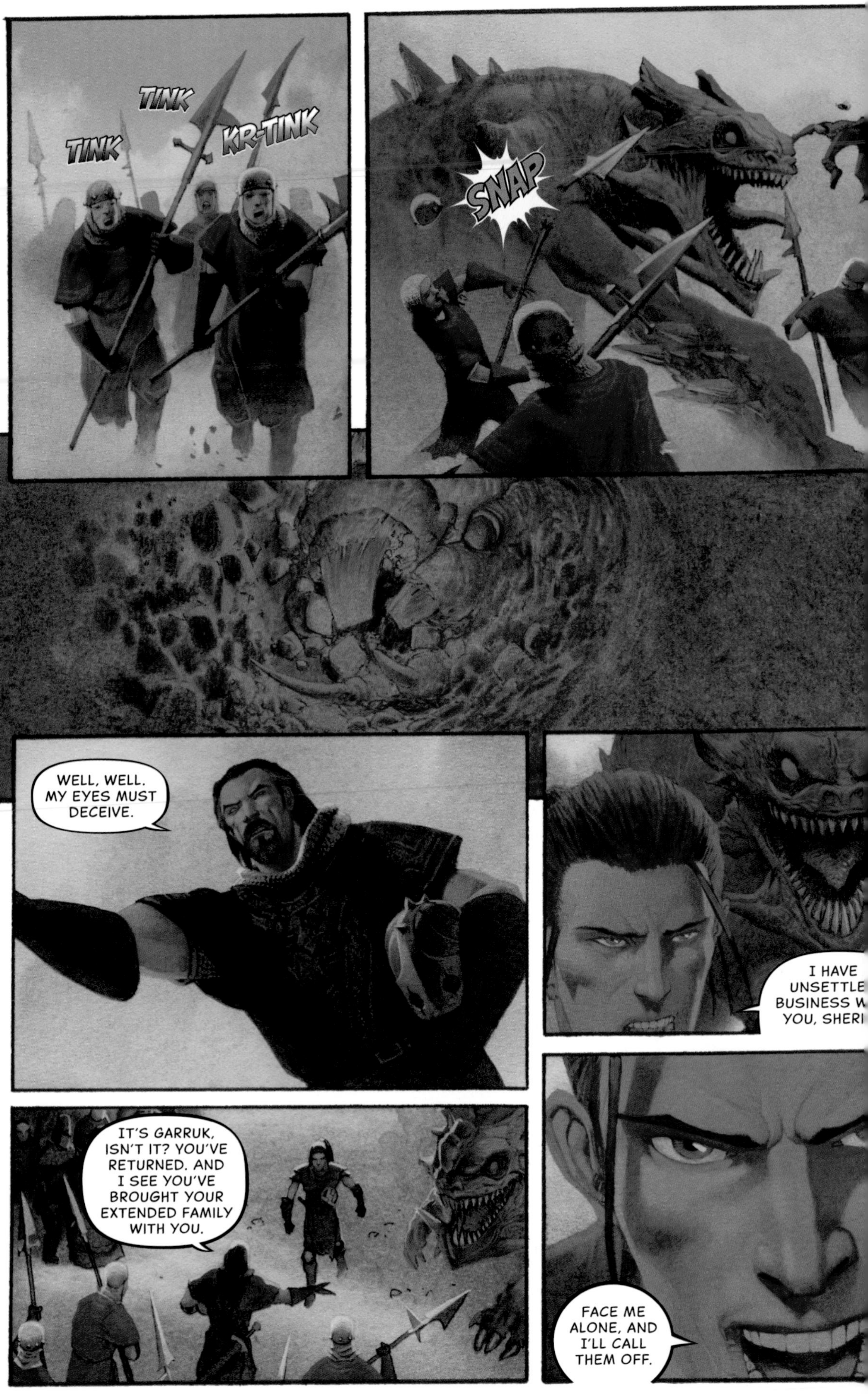
TINK
TINK
KR-TINK
SNAP
WELL, WELL. MY EYES MUST DECEIVE.
I HAVE UNSETTLE BUSINESS W YOU, SHERI
IT'S GARRUK, ISN'T IT? YOU'VE RETURNED. AND I SEE YOU'VE BROUGHT YOUR EXTENDED FAMILY WITH YOU.
FACE ME ALONE, AND I'LL CALL THEM OFF.

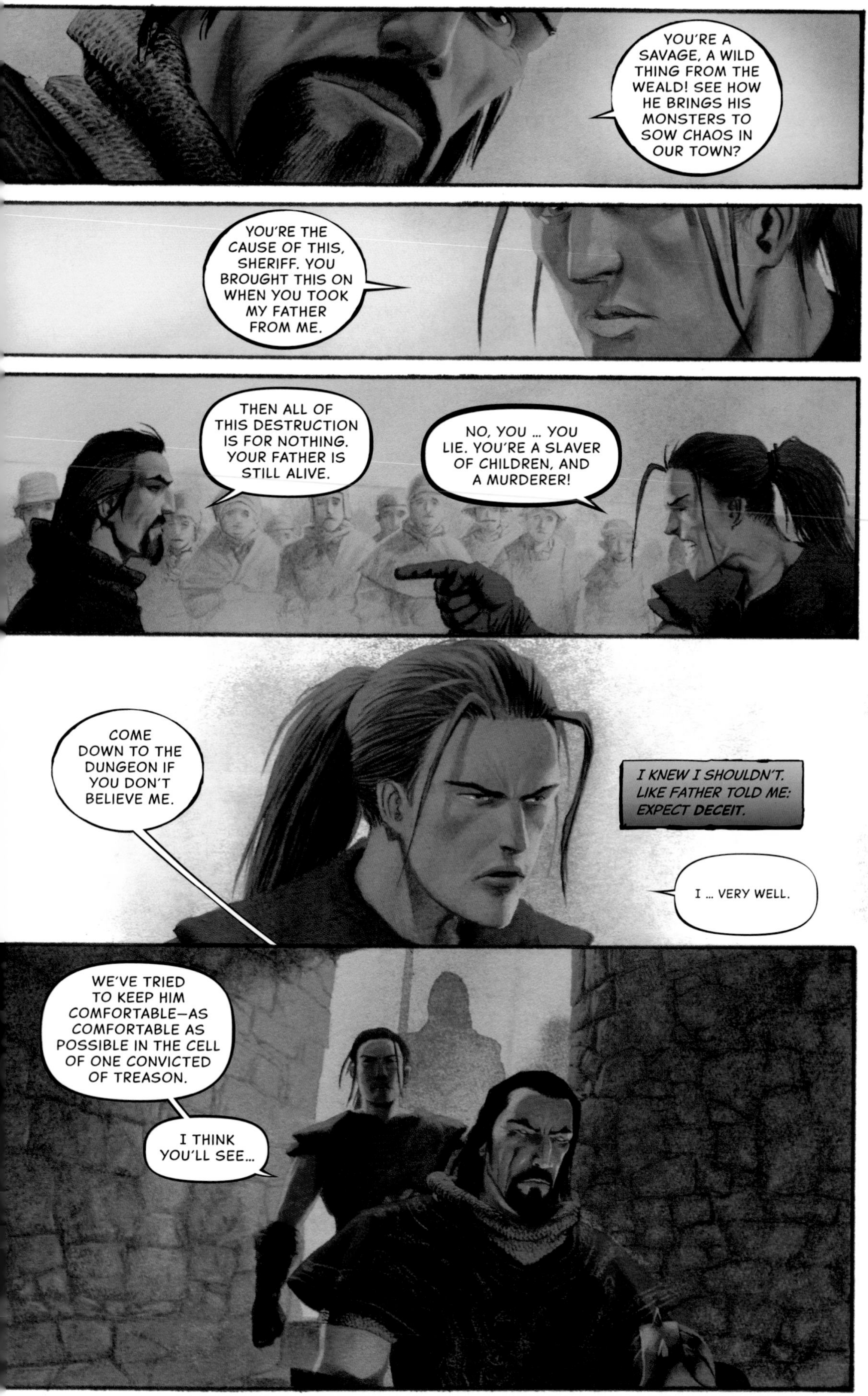
YOU'RE A SAVAGE, A WILD THING FROM THE WEALD! SEE HOW HE BRINGS HIS MONSTERS TO SOW CHAOS IN OUR TOWN?
YOU'RE THE CAUSE OF THIS, SHERIFF. YOU BROUGHT THIS ON WHEN YOU TOOK MY FATHER FROM ME.
THEN ALL OF THIS DESTRUCTION IS FOR NOTHING. YOUR FATHER IS STILL ALIVE.
NO, YOU ... YOU LIE. YOU'RE A SLAVER OF CHILDREN, AND A MURDERER!
COME DOWN TO THE DUNGEON IF YOU DON'T BELIEVE ME.
I KNEW I SHOULDN'T. LIKE FATHER TOLD ME: EXPECT DECEIT.
I ... VERY WELL.
WE'VE TRIED TO KEEP HIM COMFORTABLE—AS COMFORTABLE AS POSSIBLE IN THE CELL OF ONE CONVICTED OF TREASON.
I THINK YOU'LL SEE...

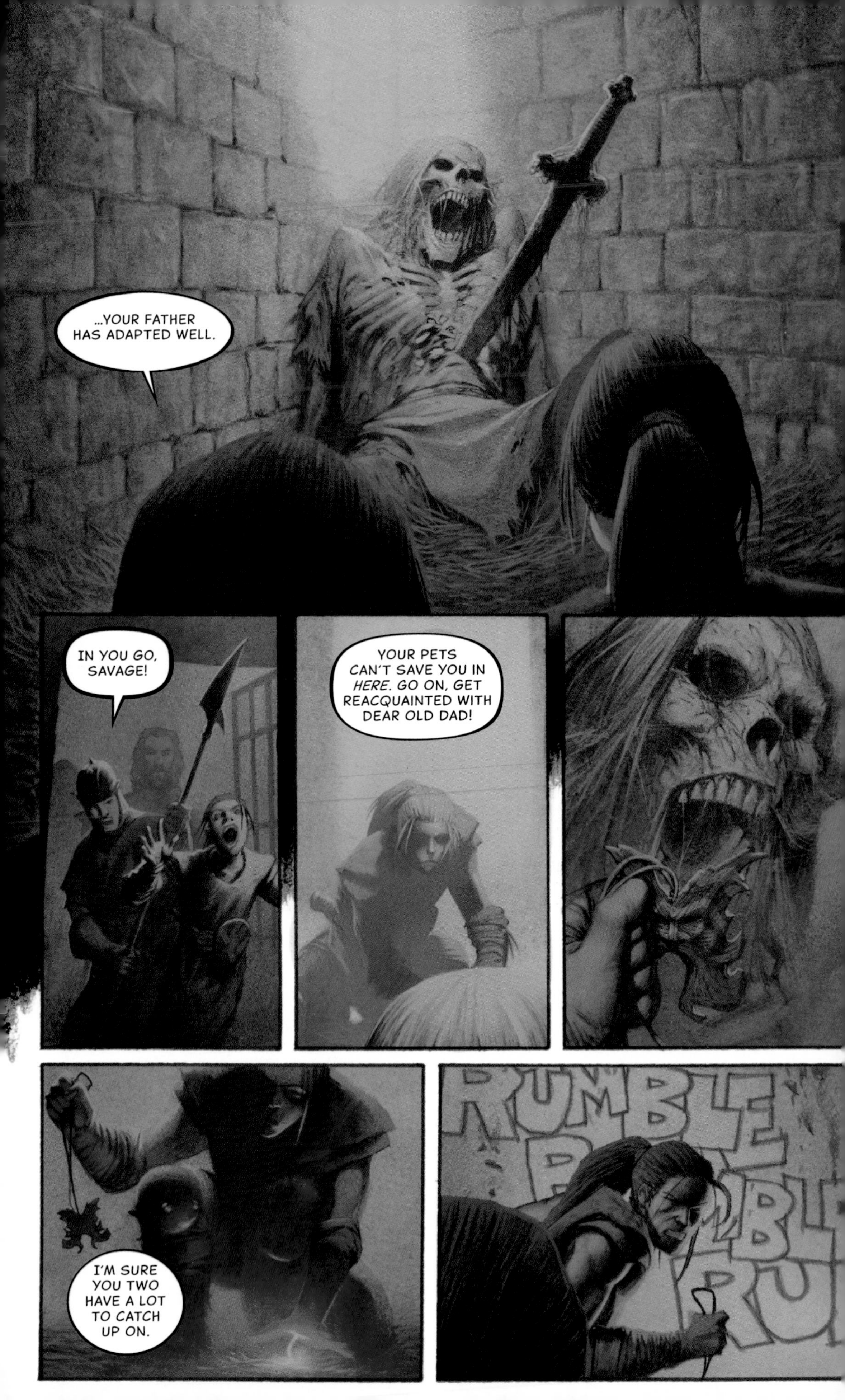
...YOUR FATHER HAS ADAPTED WELL.
IN YOU GO, SAVAGE!
YOUR PETS CAN'T SAVE YOU IN *HERE*. GO ON, GET REACQUAINTED WITH DEAR OLD DAD!
I'M SURE YOU TWO HAVE A LOT TO CATCH UP ON.
RUMBLE

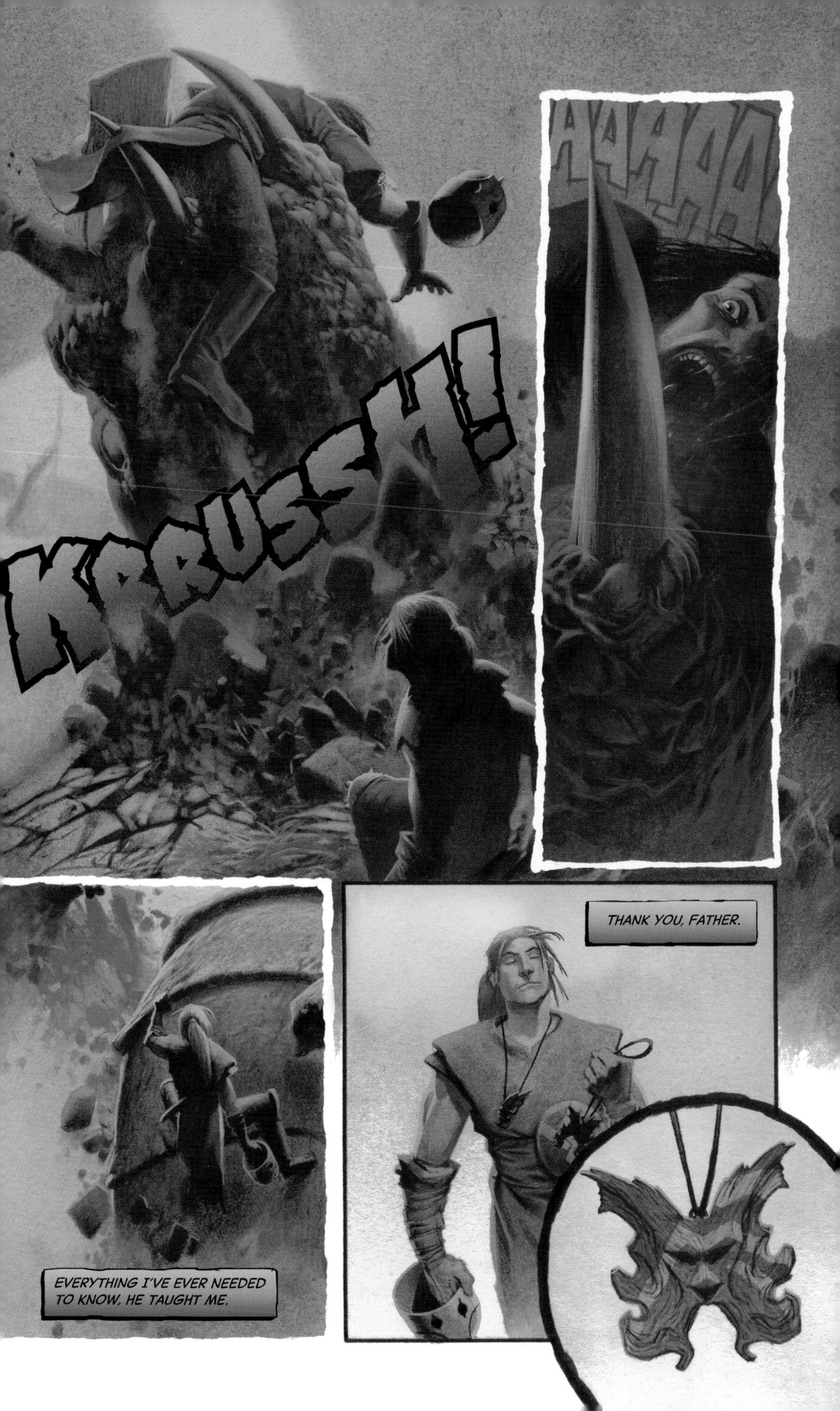
KRUSSH!
AAAHAA
EVERYTHING I'VE EVER NEEDED TO KNOW, HE TAUGHT ME.
THANK YOU, FATHER.

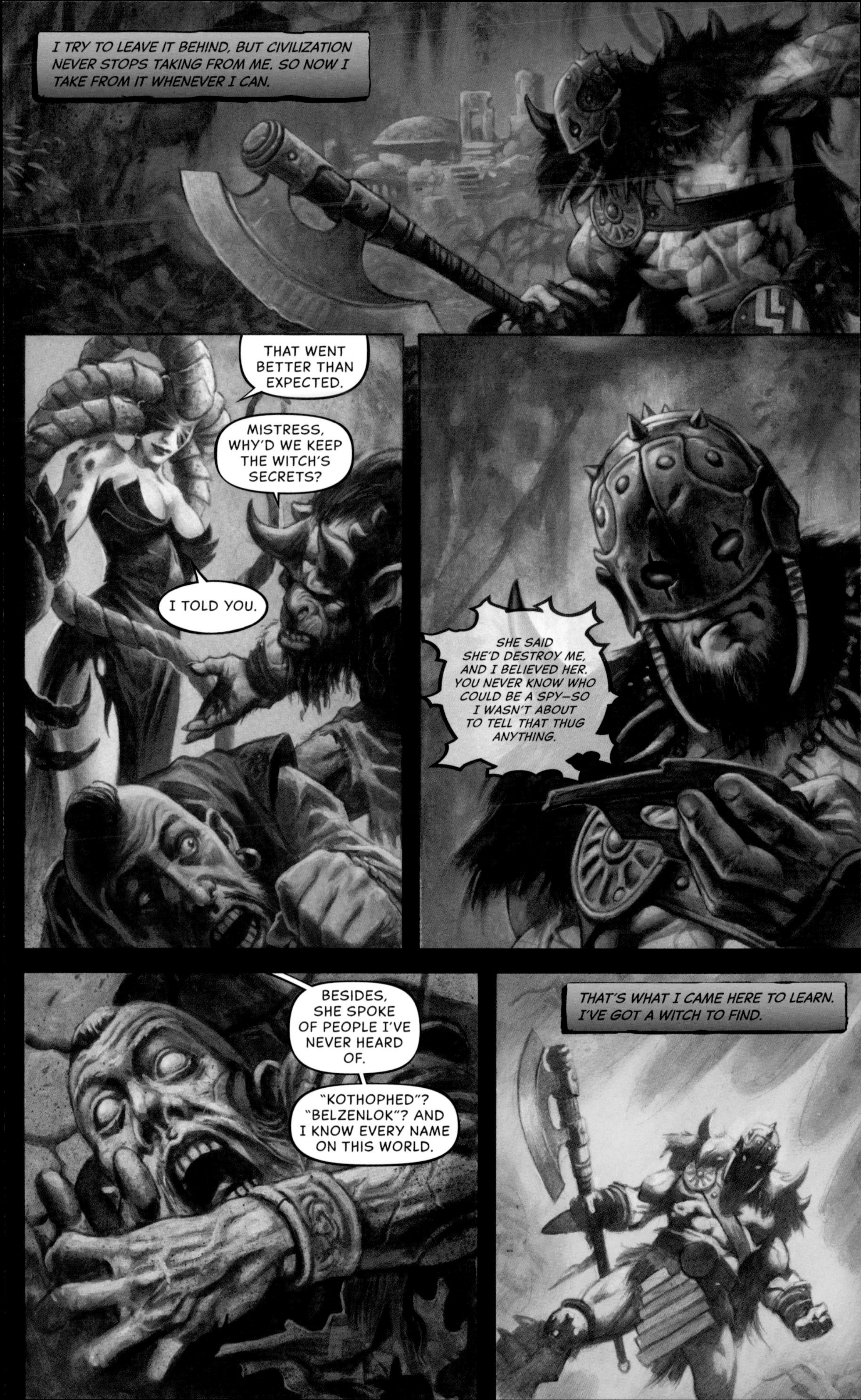
I TRY TO LEAVE IT BEHIND, BUT CIVILIZATION NEVER STOPS TAKING FROM ME. SO NOW I TAKE FROM IT WHENEVER I CAN.
THAT WENT BETTER THAN EXPECTED.
MISTRESS, WHY'D WE KEEP THE WITCH'S SECRETS?
I TOLD YOU.
SHE SAID SHE'D DESTROY ME, AND I BELIEVED HER. YOU NEVER KNOW WHO COULD BE A SPY—SO I WASN'T ABOUT TO TELL THAT THUG ANYTHING.
BESIDES, SHE SPOKE OF PEOPLE I'VE NEVER HEARD OF.
"KOTHOPHED"? "BELZENLOK"? AND I KNOW EVERY NAME ON THIS WORLD.
THAT'S WHAT I CAME HERE TO LEARN. I'VE GOT A WITCH TO FIND.

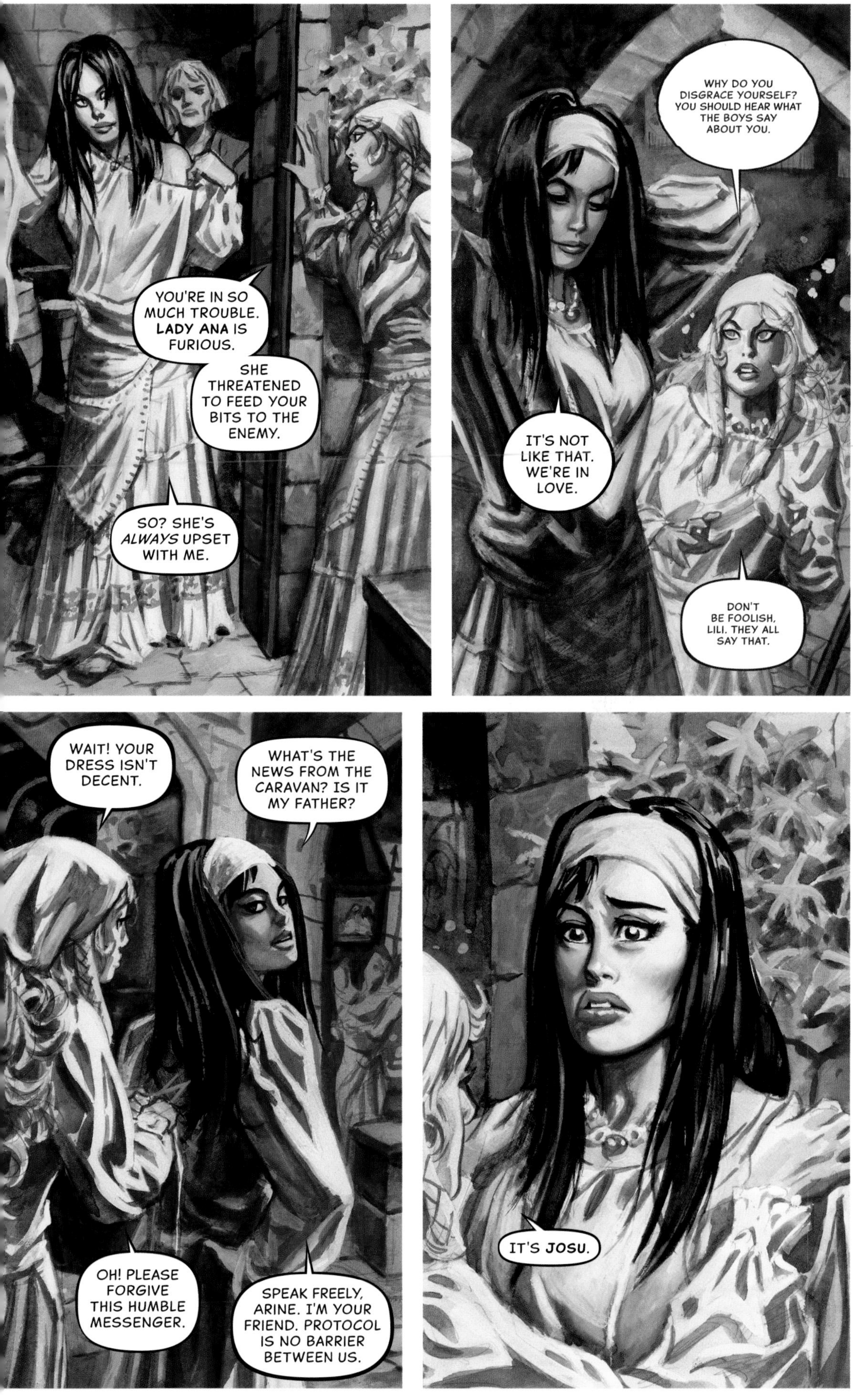
YOU'RE IN SO MUCH TROUBLE. LADY ANA IS FURIOUS.
SHE THREATENED TO FEED YOUR BITS TO THE ENEMY.
SO? SHE'S *ALWAYS* UPSET WITH ME.
WHY DO YOU DISGRACE YOURSELF? YOU SHOULD HEAR WHAT THE BOYS SAY ABOUT YOU.
IT'S NOT LIKE THAT. WE'RE IN LOVE.
DON'T BE FOOLISH, LILI. THEY ALL SAY THAT.
WAIT! YOUR DRESS ISN'T DECENT.
WHAT'S THE NEWS FROM THE CARAVAN? IS IT MY FATHER?
OH! PLEASE FORGIVE THIS HUMBLE MESSENGER.
SPEAK FREELY, ARINE. I'M YOUR FRIEND. PROTOCOL IS NO BARRIER BETWEEN US.
IT'S JOSU.

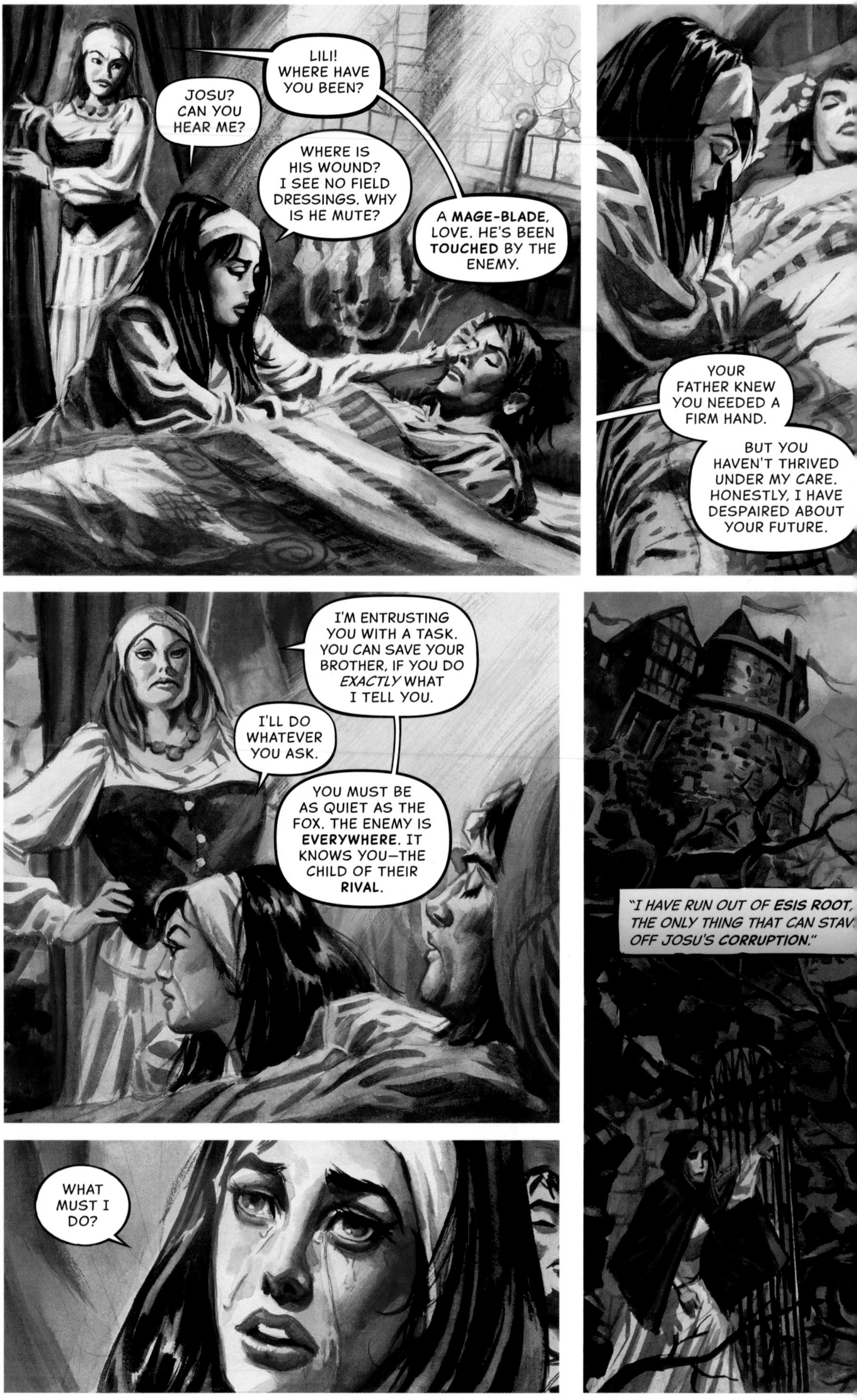
LILI! WHERE HAVE YOU BEEN?
JOSU? CAN YOU HEAR ME?
WHERE IS HIS WOUND? I SEE NO FIELD DRESSINGS. WHY IS HE MUTE?
A **MAGE-BLADE**, LOVE. HE'S BEEN **TOUCHED** BY THE ENEMY.
YOUR FATHER KNEW YOU NEEDED A FIRM HAND.
BUT YOU HAVEN'T THRIVED UNDER MY CARE. HONESTLY, I HAVE DESPAIRED ABOUT YOUR FUTURE.
I'M ENTRUSTING YOU WITH A TASK. YOU CAN SAVE YOUR BROTHER, IF YOU DO *EXACTLY* WHAT I TELL YOU.
I'LL DO WHATEVER YOU ASK.
YOU MUST BE AS QUIET AS THE FOX. THE ENEMY IS **EVERYWHERE**. IT KNOWS YOU—THE CHILD OF THEIR **RIVAL**.
WHAT MUST I DO?
*"I HAVE RUN OUT OF **ESIS ROOT**, THE ONLY THING THAT CAN STAV OFF JOSU'S **CORRUPTION**."*

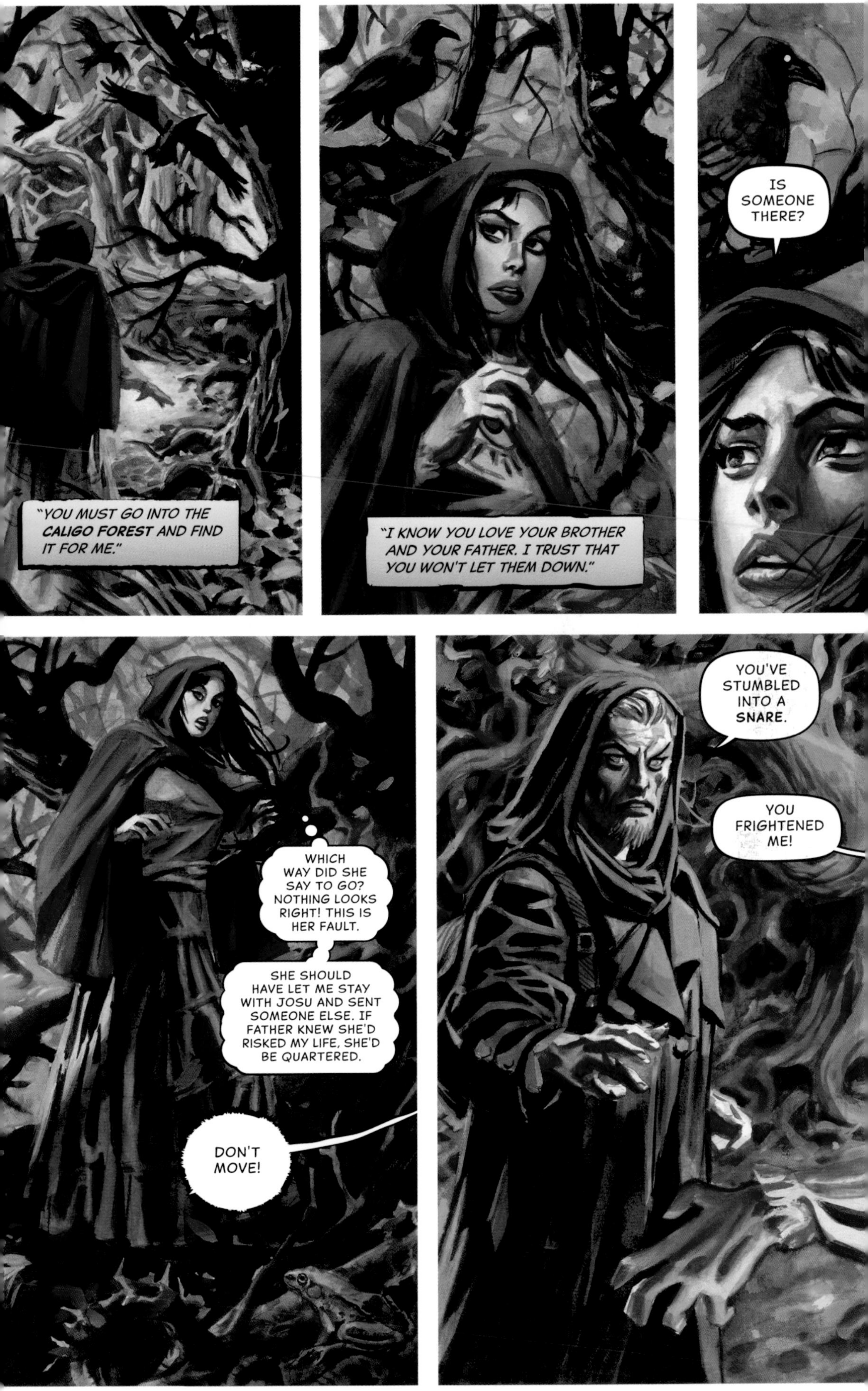

"YOU MUST GO INTO THE CALIGO FOREST AND FIND IT FOR ME."
"I KNOW YOU LOVE YOUR BROTHER AND YOUR FATHER. I TRUST THAT YOU WON'T LET THEM DOWN."
IS SOMEONE THERE?
WHICH WAY DID SHE SAY TO GO? NOTHING LOOKS RIGHT! THIS IS HER FAULT.
SHE SHOULD HAVE LET ME STAY WITH JOSU AND SENT SOMEONE ELSE. IF FATHER KNEW SHE'D RISKED MY LIFE, SHE'D BE QUARTERED.
DON'T MOVE!
YOU'VE STUMBLED INTO A SNARE.
YOU FRIGHTENED ME!

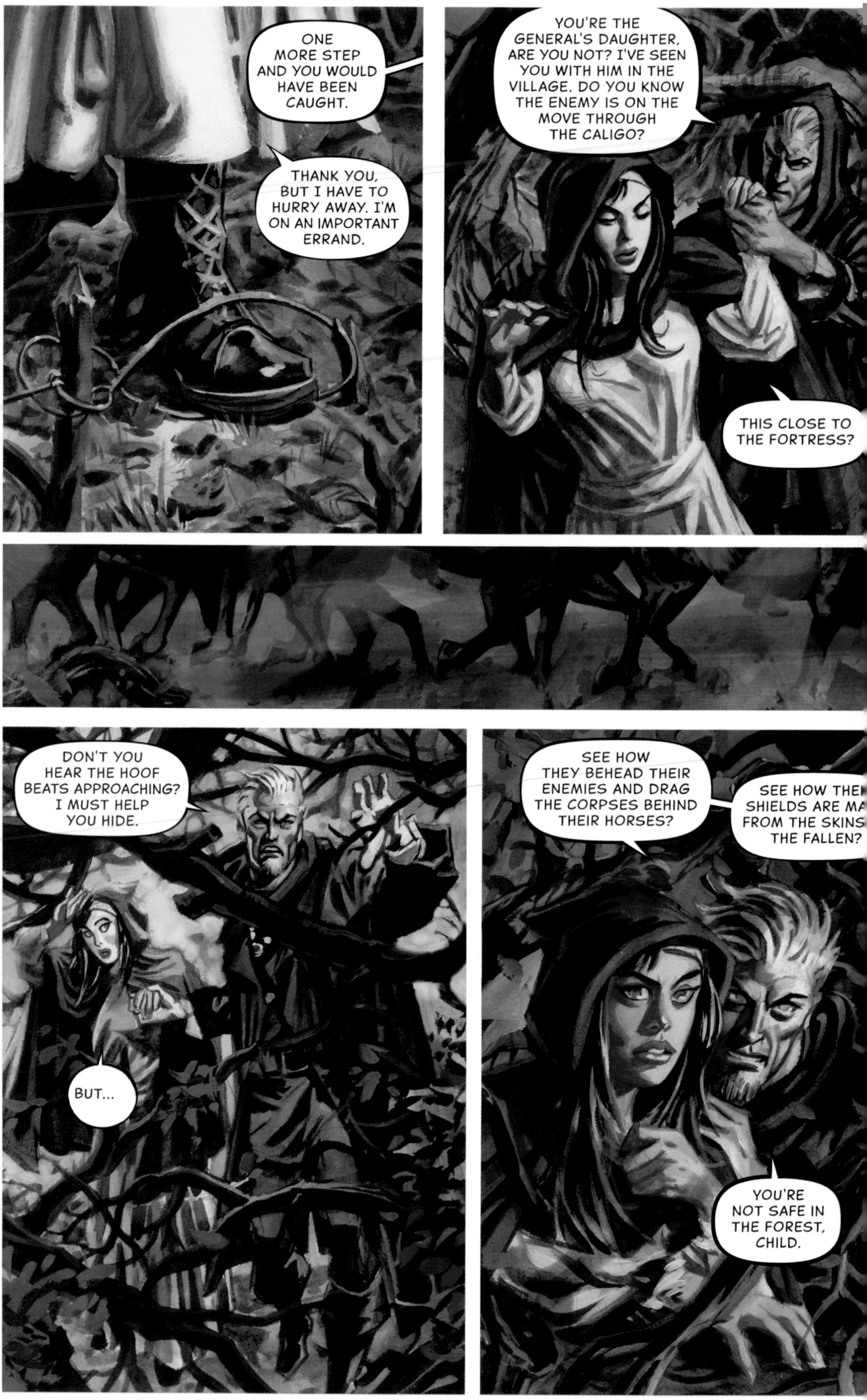
ONE MORE STEP AND YOU WOULD HAVE BEEN CAUGHT.
THANK YOU, BUT I HAVE TO HURRY AWAY. I'M ON AN IMPORTANT ERRAND.
YOU'RE THE GENERAL'S DAUGHTER, ARE YOU NOT? I'VE SEEN YOU WITH HIM IN THE VILLAGE. DO YOU KNOW THE ENEMY IS ON THE MOVE THROUGH THE CALIGO?
THIS CLOSE TO THE FORTRESS?
DON'T YOU HEAR THE HOOF BEATS APPROACHING? I MUST HELP YOU HIDE.
BUT...
SEE HOW THEY BEHEAD THEIR ENEMIES AND DRAG THE CORPSES BEHIND THEIR HORSES?
SEE HOW THE
SHIELDS ARE MA
FROM THE SKINS
THE FALLEN?
YOU'RE NOT SAFE IN THE FOREST, CHILD.

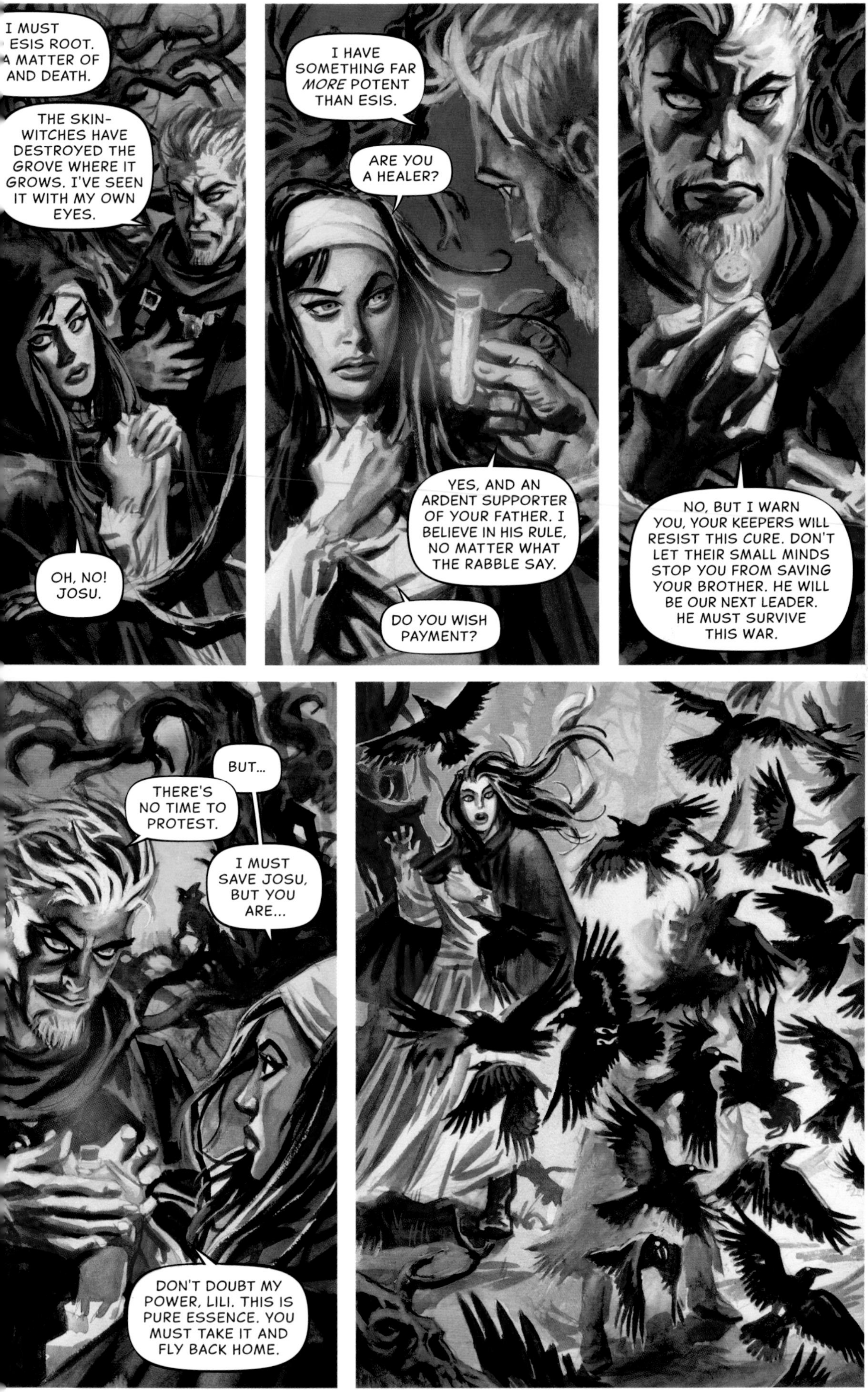
I MUST
ESIS ROOT.
A MATTER OF
AND DEATH.
THE SKIN-WITCHES HAVE DESTROYED THE GROVE WHERE IT GROWS. I'VE SEEN IT WITH MY OWN EYES.
OH, NO! JOSU.
I HAVE SOMETHING FAR *MORE* POTENT THAN ESIS.
ARE YOU A HEALER?
YES, AND AN ARDENT SUPPORTER OF YOUR FATHER. I BELIEVE IN HIS RULE, NO MATTER WHAT THE RABBLE SAY.
DO YOU WISH PAYMENT?
NO, BUT I WARN YOU, YOUR KEEPERS WILL RESIST THIS CURE. DON'T LET THEIR SMALL MINDS STOP YOU FROM SAVING YOUR BROTHER. HE WILL BE OUR NEXT LEADER. HE MUST SURVIVE THIS WAR.
BUT...
THERE'S NO TIME TO PROTEST.
I MUST SAVE JOSU, BUT YOU ARE...
DON'T DOUBT MY POWER, LILI. THIS IS PURE ESSENCE. YOU MUST TAKE IT AND FLY BACK HOME.

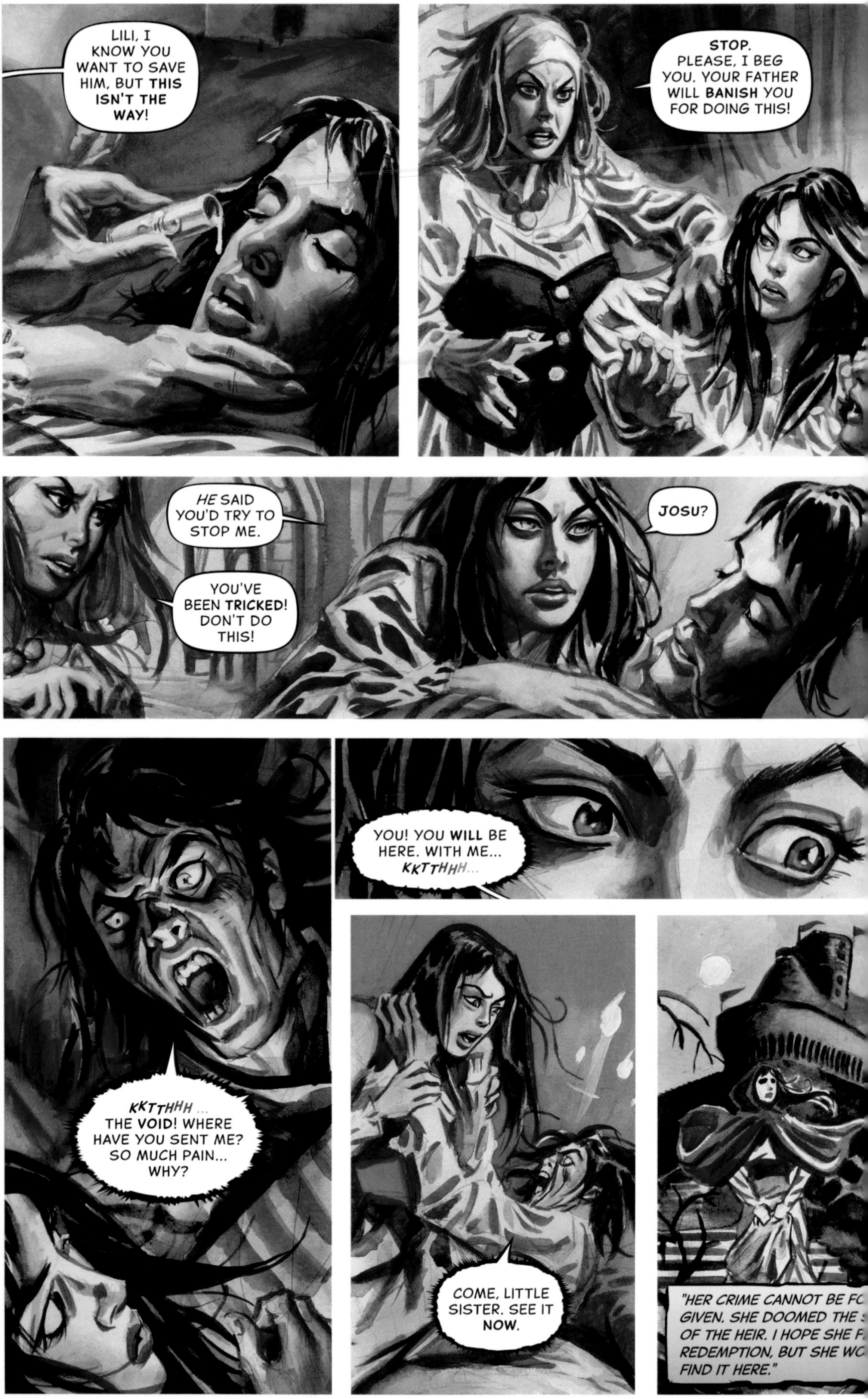
LILI, I KNOW YOU WANT TO SAVE HIM, BUT **THIS ISN'T THE WAY**!
STOP. PLEASE, I BEG YOU. YOUR FATHER WILL **BANISH** YOU FOR DOING THIS!
HE SAID YOU'D TRY TO STOP ME.
YOU'VE BEEN **TRICKED**! DON'T DO THIS!
JOSU?
KKTTHHH ... THE **VOID**! WHERE HAVE YOU SENT ME? SO MUCH PAIN... WHY?
YOU! YOU **WILL** BE HERE. WITH ME... *KKTTHHH*...
COME, LITTLE SISTER. SEE IT **NOW**.
*"HER CRIME CANNOT BE FO
GIVEN. SHE DOOMED THE
OF THE HEIR. I HOPE SHE F
REDEMPTION, BUT SHE WO
FIND IT HERE."*

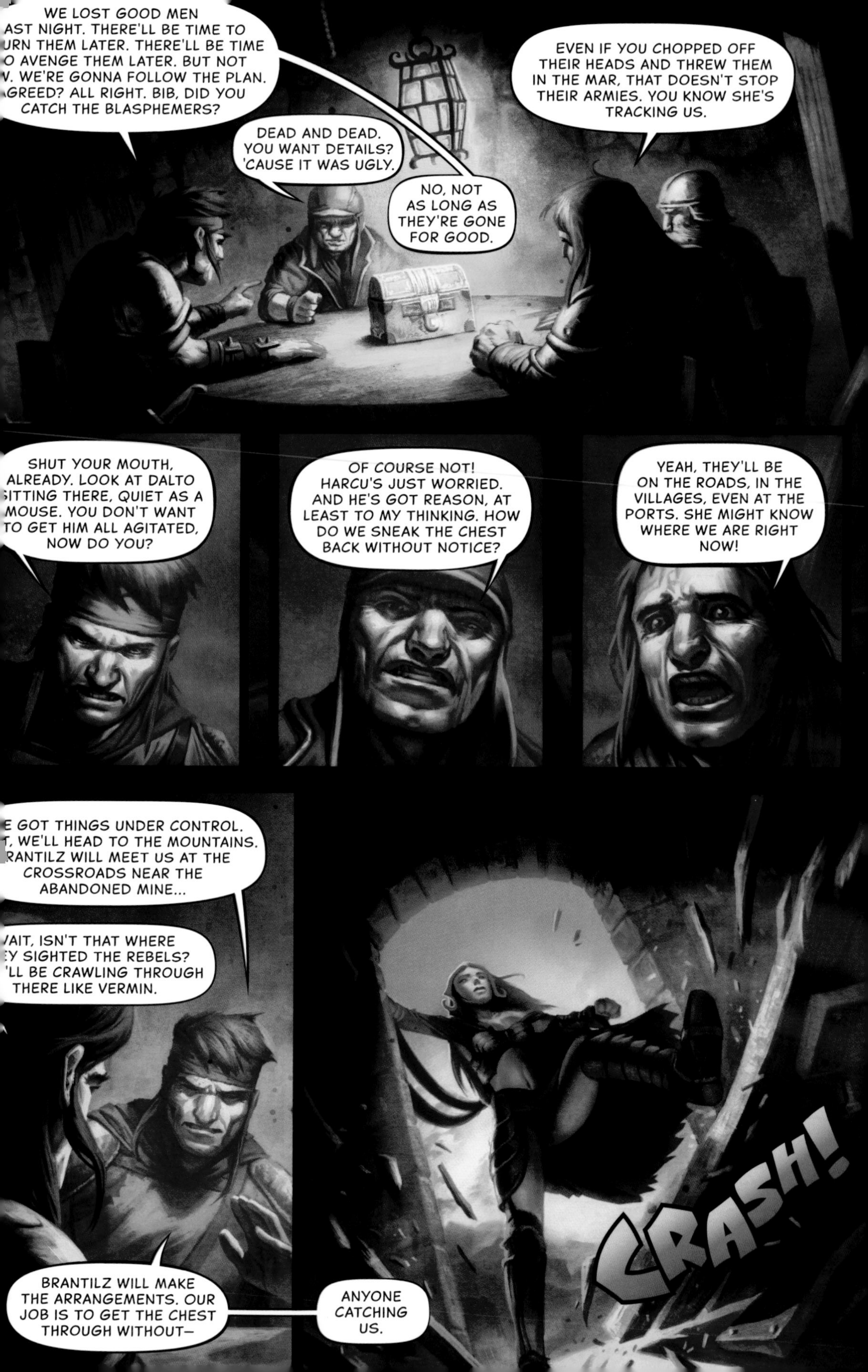
WE LOST GOOD MEN
AST NIGHT. THERE'LL BE TIME TO
URN THEM LATER. THERE'LL BE TIME
O AVENGE THEM LATER. BUT NOT
V. WE'RE GONNA FOLLOW THE PLAN.
GREED? ALL RIGHT. BIB, DID YOU
CATCH THE BLASPHEMERS?
DEAD AND DEAD. YOU WANT DETAILS? 'CAUSE IT WAS UGLY.
NO, NOT AS LONG AS THEY'RE GONE FOR GOOD.
EVEN IF YOU CHOPPED OFF THEIR HEADS AND THREW THEM IN THE MAR, THAT DOESN'T STOP THEIR ARMIES. YOU KNOW SHE'S TRACKING US.
SHUT YOUR MOUTH, ALREADY. LOOK AT DALTO SITTING THERE, QUIET AS A MOUSE. YOU DON'T WANT TO GET HIM ALL AGITATED, NOW DO YOU?
OF COURSE NOT! HARCU'S JUST WORRIED. AND HE'S GOT REASON, AT LEAST TO MY THINKING. HOW DO WE SNEAK THE CHEST BACK WITHOUT NOTICE?
YEAH, THEY'LL BE ON THE ROADS, IN THE VILLAGES, EVEN AT THE PORTS. SHE MIGHT KNOW WHERE WE ARE RIGHT NOW!
E GOT THINGS UNDER CONTROL.
T, WE'LL HEAD TO THE MOUNTAINS.
RANTILZ WILL MEET US AT THE
CROSSROADS NEAR THE
ABANDONED MINE...
AIT, ISN'T THAT WHERE
EY SIGHTED THE REBELS?
'LL BE CRAWLING THROUGH
THERE LIKE VERMIN.
BRANTILZ WILL MAKE THE ARRANGEMENTS. OUR JOB IS TO GET THE CHEST THROUGH WITHOUT—
ANYONE CATCHING US.
CRASH!

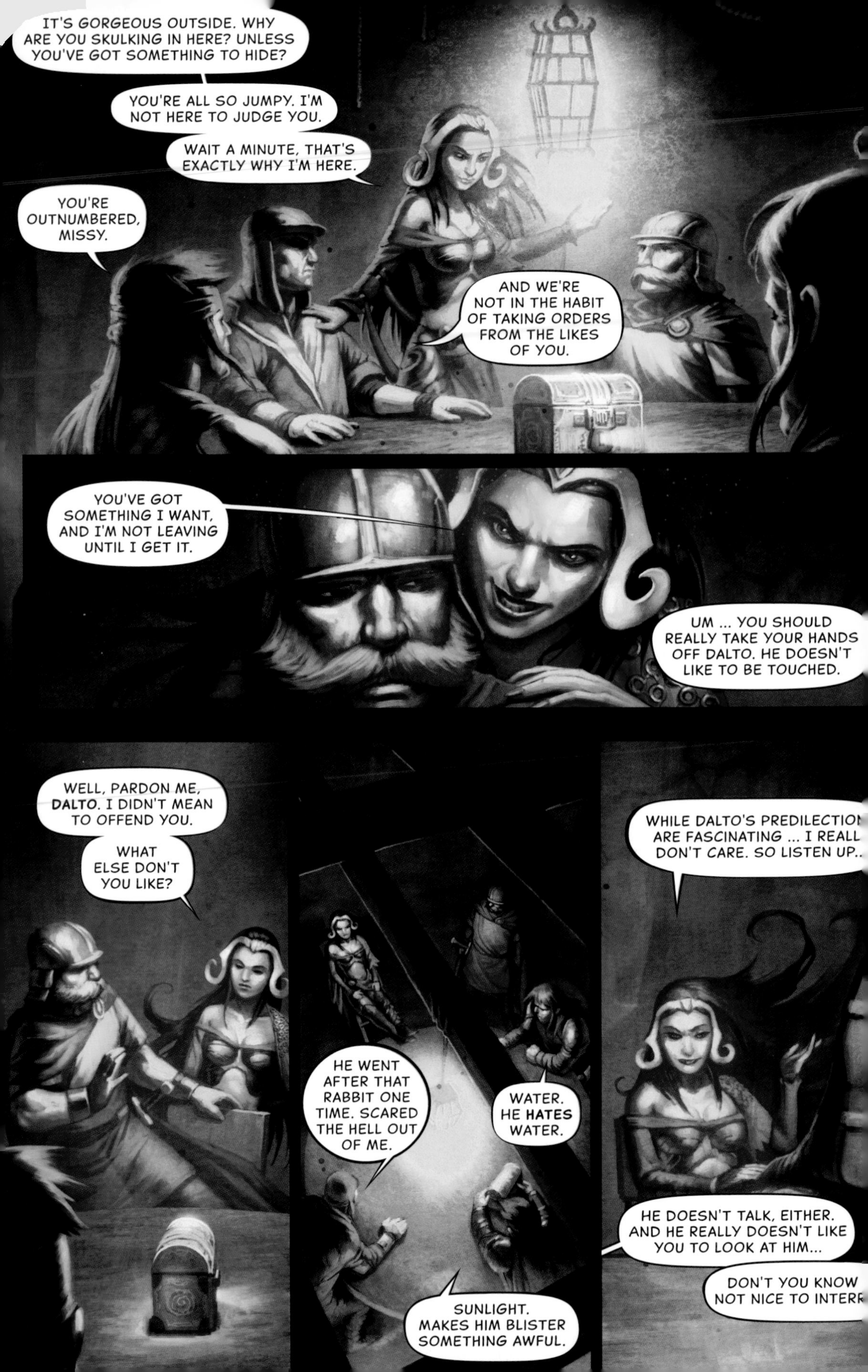
IT'S GORGEOUS OUTSIDE. WHY ARE YOU SKULKING IN HERE? UNLESS YOU'VE GOT SOMETHING TO HIDE?
YOU'RE ALL SO JUMPY. I'M NOT HERE TO JUDGE YOU.
WAIT A MINUTE, THAT'S EXACTLY WHY I'M HERE.
YOU'RE OUTNUMBERED, MISSY.
AND WE'RE NOT IN THE HABIT OF TAKING ORDERS FROM THE LIKES OF YOU.
YOU'VE GOT SOMETHING I WANT, AND I'M NOT LEAVING UNTIL I GET IT.
UM ... YOU SHOULD REALLY TAKE YOUR HANDS OFF DALTO. HE DOESN'T LIKE TO BE TOUCHED.
WELL, PARDON ME, **DALTO**. I DIDN'T MEAN TO OFFEND YOU.
WHAT ELSE DON'T YOU LIKE?
HE WENT AFTER THAT RABBIT ONE TIME. SCARED THE HELL OUT OF ME.
WATER. HE **HATES** WATER.
SUNLIGHT. MAKES HIM BLISTER SOMETHING AWFUL.
WHILE DALTO'S PREDILECTION ARE FASCINATING ... I REALL DON'T CARE. SO LISTEN UP..
HE DOESN'T TALK, EITHER. AND HE REALLY DOESN'T LIKE YOU TO LOOK AT HIM...
DON'T YOU KNOW NOT NICE TO INTERR

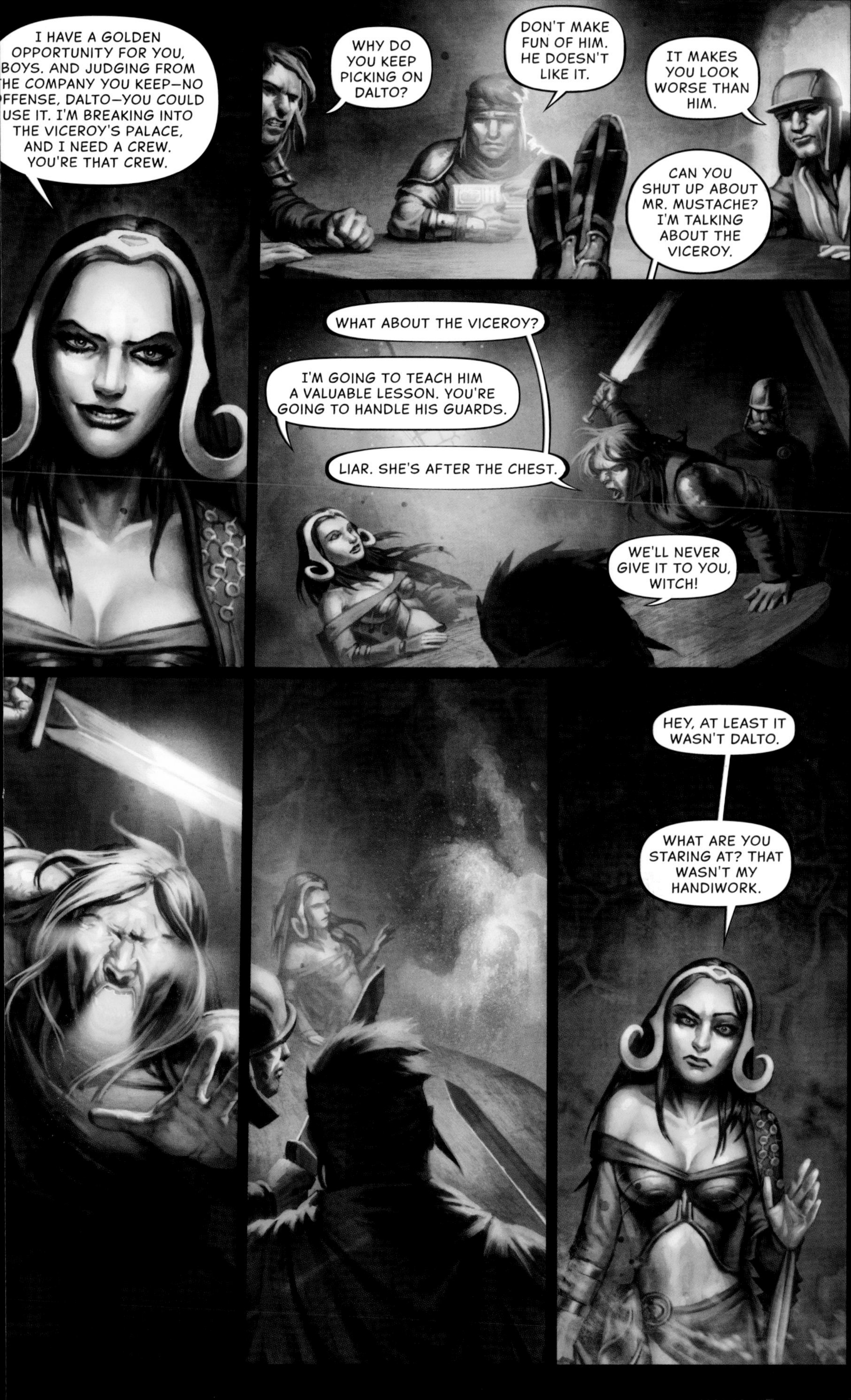
I HAVE A GOLDEN OPPORTUNITY FOR YOU, BOYS. AND JUDGING FROM THE COMPANY YOU KEEP—NO OFFENSE, DALTO—YOU COULD USE IT. I'M BREAKING INTO THE VICEROY'S PALACE, AND I NEED A CREW. YOU'RE THAT CREW.
WHY DO YOU KEEP PICKING ON DALTO?
DON'T MAKE FUN OF HIM. HE DOESN'T LIKE IT.
IT MAKES YOU LOOK WORSE THAN HIM.
CAN YOU SHUT UP ABOUT MR. MUSTACHE? I'M TALKING ABOUT THE VICEROY.
WHAT ABOUT THE VICEROY?
I'M GOING TO TEACH HIM A VALUABLE LESSON. YOU'RE GOING TO HANDLE HIS GUARDS.
LIAR. SHE'S AFTER THE CHEST.
WE'LL NEVER GIVE IT TO YOU, WITCH!
HEY, AT LEAST IT WASN'T DALTO.
WHAT ARE YOU STARING AT? THAT WASN'T MY HANDIWORK.

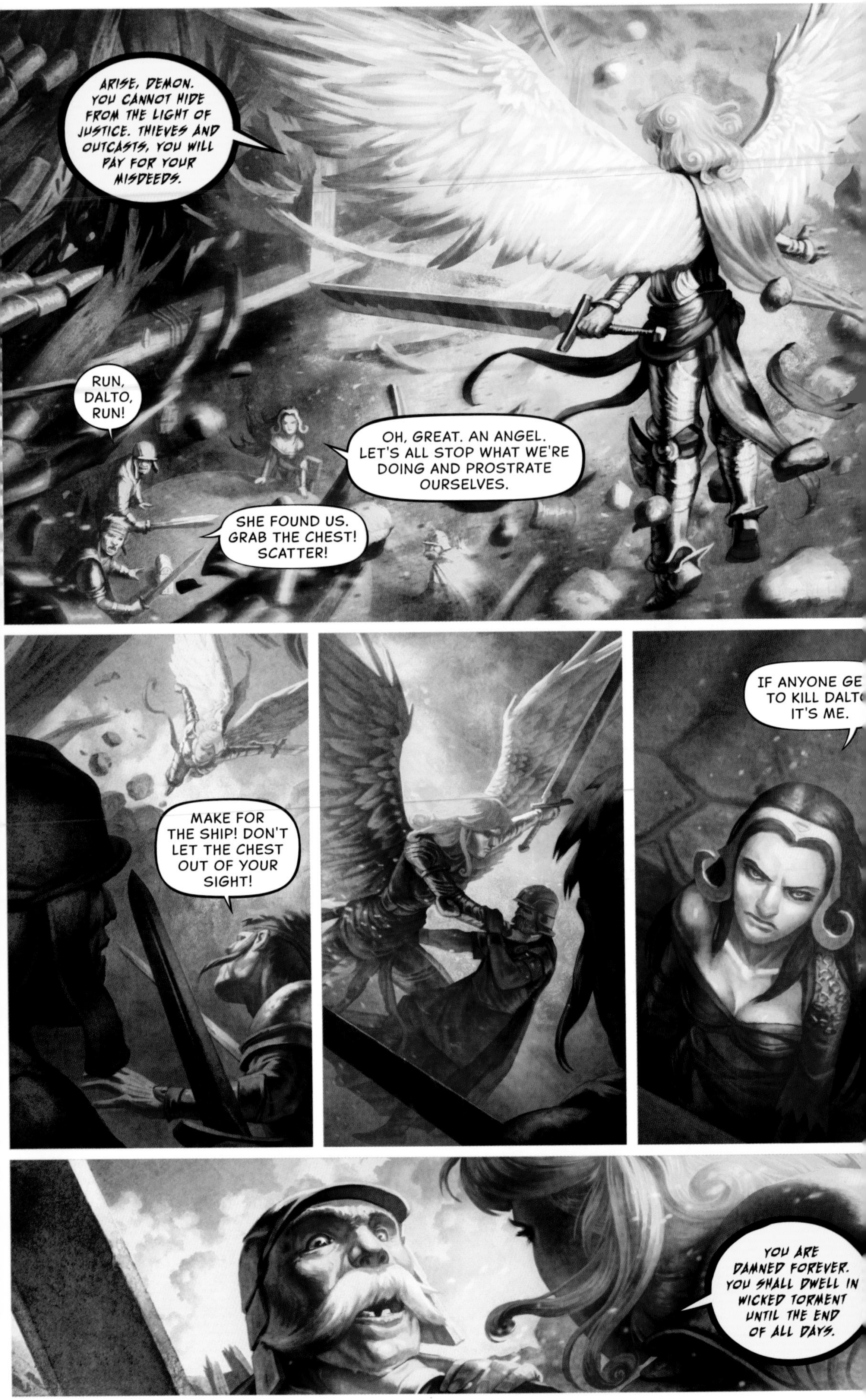
ARISE, DEMON. YOU CANNOT HIDE FROM THE LIGHT OF JUSTICE. THIEVES AND OUTCASTS, YOU WILL PAY FOR YOUR MISDEEDS.
RUN, DALTO, RUN!
OH, GREAT. AN ANGEL. LET'S ALL STOP WHAT WE'RE DOING AND PROSTRATE OURSELVES.
SHE FOUND US. GRAB THE CHEST! SCATTER!
MAKE FOR THE SHIP! DON'T LET THE CHEST OUT OF YOUR SIGHT!
IF ANYONE GE TO KILL DALT IT'S ME.
YOU ARE DAMNED FOREVER. YOU SHALL DWELL IN WICKED TORMENT UNTIL THE END OF ALL DAYS.

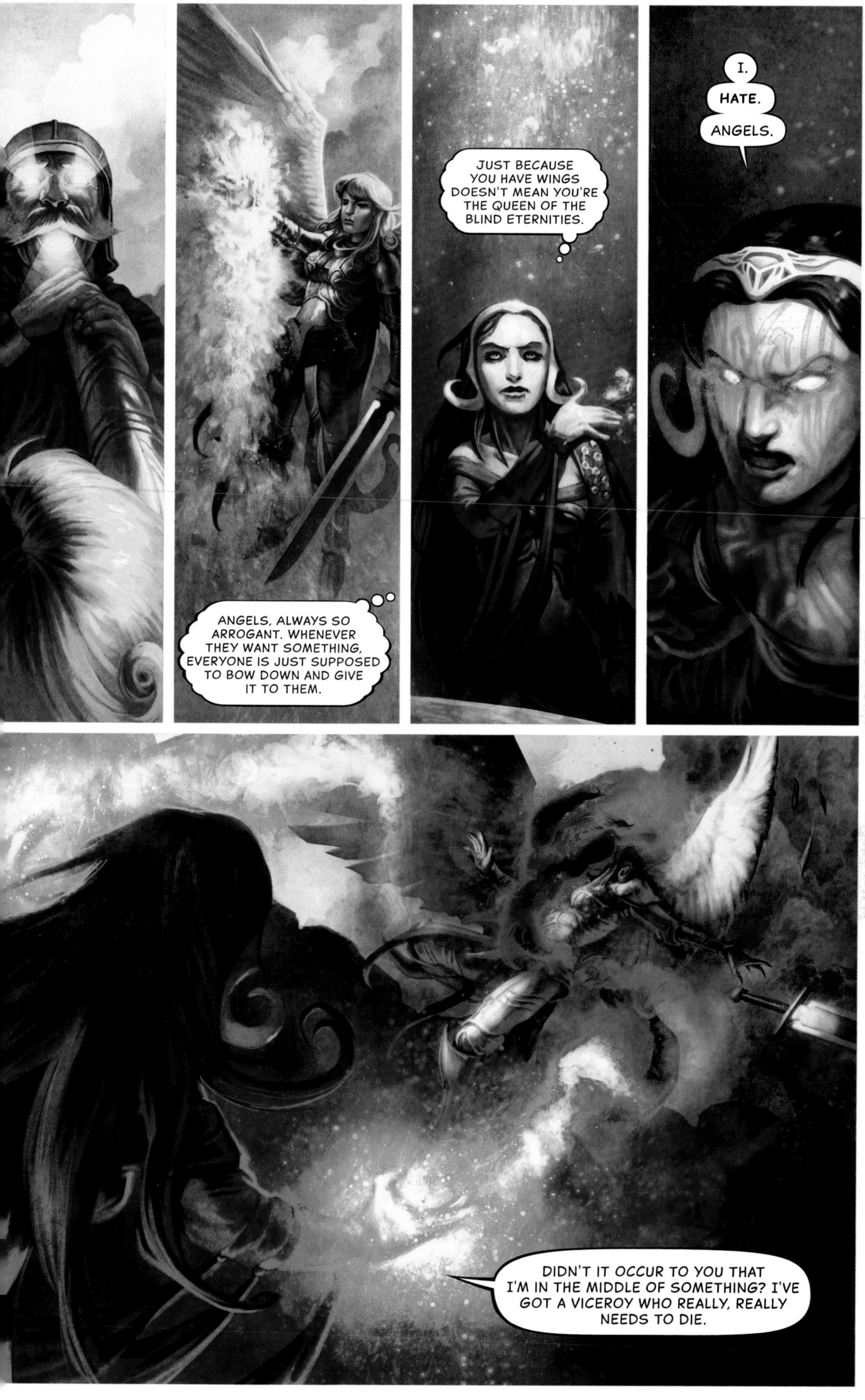
ANGELS, ALWAYS SO ARROGANT. WHENEVER THEY WANT SOMETHING, EVERYONE IS JUST SUPPOSED TO BOW DOWN AND GIVE IT TO THEM.
JUST BECAUSE YOU HAVE WINGS DOESN'T MEAN YOU'RE THE QUEEN OF THE BLIND ETERNITIES.
I.
HATE.
ANGELS.
DIDN'T IT OCCUR TO YOU THAT I'M IN THE MIDDLE OF SOMETHING? I'VE GOT A VICEROY WHO REALLY, REALLY NEEDS TO DIE.

THE BLESSED MUST COMPLETE THEIR WORK. THE EVIL MUST NOT BE RELEASED. DO NOT BIND ME. FOR THE SAKE OF YOUR SOUL, LET ME PASS.

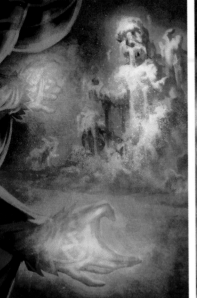

DALTO?

THE RIGHTEOUS WILL ... TRIUMPH. CHOKING FILTH OF DEAD IS ... NOT ENOU SILENCE THE BLESS

HRPFF

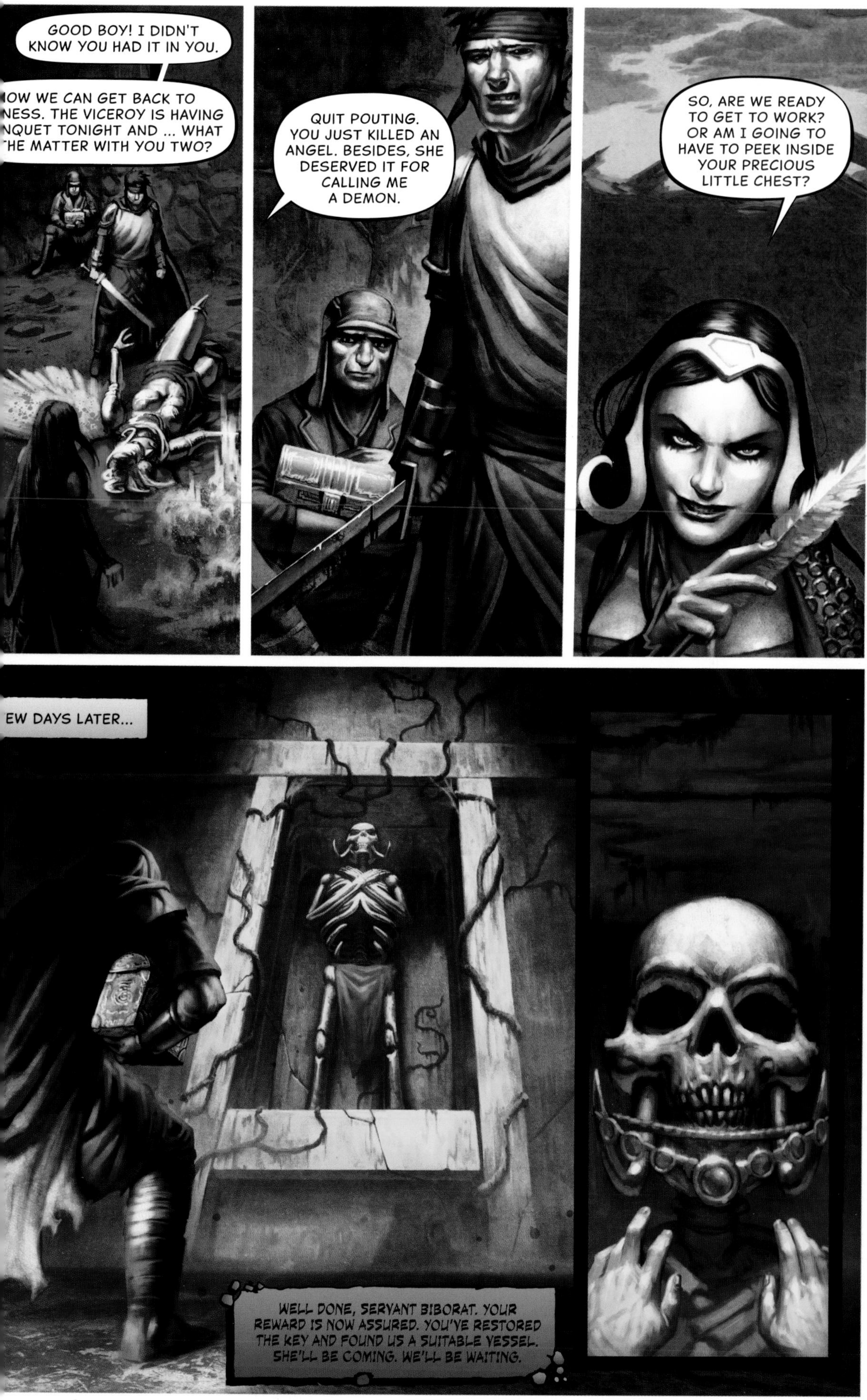
GOOD BOY! I DIDN'T KNOW YOU HAD IT IN YOU.
IOW WE CAN GET BACK TO NESS. THE VICEROY IS HAVING NQUET TONIGHT AND ... WHAT 'HE MATTER WITH YOU TWO?
QUIT POUTING. YOU JUST KILLED AN ANGEL. BESIDES, SHE DESERVED IT FOR CALLING ME A DEMON.
SO, ARE WE READY TO GET TO WORK? OR AM I GOING TO HAVE TO PEEK INSIDE YOUR PRECIOUS LITTLE CHEST?
EW DAYS LATER...
WELL DONE, SERVANT BIBORAT. YOUR REWARD IS NOW ASSURED. YOU'VE RESTORED THE KEY AND FOUND US A SUITABLE VESSEL. SHE'LL BE COMING. WE'LL BE WAITING.

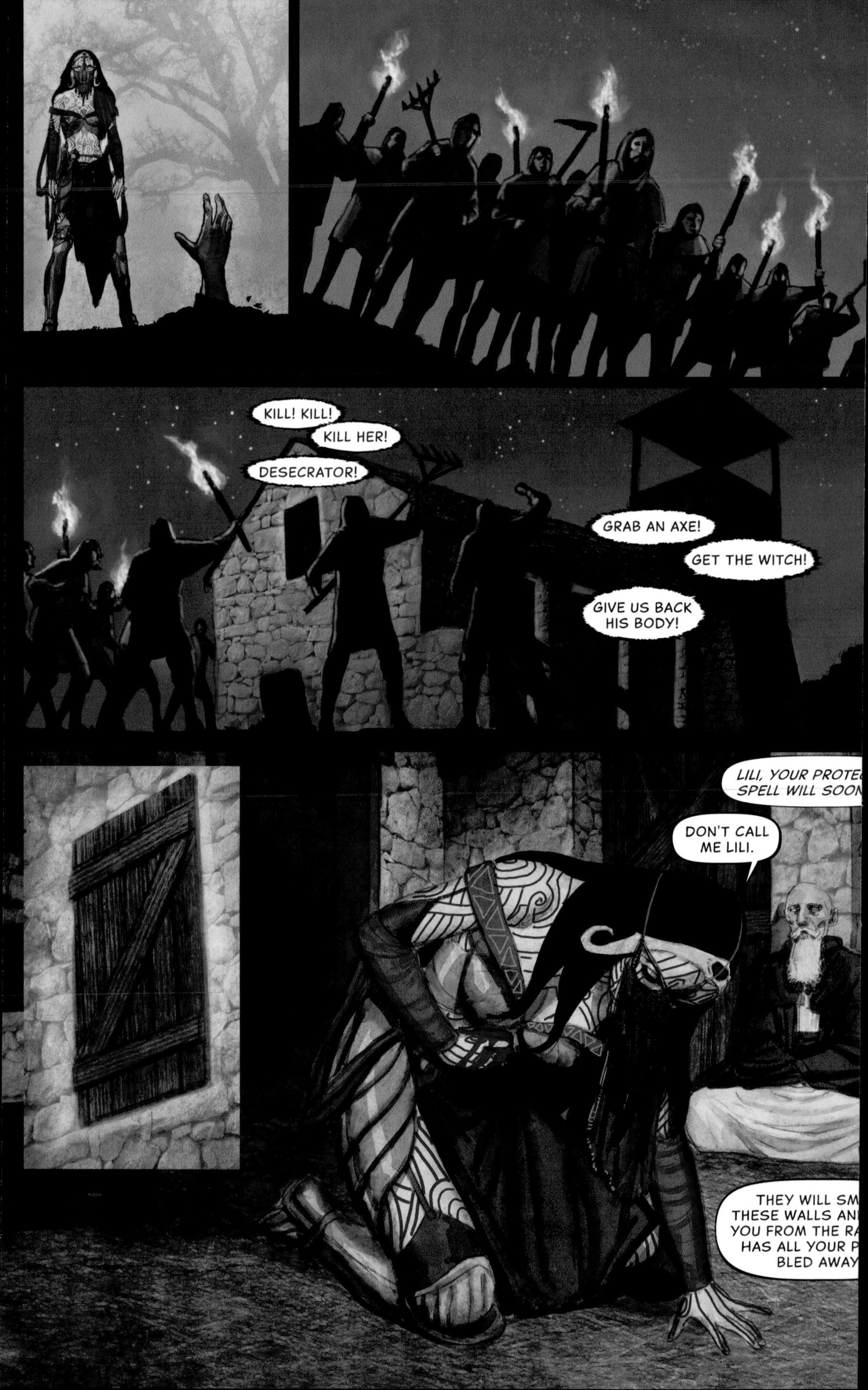
KILL! KILL!
KILL HER!
DESECRATOR!
GRAB AN AXE!
GET THE WITCH!
GIVE US BACK HIS BODY!
LILI, YOUR PROTE SPELL WILL SOON
DON'T CALL ME LILI.
THEY WILL SM THESE WALLS AN YOU FROM THE RA HAS ALL YOUR P BLED AWAY

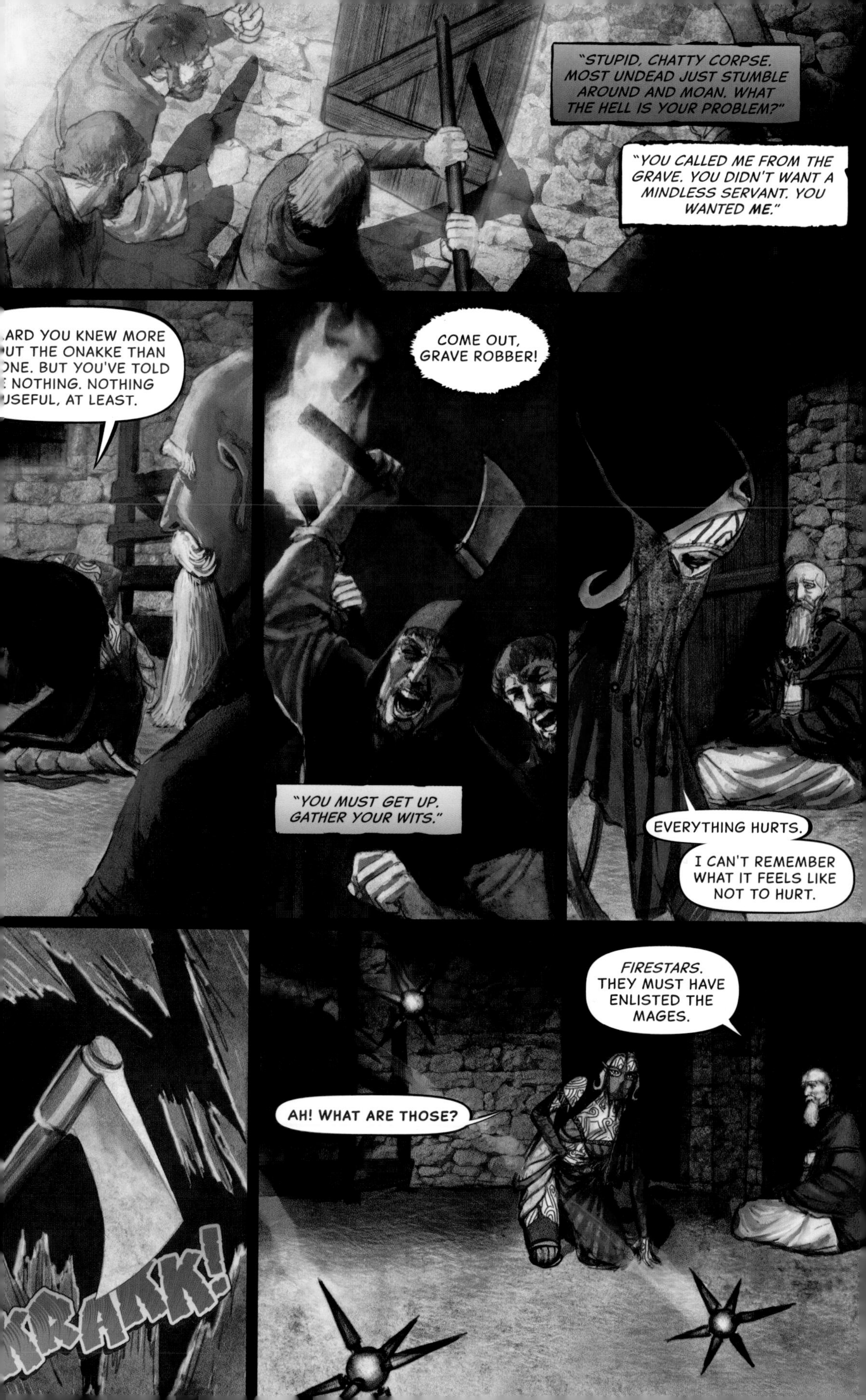

"STUPID, CHATTY CORPSE. MOST UNDEAD JUST STUMBLE AROUND AND MOAN. WHAT THE HELL IS YOUR PROBLEM?"
"YOU CALLED ME FROM THE GRAVE. YOU DIDN'T WANT A MINDLESS SERVANT. YOU WANTED *ME*."
ARD YOU KNEW MORE UT THE ONAKKE THAN ONE. BUT YOU'VE TOLD NOTHING. NOTHING USEFUL, AT LEAST.
COME OUT, GRAVE ROBBER!
"YOU MUST GET UP. GATHER YOUR WITS."
EVERYTHING HURTS.
I CAN'T REMEMBER WHAT IT FEELS LIKE NOT TO HURT.
AH! WHAT ARE THOSE?
FIRESTARS. THEY MUST HAVE ENLISTED THE MAGES.

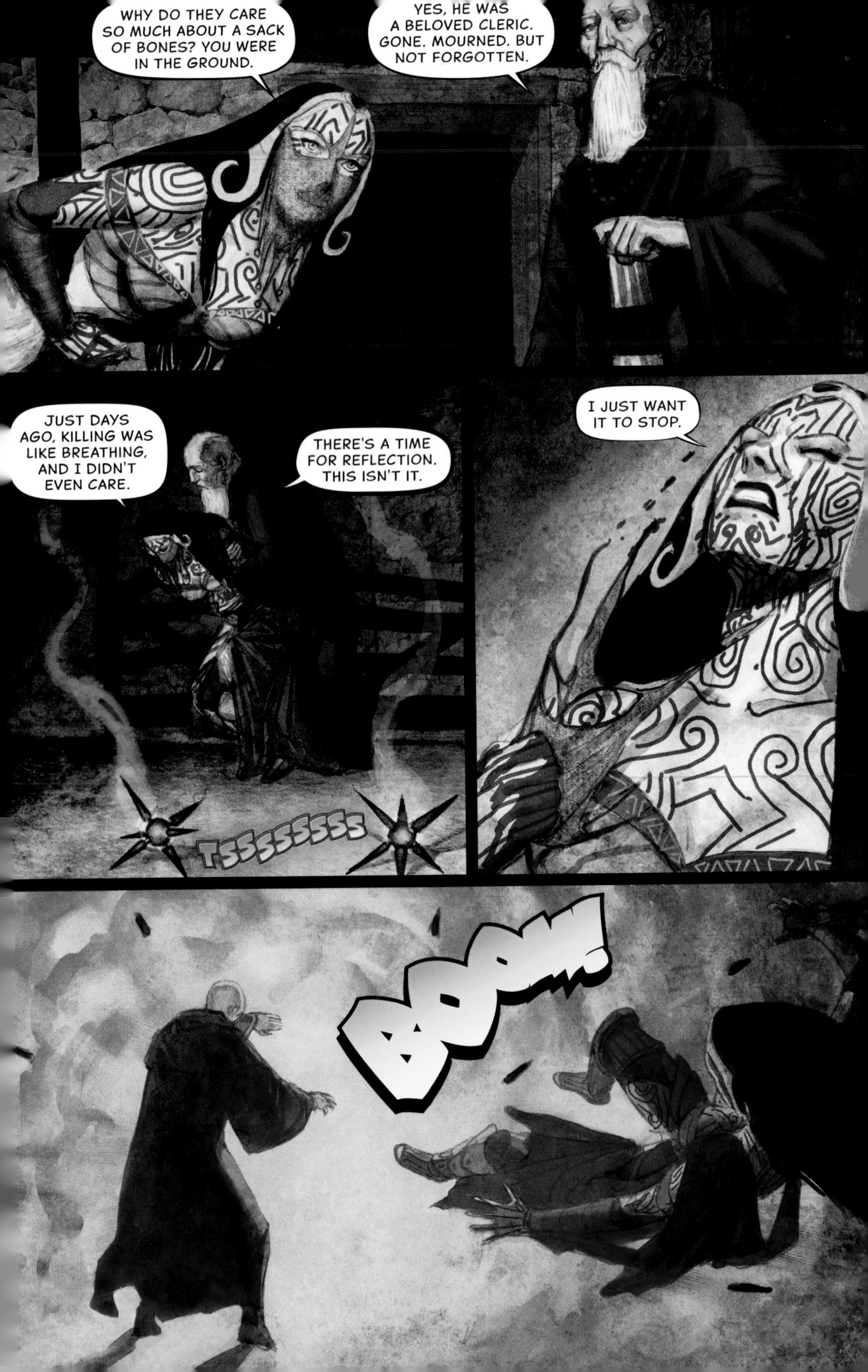
WHY DO THEY CARE SO MUCH ABOUT A SACK OF BONES? YOU WERE IN THE GROUND.
YES, HE WAS A BELOVED CLERIC. GONE. MOURNED. BUT NOT FORGOTTEN.
JUST DAYS AGO, KILLING WAS LIKE BREATHING, AND I DIDN'T EVEN CARE.
THERE'S A TIME FOR REFLECTION. THIS ISN'T IT.
TSSSSSSSS
I JUST WANT IT TO STOP.
BOOM!

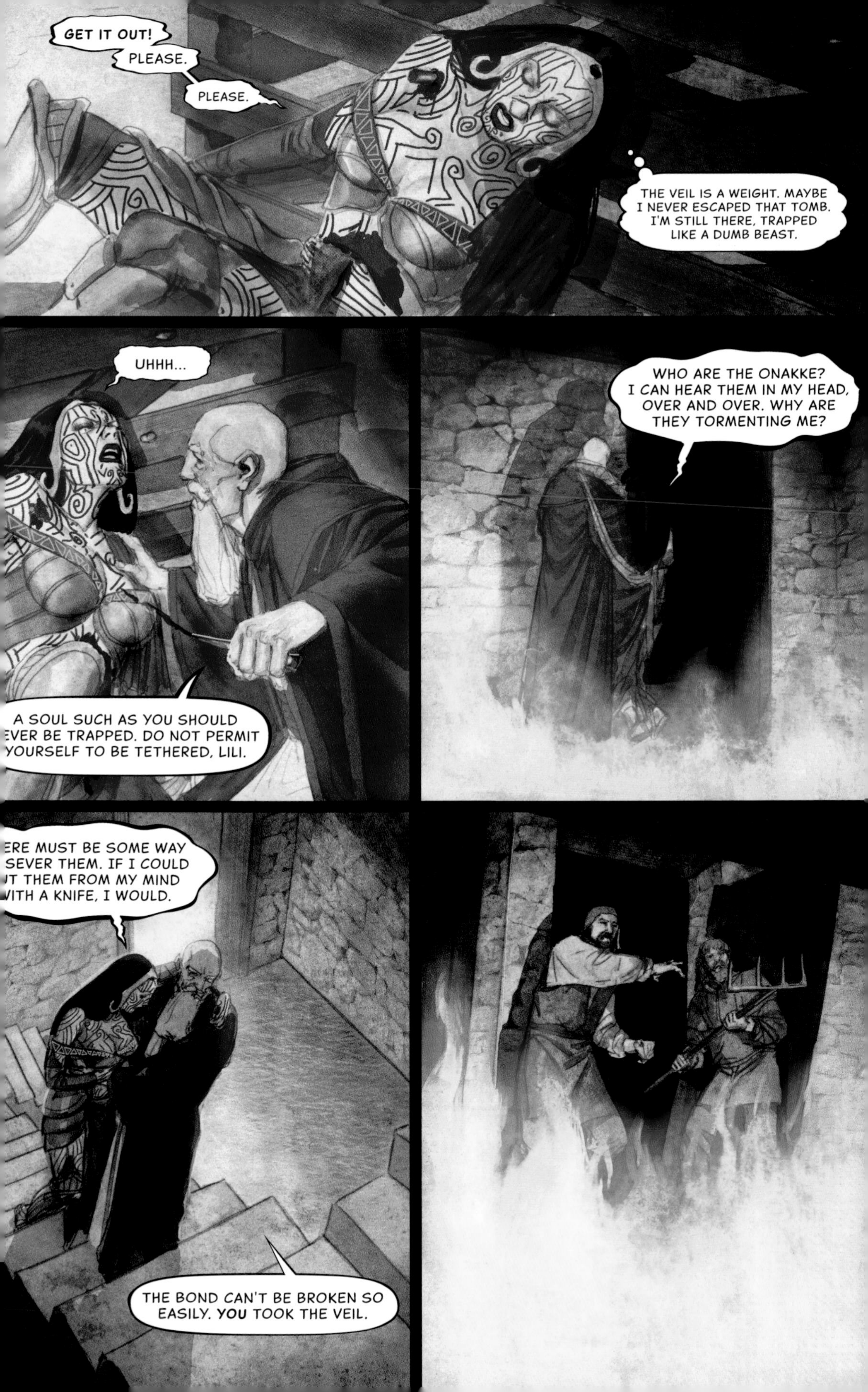
GET IT OUT!
PLEASE.
PLEASE.
THE VEIL IS A WEIGHT. MAYBE I NEVER ESCAPED THAT TOMB. I'M STILL THERE, TRAPPED LIKE A DUMB BEAST.
UHHH...
A SOUL SUCH AS YOU SHOULD EVER BE TRAPPED. DO NOT PERMIT YOURSELF TO BE TETHERED, LILI.
WHO ARE THE ONAKKE? I CAN HEAR THEM IN MY HEAD, OVER AND OVER. WHY ARE THEY TORMENTING ME?
ERE MUST BE SOME WAY SEVER THEM. IF I COULD IT THEM FROM MY MIND WITH A KNIFE, I WOULD.
THE BOND CAN'T BE BROKEN SO EASILY. YOU TOOK THE VEIL.

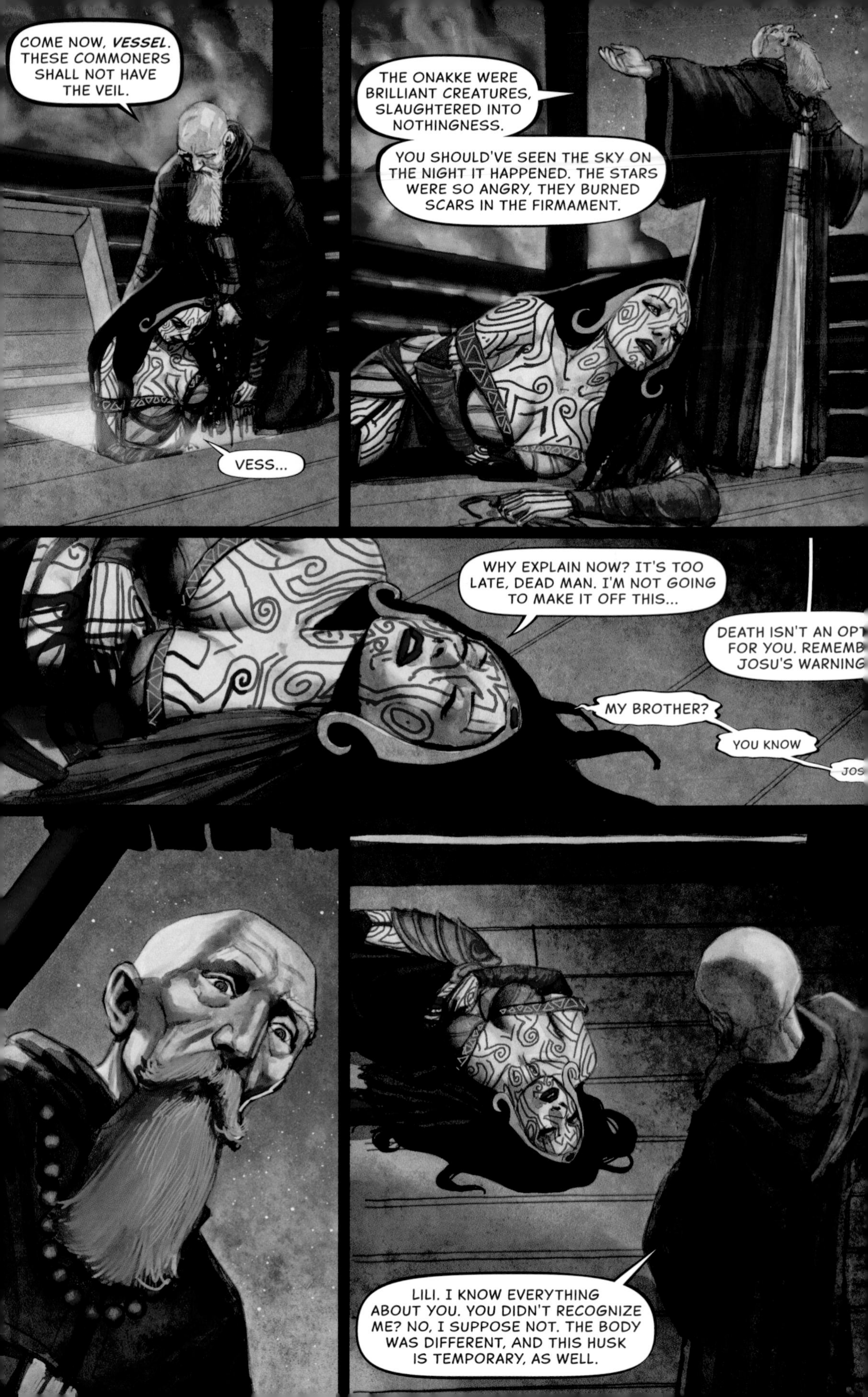
COME NOW, *VESSEL*. THESE COMMONERS SHALL NOT HAVE THE VEIL.
VESS...
THE ONAKKE WERE BRILLIANT CREATURES, SLAUGHTERED INTO NOTHINGNESS.
YOU SHOULD'VE SEEN THE SKY ON THE NIGHT IT HAPPENED. THE STARS WERE SO ANGRY, THEY BURNED SCARS IN THE FIRMAMENT.
WHY EXPLAIN NOW? IT'S TOO LATE, DEAD MAN. I'M NOT GOING TO MAKE IT OFF THIS...
DEATH ISN'T AN OPT FOR YOU. REMEMB JOSU'S WARNING
MY BROTHER?
YOU KNOW
JOS
LILI. I KNOW EVERYTHING ABOUT YOU. YOU DIDN'T RECOGNIZE ME? NO, I SUPPOSE NOT. THE BODY WAS DIFFERENT, AND THIS HUSK IS TEMPORARY, AS WELL.

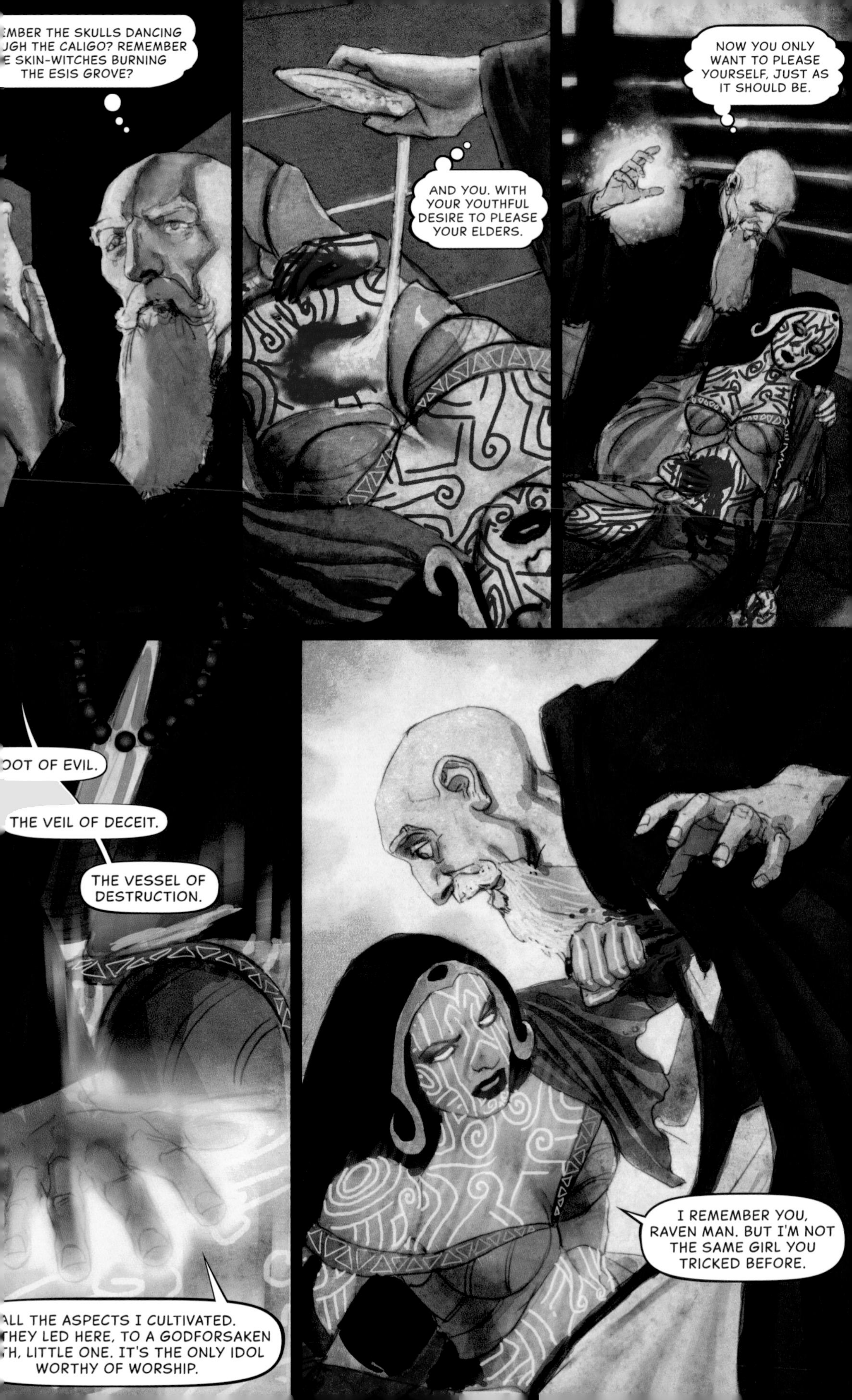
EMBER THE SKULLS DANCING UGH THE CALIGO? REMEMBER E SKIN-WITCHES BURNING THE ESIS GROVE?
AND YOU. WITH YOUR YOUTHFUL DESIRE TO PLEASE YOUR ELDERS.
NOW YOU ONLY WANT TO PLEASE YOURSELF, JUST AS IT SHOULD BE.
OOT OF EVIL.
THE VEIL OF DECEIT.
THE VESSEL OF DESTRUCTION.
ALL THE ASPECTS I CULTIVATED. THEY LED HERE, TO A GODFORSAKEN TH, LITTLE ONE. IT'S THE ONLY IDOL WORTHY OF WORSHIP.
I REMEMBER YOU, RAVEN MAN. BUT I'M NOT THE SAME GIRL YOU TRICKED BEFORE.

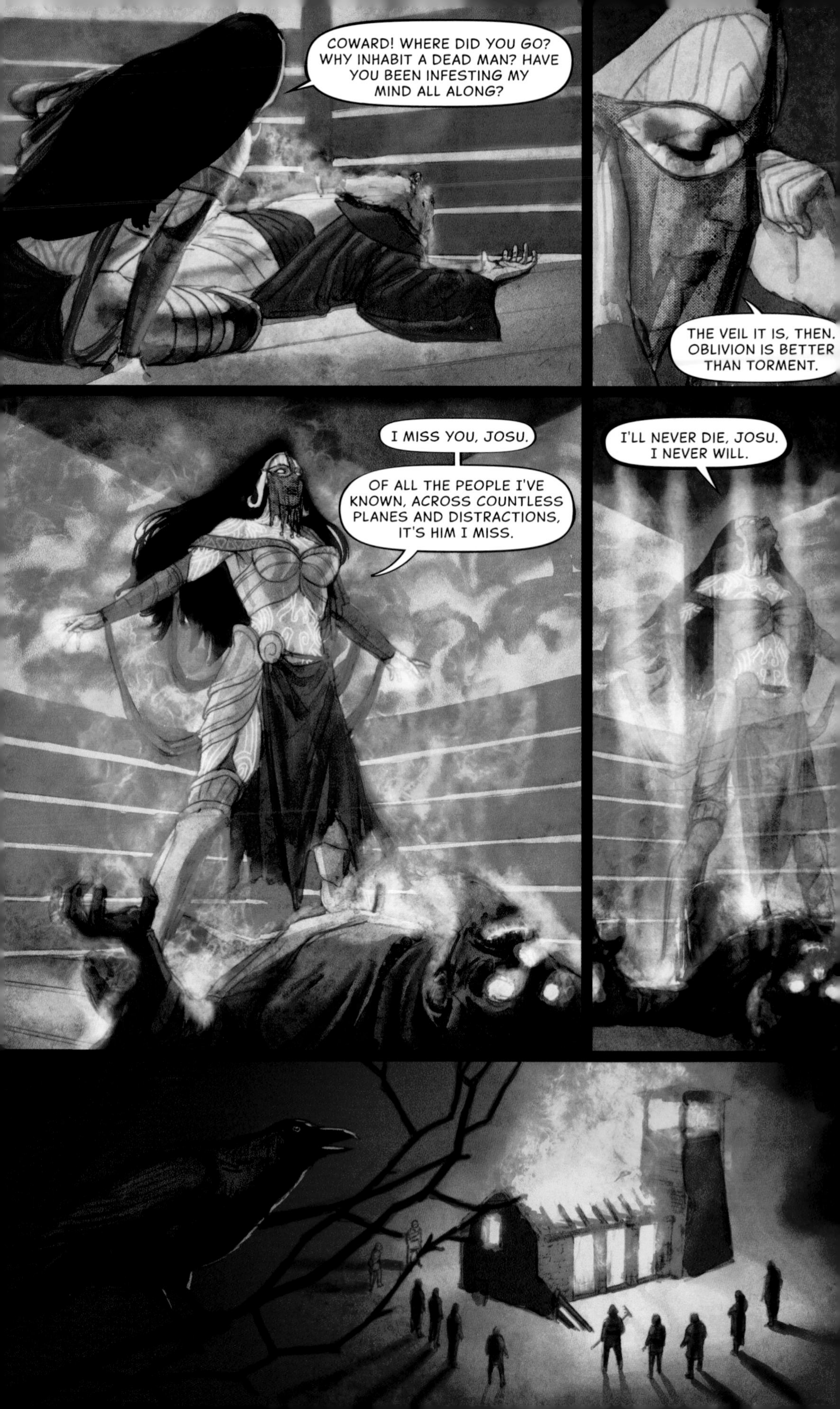
COWARD! WHERE DID YOU GO? WHY INHABIT A DEAD MAN? HAVE YOU BEEN INFESTING MY MIND ALL ALONG?
THE VEIL IT IS, THEN. OBLIVION IS BETTER THAN TORMENT.
I MISS YOU, JOSU.
OF ALL THE PEOPLE I'VE KNOWN, ACROSS COUNTLESS PLANES AND DISTRACTIONS, IT'S HIM I MISS.
I'LL NEVER DIE, JOSU. I NEVER WILL.

GATHERING FORCES

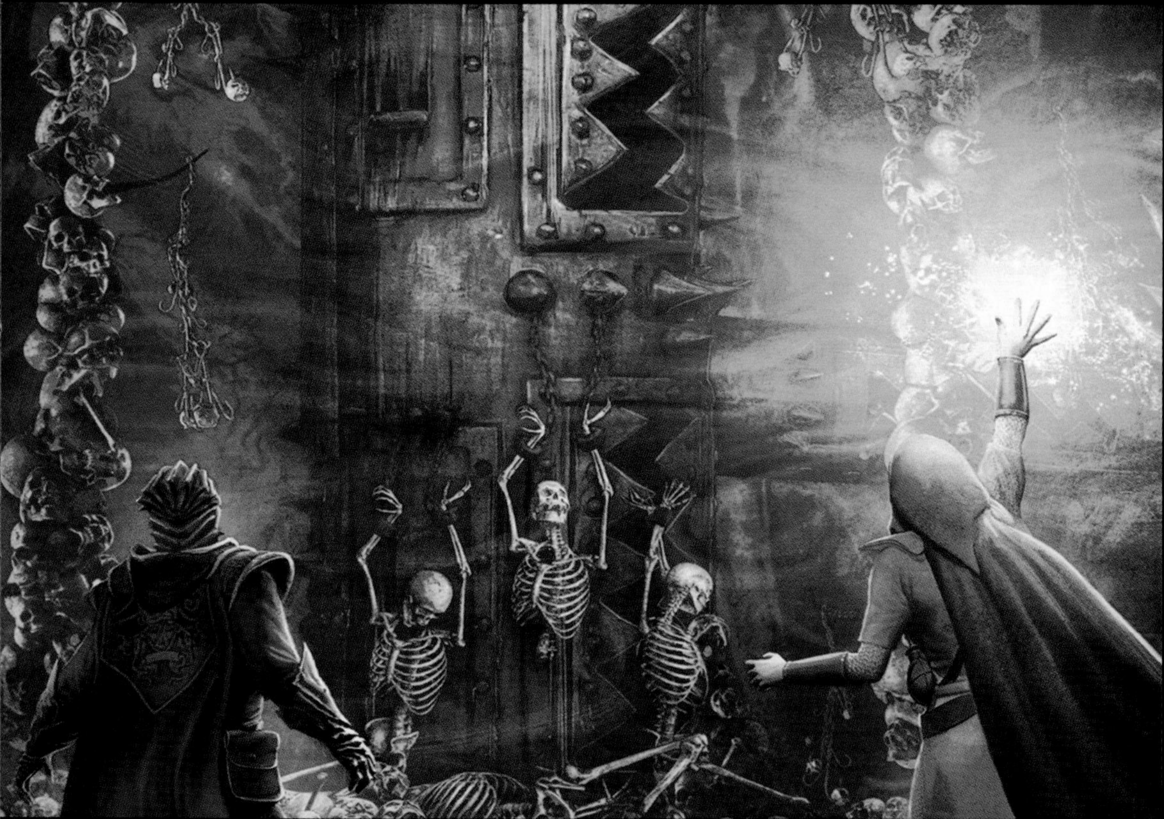

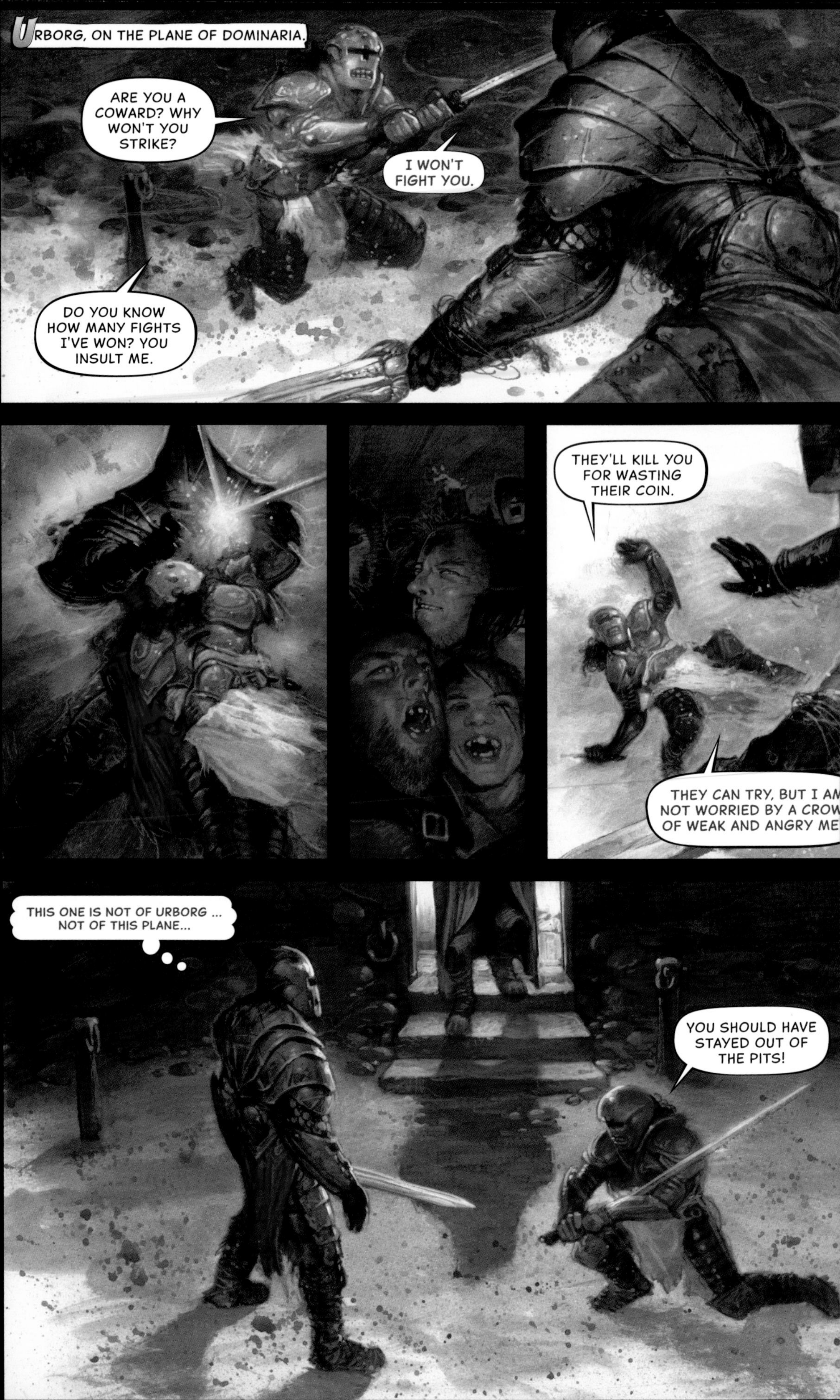
URBORG, ON THE PLANE OF DOMINARIA.
ARE YOU A COWARD? WHY WON'T YOU STRIKE?
I WON'T FIGHT YOU.
DO YOU KNOW HOW MANY FIGHTS I'VE WON? YOU INSULT ME.
THEY'LL KILL YOU FOR WASTING THEIR COIN.
THEY CAN TRY, BUT I AM NOT WORRIED BY A CROW OF WEAK AND ANGRY ME
THIS ONE IS NOT OF URBORG ... NOT OF THIS PLANE...
YOU SHOULD HAVE STAYED OUT OF THE PITS!

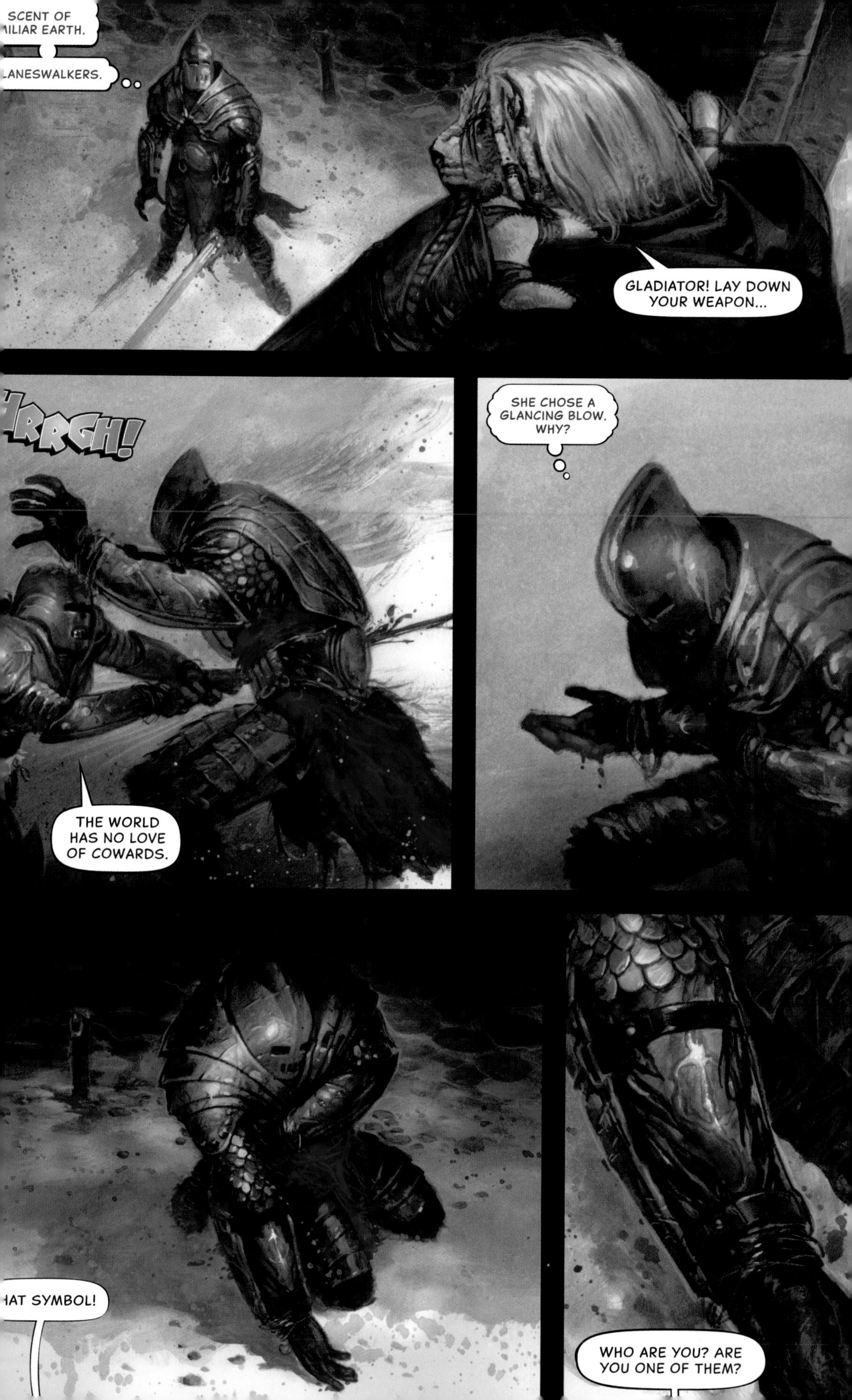
SCENT OF
ILIAR EARTH.
LANESWALKERS.
GLADIATOR! LAY DOWN YOUR WEAPON...
HRRGH!
THE WORLD HAS NO LOVE OF COWARDS.
SHE CHOSE A GLANCING BLOW. WHY?
HAT SYMBOL!
WHO ARE YOU? ARE YOU ONE OF THEM?

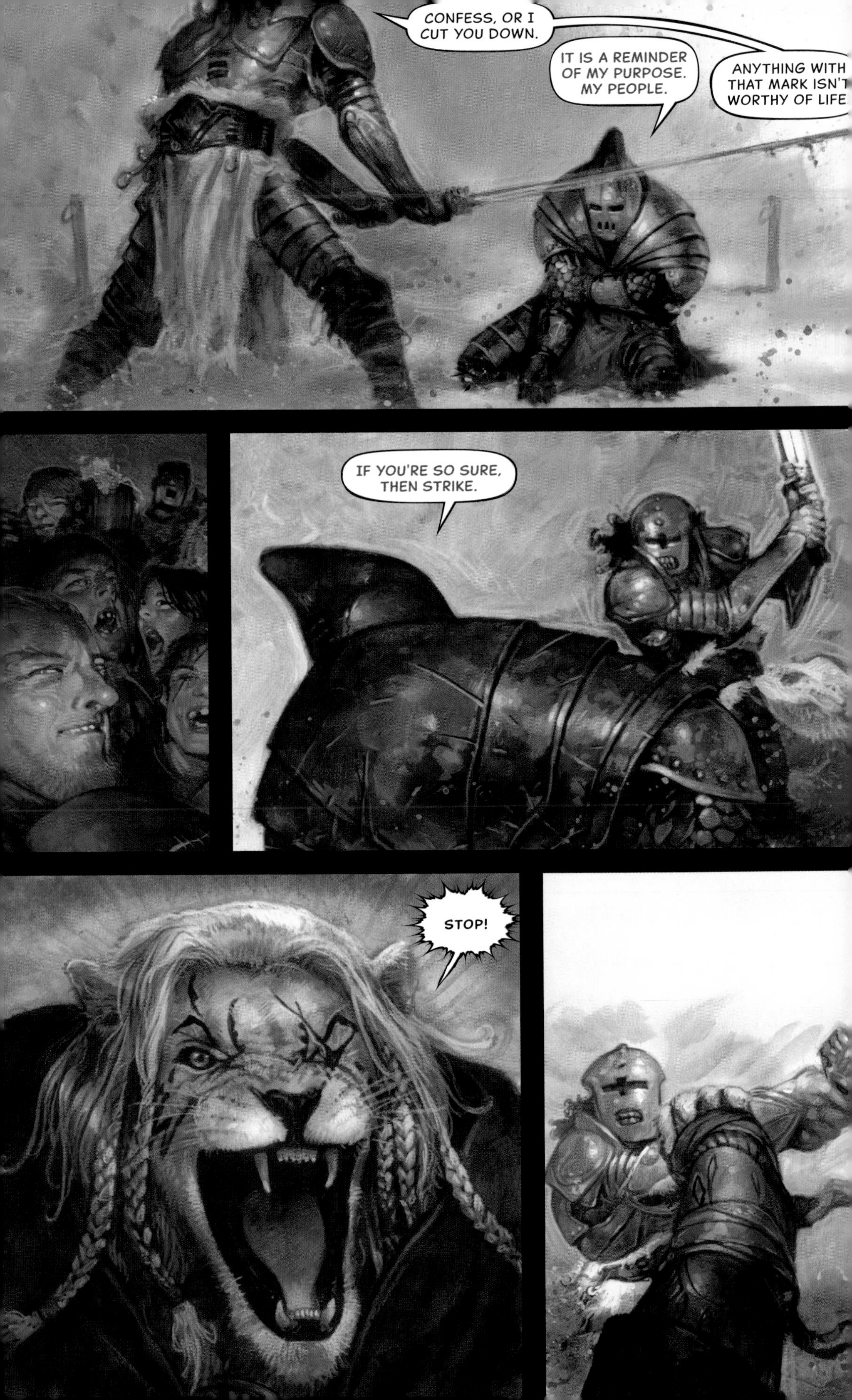
CONFESS, OR I CUT YOU DOWN.
IT IS A REMINDER OF MY PURPOSE. MY PEOPLE.
ANYTHING WITH THAT MARK ISN'T WORTHY OF LIFE
IF YOU'RE SO SURE, THEN STRIKE.
STOP!

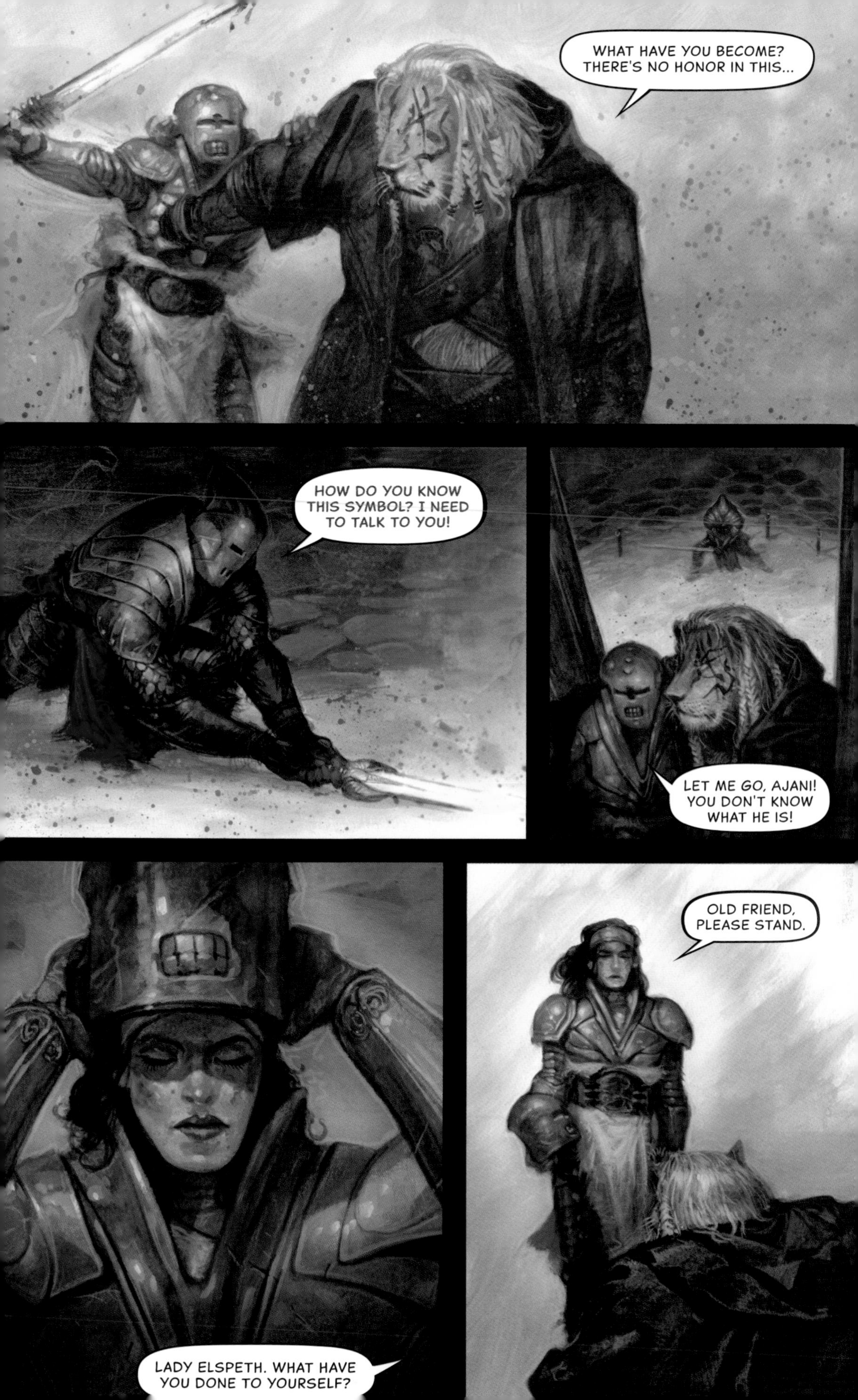
WHAT HAVE YOU BECOME? THERE'S NO HONOR IN THIS...
HOW DO YOU KNOW THIS SYMBOL? I NEED TO TALK TO YOU!
LET ME GO, AJANI! YOU DON'T KNOW WHAT HE IS!
LADY ELSPETH. WHAT HAVE YOU DONE TO YOURSELF?
OLD FRIEND, PLEASE STAND.

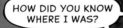

HOW DID YOU KNOW WHERE I WAS?

I SPOKE WITH YOUR FRIEND, ARAN. WHY URBORG, OF ALL PLACES?

I'D SPENT TIME HERE IN MY YOUTH, BEFORE I FOUND BANT. I KNEW WHAT TO EXPECT.

THERE ARE BETTER PLACES THAN THIS.

PERHAPS, BUT I / WEARY OF SEARCH AND DISAPPOINTM

ALARA IS BROKEN, BUT IT'S NOT LOST. YOU COULD BE A GREAT AID AND COMFORT.

BANT IS LOST FOREVER. ALARA IS NOT MY HOME.

VALERON'S TWELVE TREES S STAND. BANT HAS BECOME P OF SOMETHING LARGER.

WHAT'S LEFT OF BANT WILL OVERRUN, CONSUMED BY T UNDEAD. YOU KNOW THA

THAT IS NOT INEVITABLE. EVIL DOESN'T ALWAYS TRIUMPH.

BANT CAN STILL BE S COME BACK. TOGET WE ARE STRONGE

I CANNOT. I WILL NOT LEAD THEM. AND I CAN'T FACE THE EXPECTATION IN THEIR EYES.

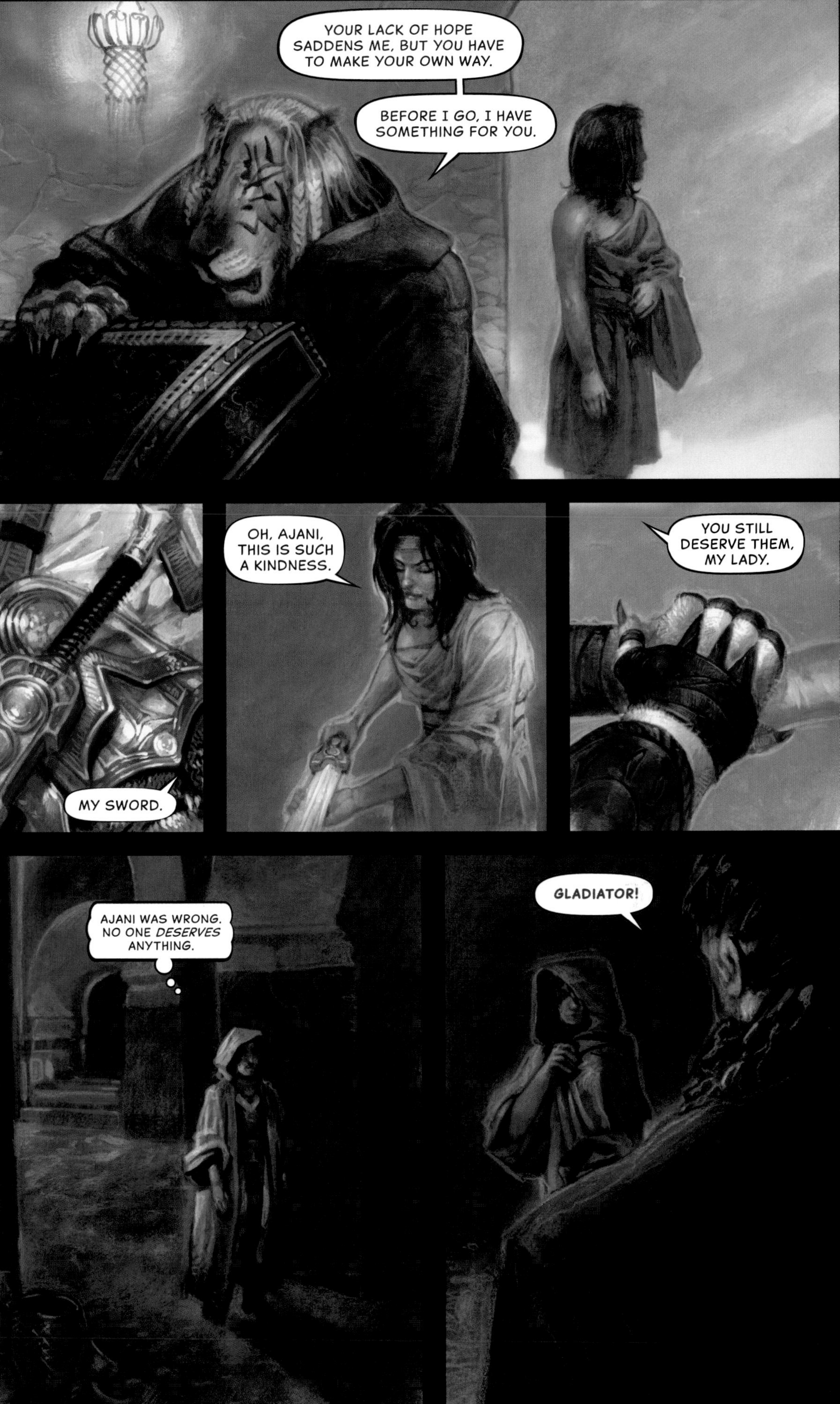
YOUR LACK OF HOPE SADDENS ME, BUT YOU HAVE TO MAKE YOUR OWN WAY.
BEFORE I GO, I HAVE SOMETHING FOR YOU.
MY SWORD.
OH, AJANI, THIS IS SUCH A KINDNESS.
YOU STILL DESERVE THEM, MY LADY.
AJANI WAS WRONG. NO ONE *DESERVES* ANYTHING.
GLADIATOR!

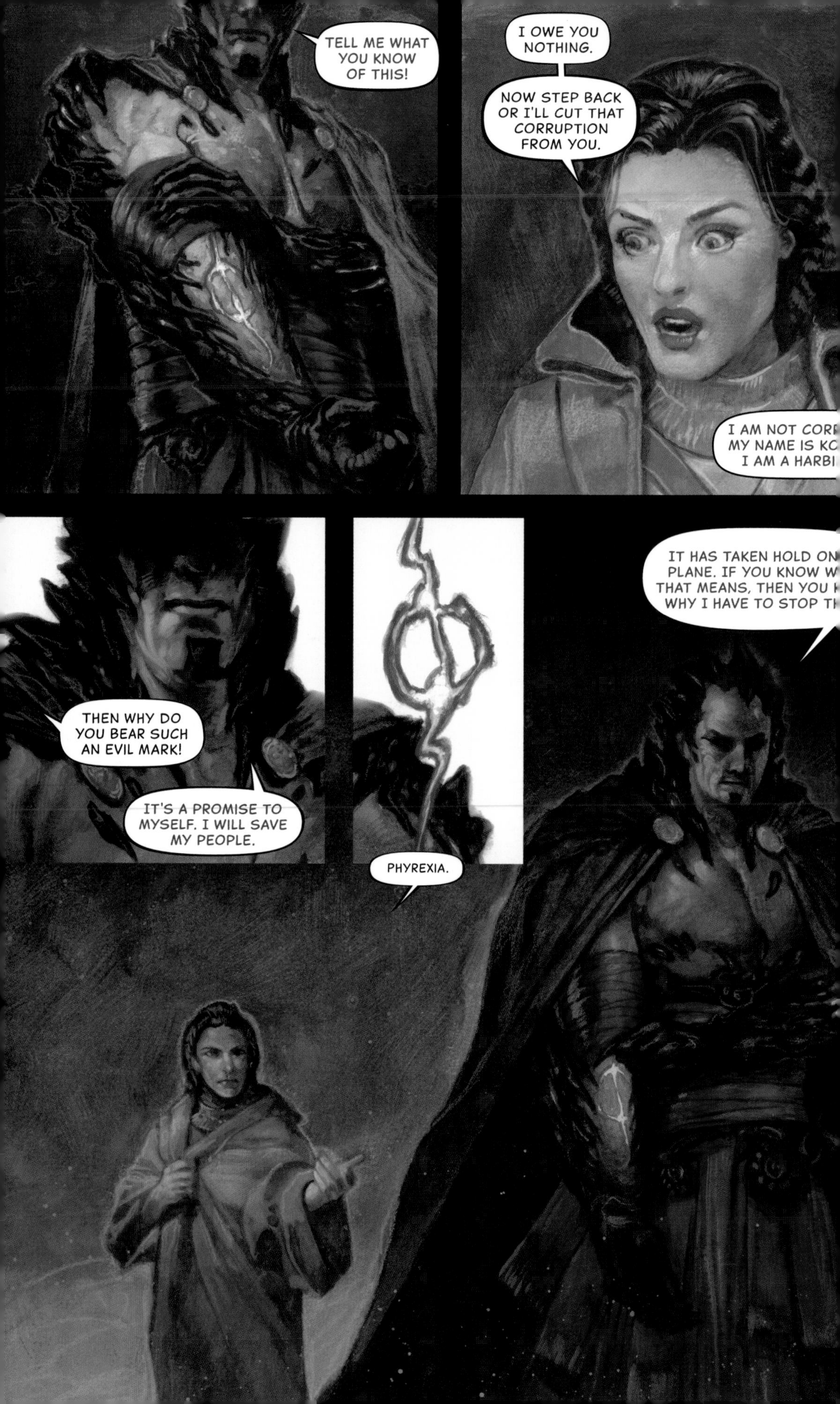
TELL ME WHAT YOU KNOW OF THIS!
I OWE YOU NOTHING.
NOW STEP BACK OR I'LL CUT THAT CORRUPTION FROM YOU.
I AM NOT COR
MY NAME IS KO
I AM A HARBI
THEN WHY DO YOU BEAR SUCH AN EVIL MARK!
IT'S A PROMISE TO MYSELF. I WILL SAVE MY PEOPLE.
PHYREXIA.
IT HAS TAKEN HOLD ON
PLANE. IF YOU KNOW W
THAT MEANS, THEN YOU
WHY I HAVE TO STOP T

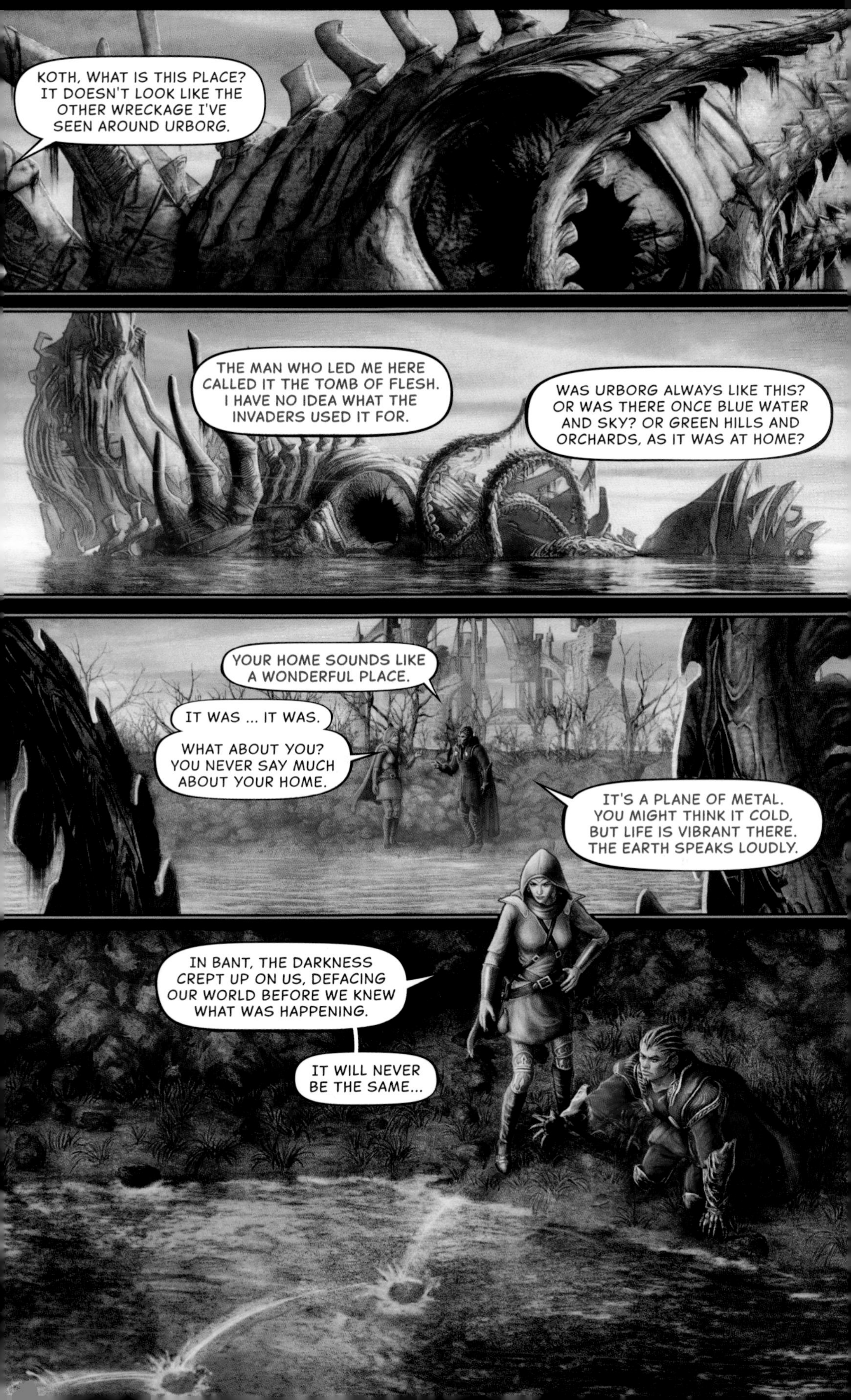
KOTH, WHAT IS THIS PLACE? IT DOESN'T LOOK LIKE THE OTHER WRECKAGE I'VE SEEN AROUND URBORG.
THE MAN WHO LED ME HERE CALLED IT THE TOMB OF FLESH. I HAVE NO IDEA WHAT THE INVADERS USED IT FOR.
WAS URBORG ALWAYS LIKE THIS? OR WAS THERE ONCE BLUE WATER AND SKY? OR GREEN HILLS AND ORCHARDS, AS IT WAS AT HOME?
YOUR HOME SOUNDS LIKE A WONDERFUL PLACE.
IT WAS ... IT WAS.
WHAT ABOUT YOU? YOU NEVER SAY MUCH ABOUT YOUR HOME.
IT'S A PLANE OF METAL. YOU MIGHT THINK IT COLD, BUT LIFE IS VIBRANT THERE. THE EARTH SPEAKS LOUDLY.
IN BANT, THE DARKNESS CREPT UP ON US, DEFACING OUR WORLD BEFORE WE KNEW WHAT WAS HAPPENING.
IT WILL NEVER BE THE SAME...

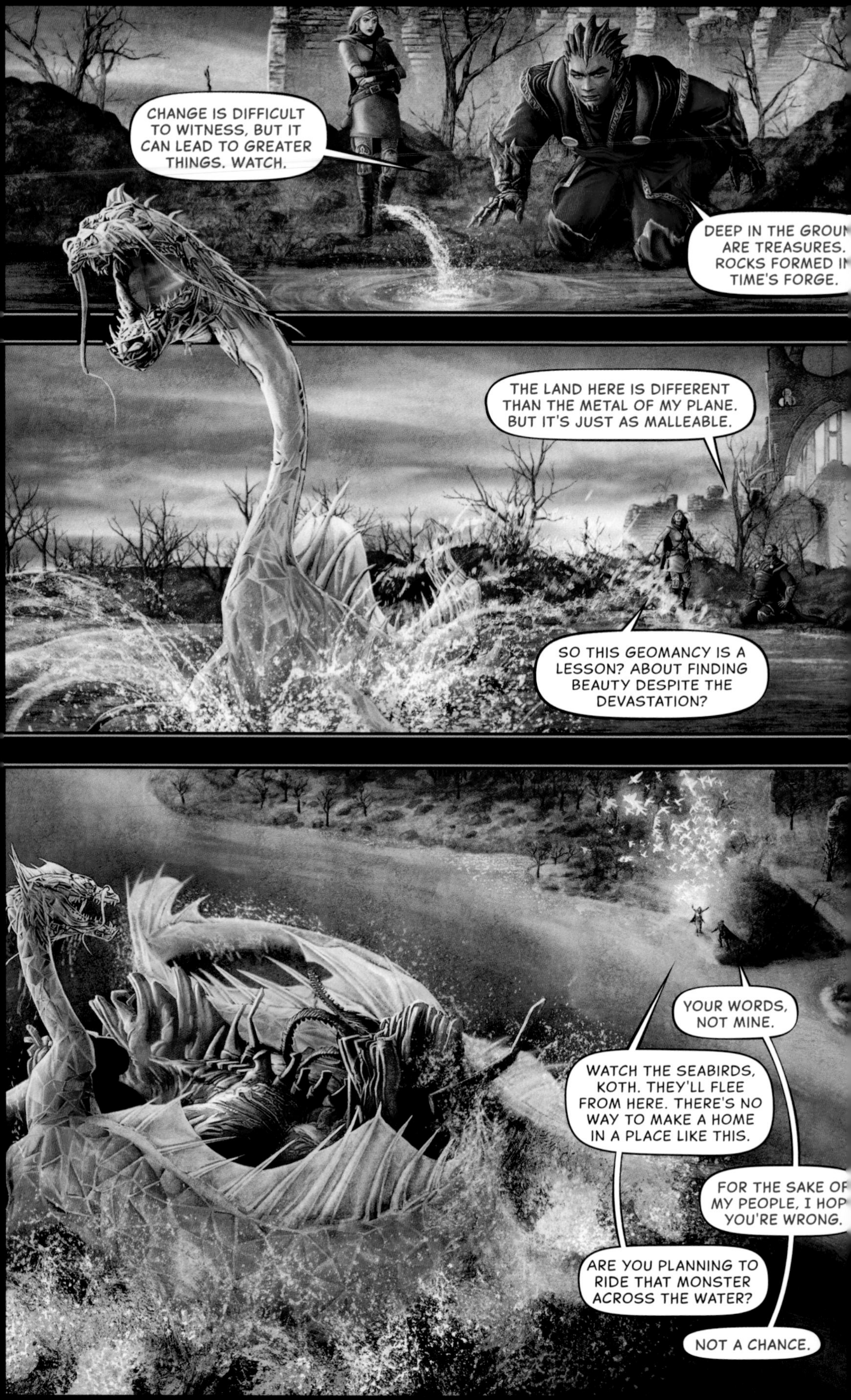
CHANGE IS DIFFICULT TO WITNESS, BUT IT CAN LEAD TO GREATER THINGS. WATCH.
DEEP IN THE GROUN ARE TREASURES. ROCKS FORMED I TIME'S FORGE.
THE LAND HERE IS DIFFERENT THAN THE METAL OF MY PLANE. BUT IT'S JUST AS MALLEABLE.
SO THIS GEOMANCY IS A LESSON? ABOUT FINDING BEAUTY DESPITE THE DEVASTATION?
YOUR WORDS, NOT MINE.
WATCH THE SEABIRDS, KOTH. THEY'LL FLEE FROM HERE. THERE'S NO WAY TO MAKE A HOME IN A PLACE LIKE THIS.
FOR THE SAKE OF MY PEOPLE, I HOP YOU'RE WRONG.
ARE YOU PLANNING TO RIDE THAT MONSTER ACROSS THE WATER?
NOT A CHANCE.

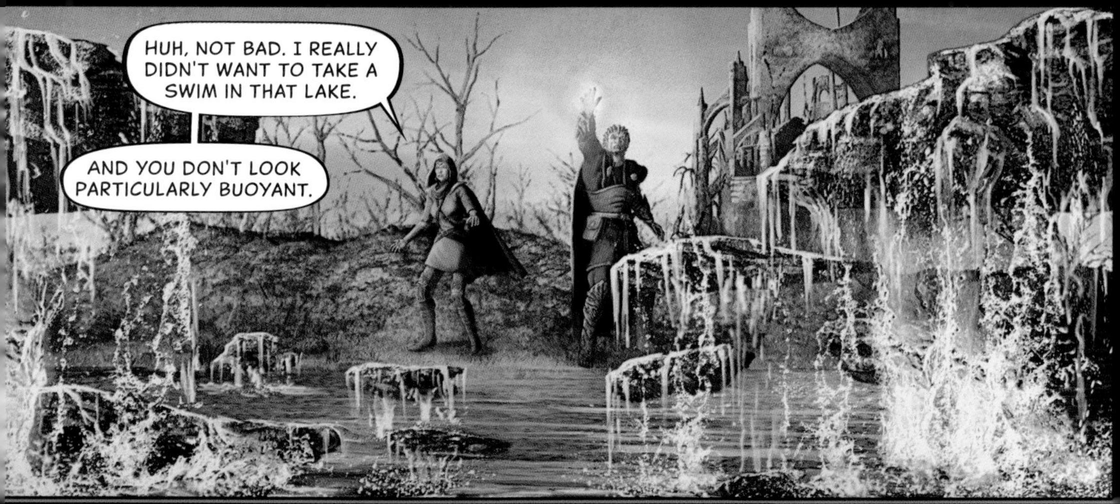
HUH, NOT BAD. I REALLY DIDN'T WANT TO TAKE A SWIM IN THAT LAKE.
AND YOU DON'T LOOK PARTICULARLY BUOYANT.

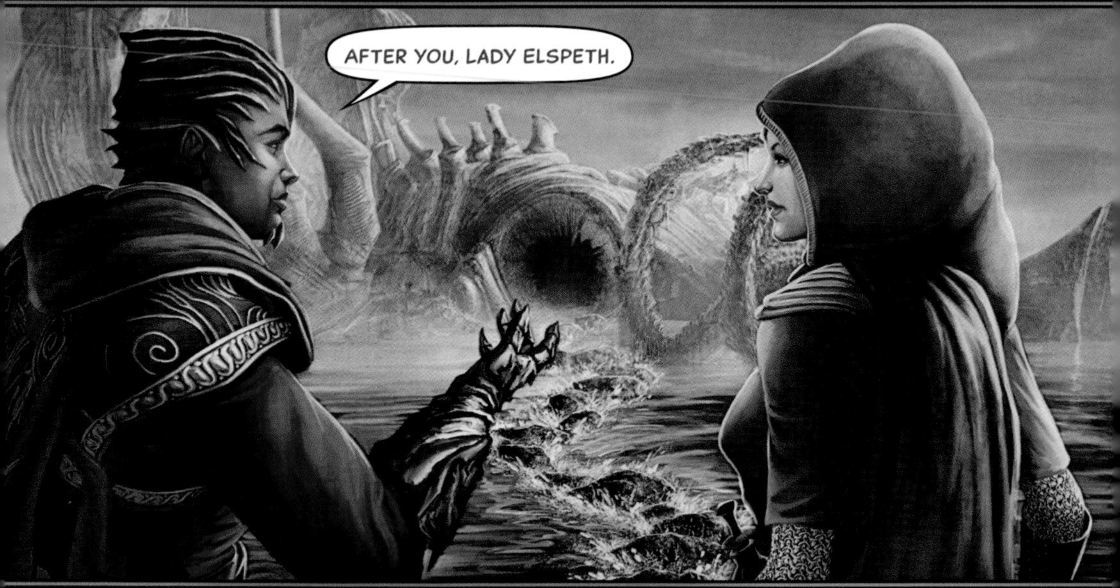
AFTER YOU, LADY ELSPETH.

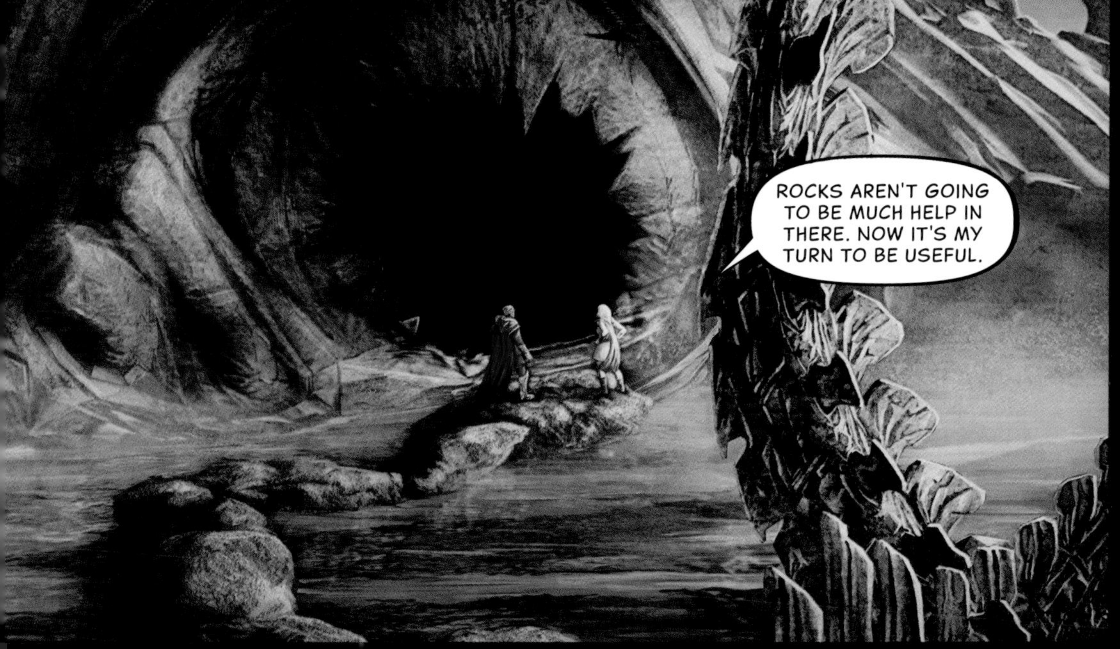
ROCKS AREN'T GOING TO BE MUCH HELP IN THERE. NOW IT'S MY TURN TO BE USEFUL.

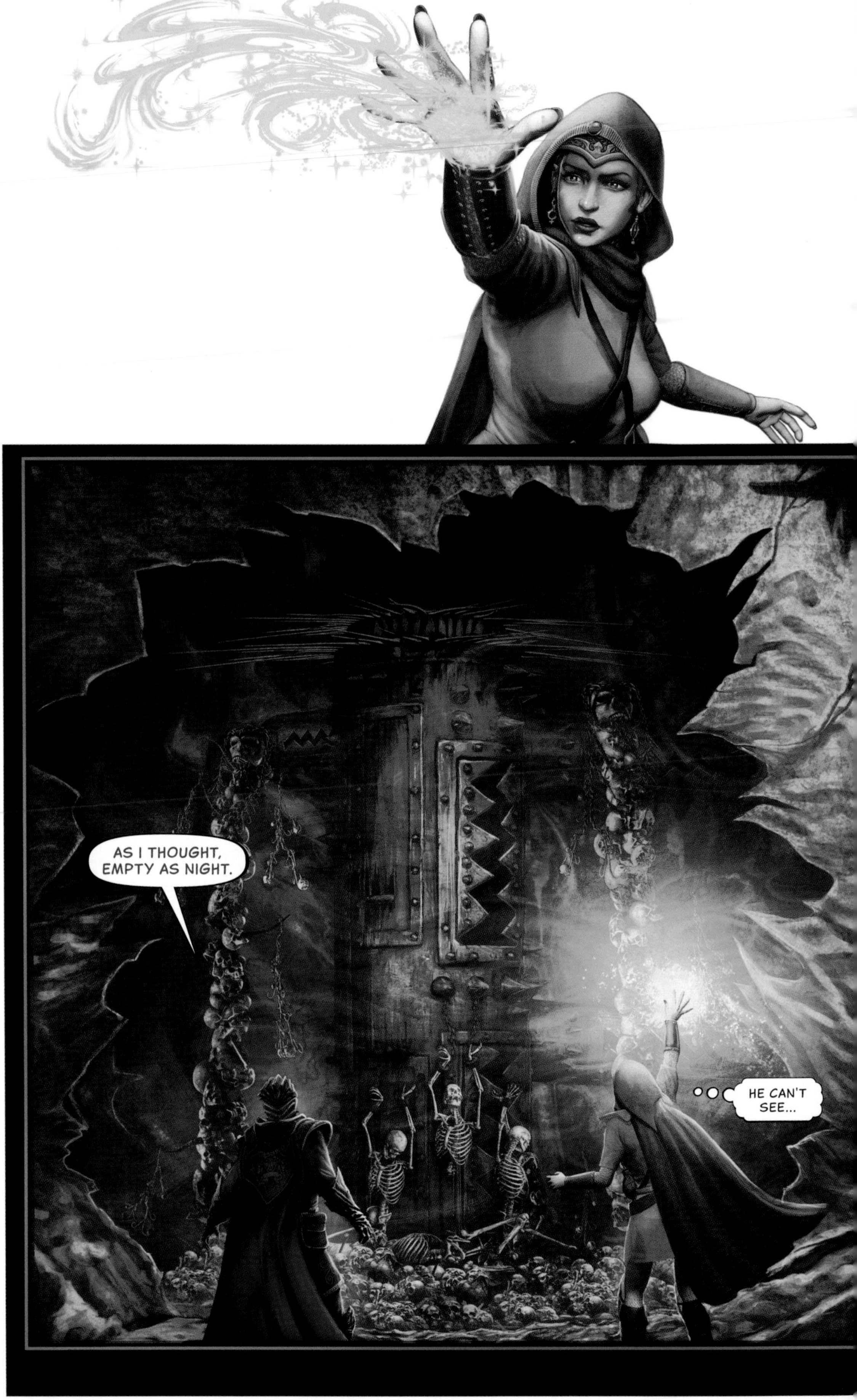
AS I THOUGHT, EMPTY AS NIGHT.
HE CAN'T SEE...

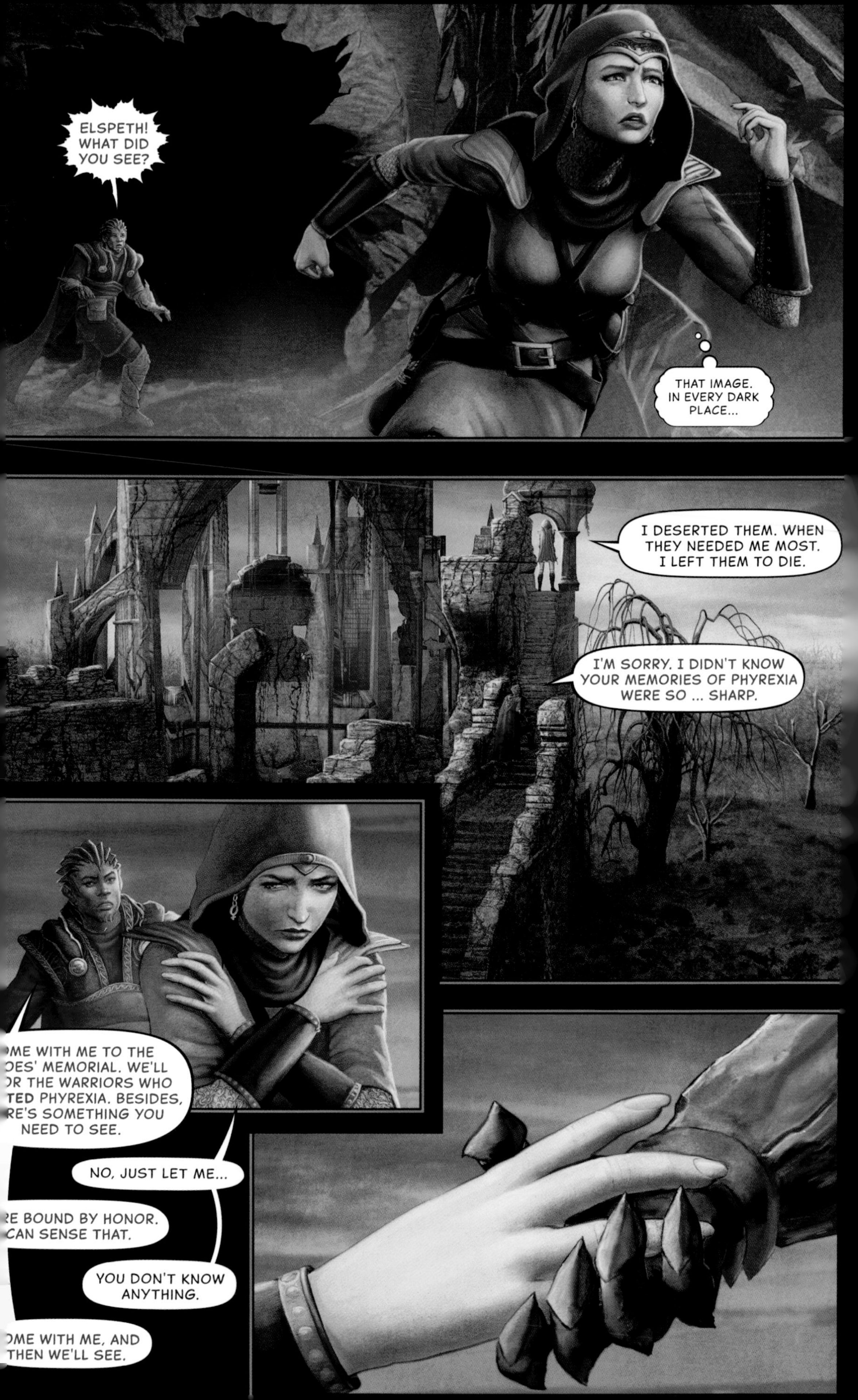
ELSPETH! WHAT DID YOU SEE?
THAT IMAGE. IN EVERY DARK PLACE...
I DESERTED THEM. WHEN THEY NEEDED ME MOST. I LEFT THEM TO DIE.
I'M SORRY. I DIDN'T KNOW YOUR MEMORIES OF PHYREXIA WERE SO ... SHARP.
OME WITH ME TO THE OES' MEMORIAL. WE'LL OR THE WARRIORS WHO TED PHYREXIA. BESIDES, RE'S SOMETHING YOU NEED TO SEE.
NO, JUST LET ME...
E BOUND BY HONOR. CAN SENSE THAT.
YOU DON'T KNOW ANYTHING.
OME WITH ME, AND THEN WE'LL SEE.

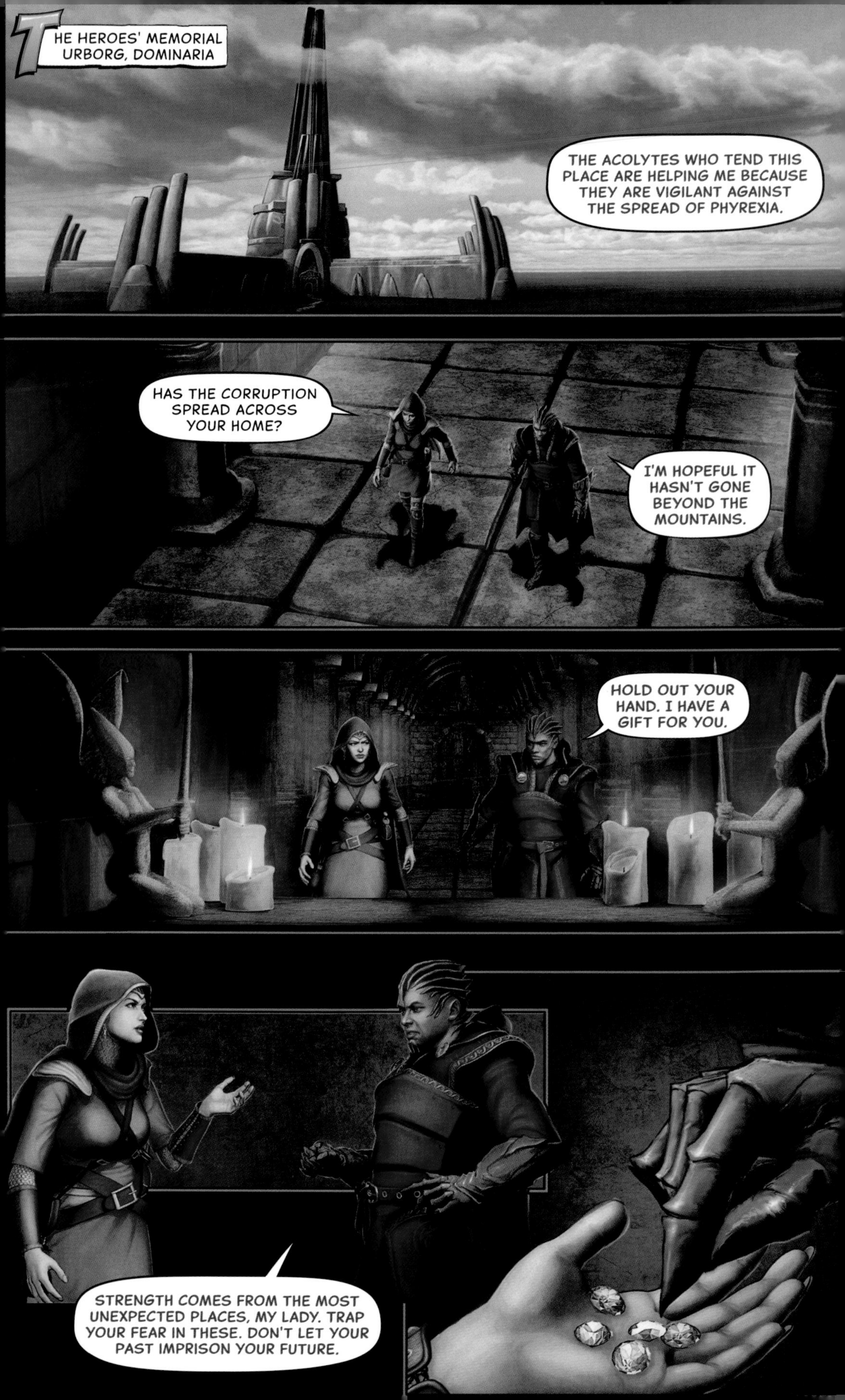
THE HEROES' MEMORIAL
URBORG, DOMINARIA
THE ACOLYTES WHO TEND THIS PLACE ARE HELPING ME BECAUSE THEY ARE VIGILANT AGAINST THE SPREAD OF PHYREXIA.
HAS THE CORRUPTION SPREAD ACROSS YOUR HOME?
I'M HOPEFUL IT HASN'T GONE BEYOND THE MOUNTAINS.
HOLD OUT YOUR HAND. I HAVE A GIFT FOR YOU.
STRENGTH COMES FROM THE MOST UNEXPECTED PLACES, MY LADY. TRAP YOUR FEAR IN THESE. DON'T LET YOUR PAST IMPRISON YOUR FUTURE.

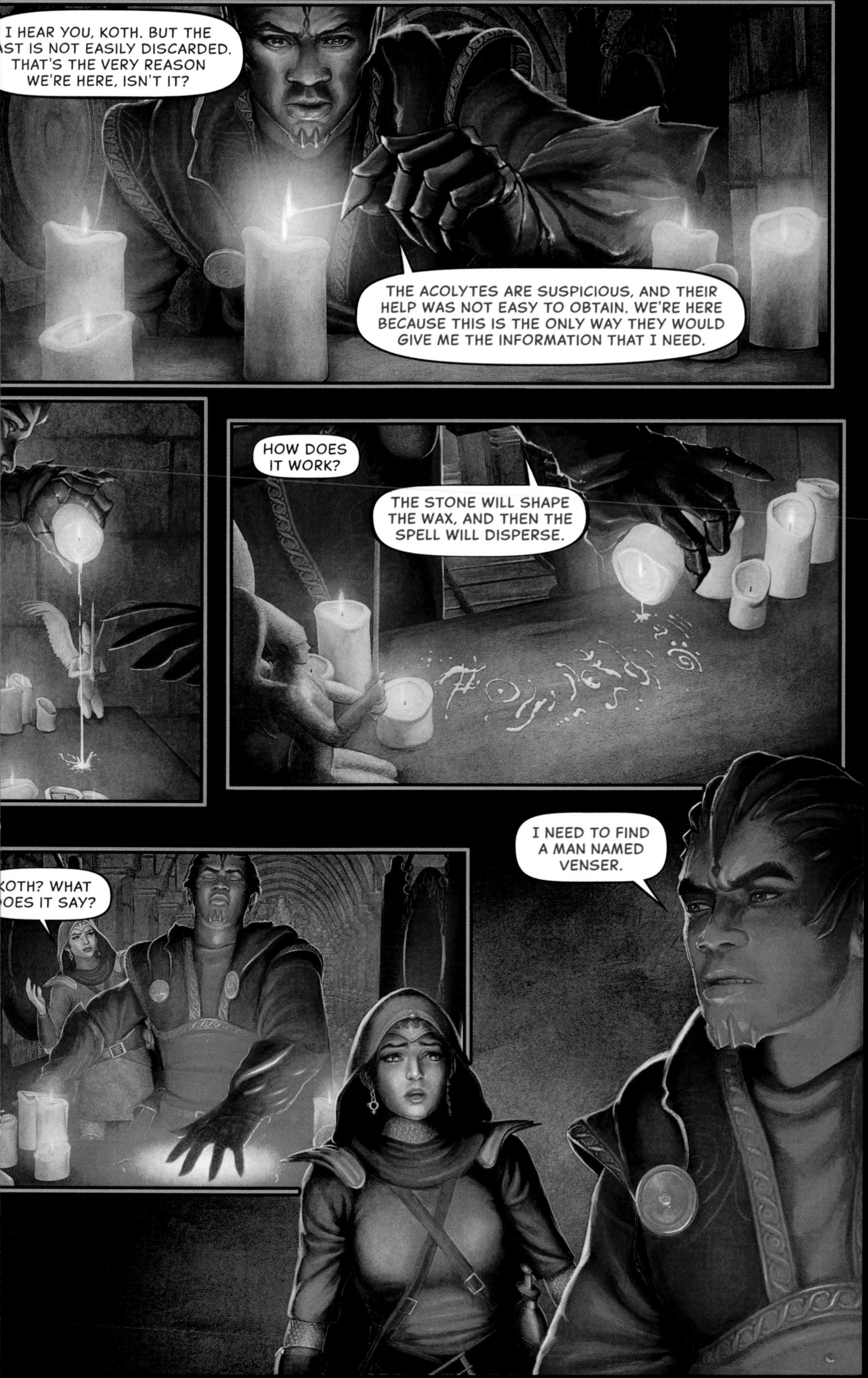
I HEAR YOU, KOTH. BUT THE AST IS NOT EASILY DISCARDED. THAT'S THE VERY REASON WE'RE HERE, ISN'T IT?
THE ACOLYTES ARE SUSPICIOUS, AND THEIR HELP WAS NOT EASY TO OBTAIN. WE'RE HERE BECAUSE THIS IS THE ONLY WAY THEY WOULD GIVE ME THE INFORMATION THAT I NEED.
HOW DOES IT WORK?
THE STONE WILL SHAPE THE WAX, AND THEN THE SPELL WILL DISPERSE.
KOTH? WHAT OES IT SAY?
I NEED TO FIND A MAN NAMED VENSER.

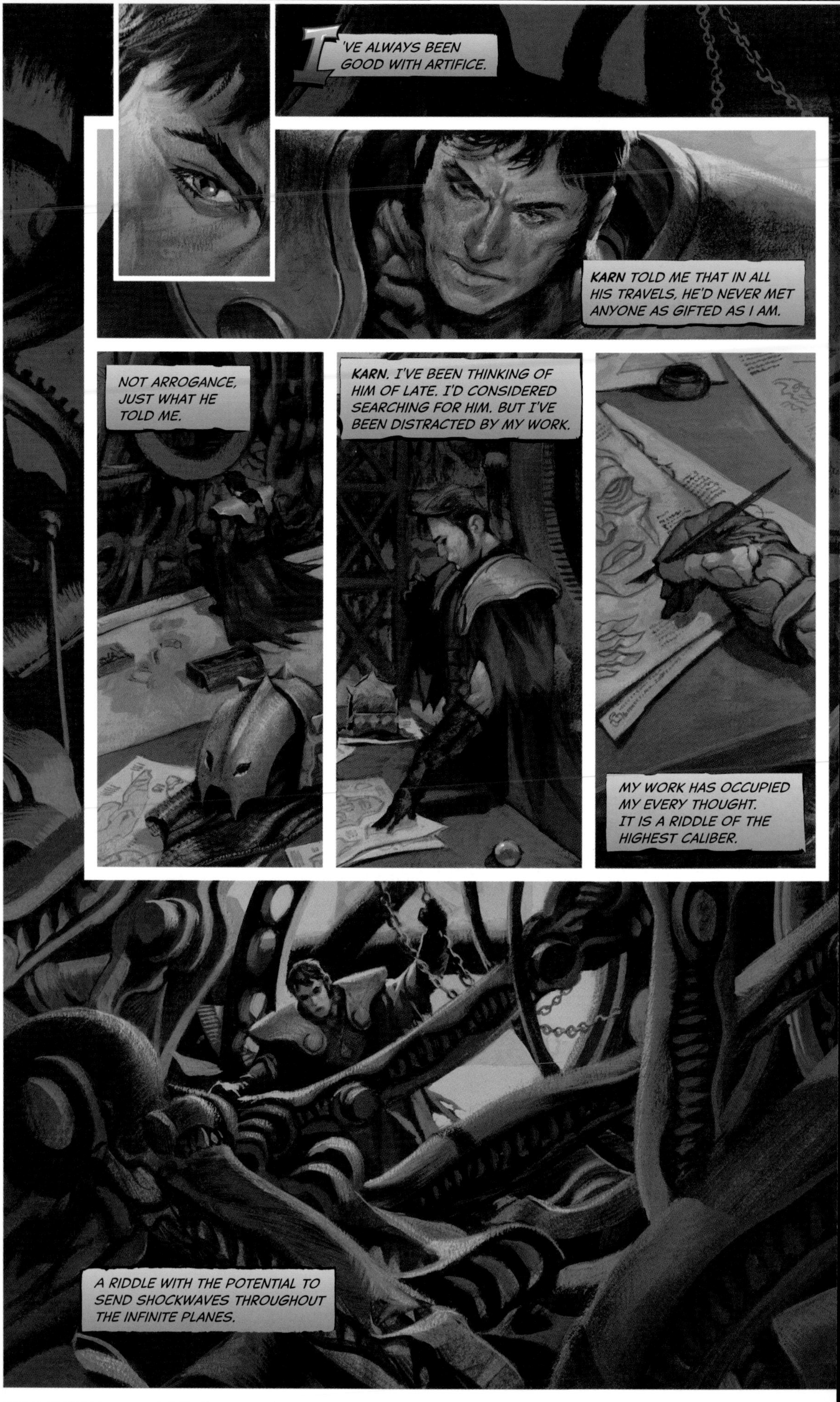
I'VE ALWAYS BEEN GOOD WITH ARTIFICE.
KARN TOLD ME THAT IN ALL HIS TRAVELS, HE'D NEVER MET ANYONE AS GIFTED AS I AM.
NOT ARROGANCE, JUST WHAT HE TOLD ME.
KARN. I'VE BEEN THINKING OF HIM OF LATE. I'D CONSIDERED SEARCHING FOR HIM. BUT I'VE BEEN DISTRACTED BY MY WORK.
MY WORK HAS OCCUPIED MY EVERY THOUGHT. IT IS A RIDDLE OF THE HIGHEST CALIBER.
A RIDDLE WITH THE POTENTIAL TO SEND SHOCKWAVES THROUGHOUT THE INFINITE PLANES.

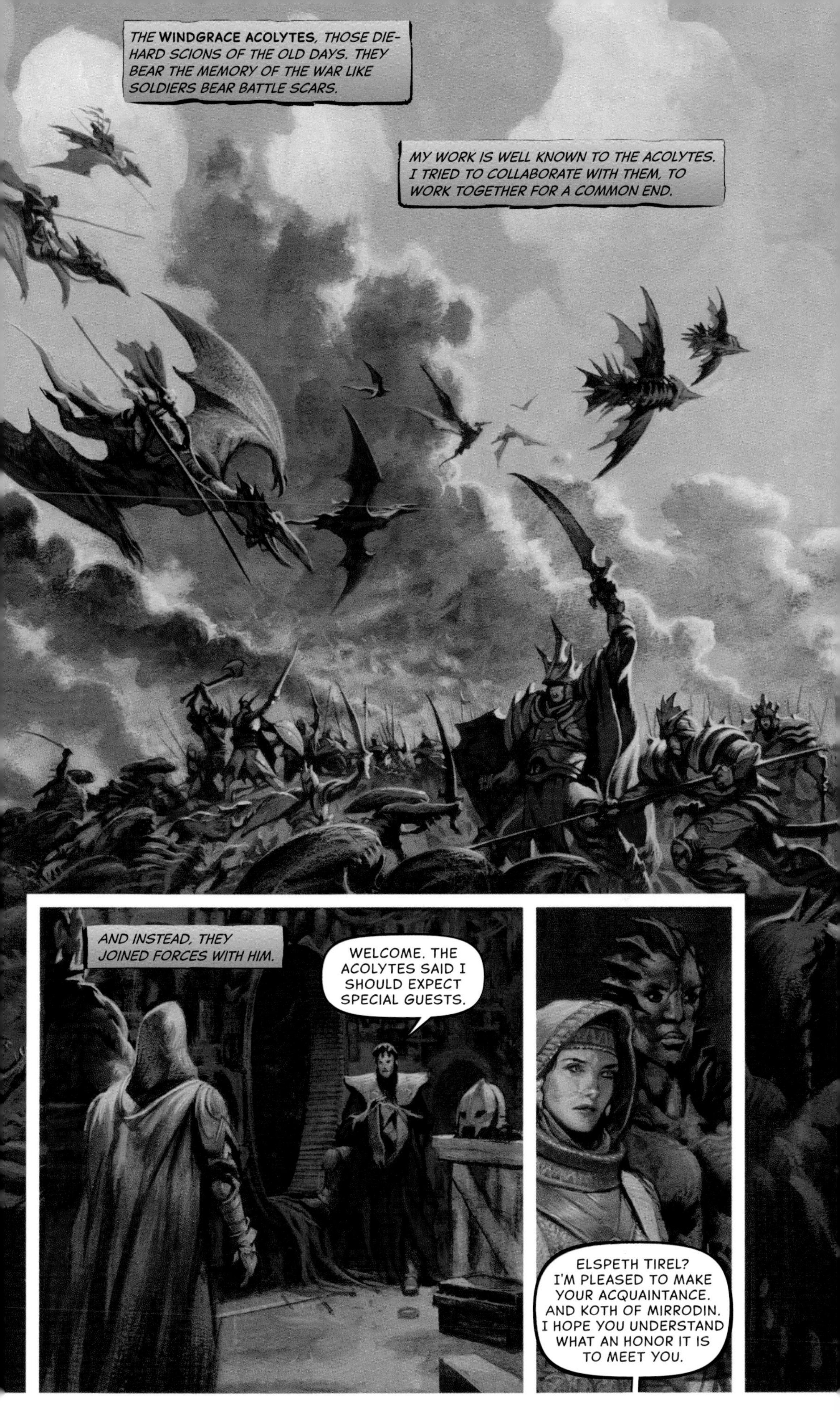
THE WINDGRACE ACOLYTES, THOSE DIE-HARD SCIONS OF THE OLD DAYS. THEY BEAR THE MEMORY OF THE WAR LIKE SOLDIERS BEAR BATTLE SCARS.
MY WORK IS WELL KNOWN TO THE ACOLYTES. I TRIED TO COLLABORATE WITH THEM, TO WORK TOGETHER FOR A COMMON END.
AND INSTEAD, THEY JOINED FORCES WITH HIM.
WELCOME. THE ACOLYTES SAID I SHOULD EXPECT SPECIAL GUESTS.
ELSPETH TIREL? I'M PLEASED TO MAKE YOUR ACQUAINTANCE. AND KOTH OF MIRRODIN. I HOPE YOU UNDERSTAND WHAT AN HONOR IT IS TO MEET YOU.

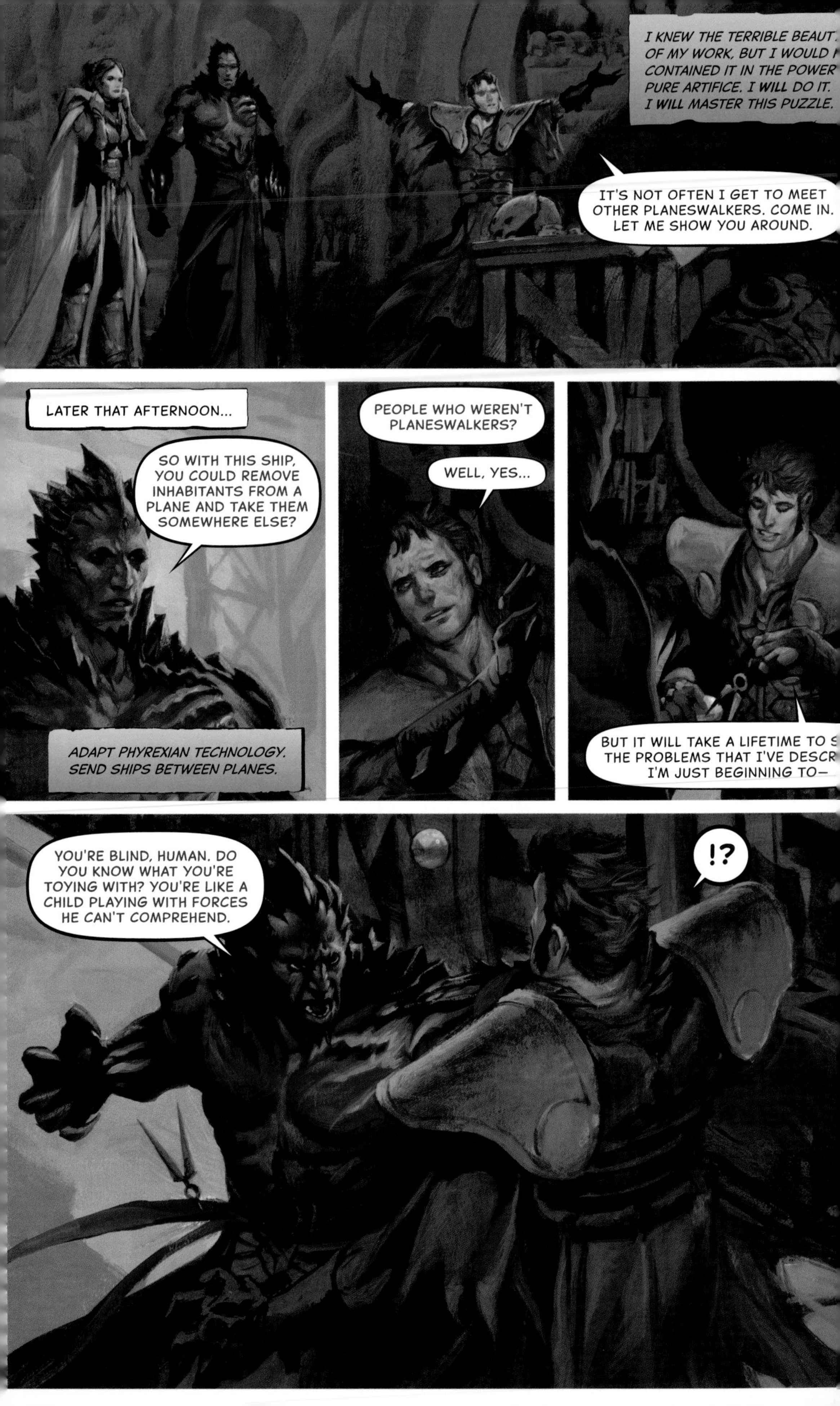
I KNEW THE TERRIBLE BEAUT
OF MY WORK, BUT I WOULD
CONTAINED IT IN THE POWER
PURE ARTIFICE. I WILL DO IT.
I WILL MASTER THIS PUZZLE.
IT'S NOT OFTEN I GET TO MEET OTHER PLANESWALKERS. COME IN. LET ME SHOW YOU AROUND.
LATER THAT AFTERNOON...
SO WITH THIS SHIP, YOU COULD REMOVE INHABITANTS FROM A PLANE AND TAKE THEM SOMEWHERE ELSE?
ADAPT PHYREXIAN TECHNOLOGY. SEND SHIPS BETWEEN PLANES.
PEOPLE WHO WEREN'T PLANESWALKERS?
WELL, YES...
BUT IT WILL TAKE A LIFETIME TO
THE PROBLEMS THAT I'VE DESCR
I'M JUST BEGINNING TO—
YOU'RE BLIND, HUMAN. DO YOU KNOW WHAT YOU'RE TOYING WITH? YOU'RE LIKE A CHILD PLAYING WITH FORCES HE CAN'T COMPREHEND.
!?

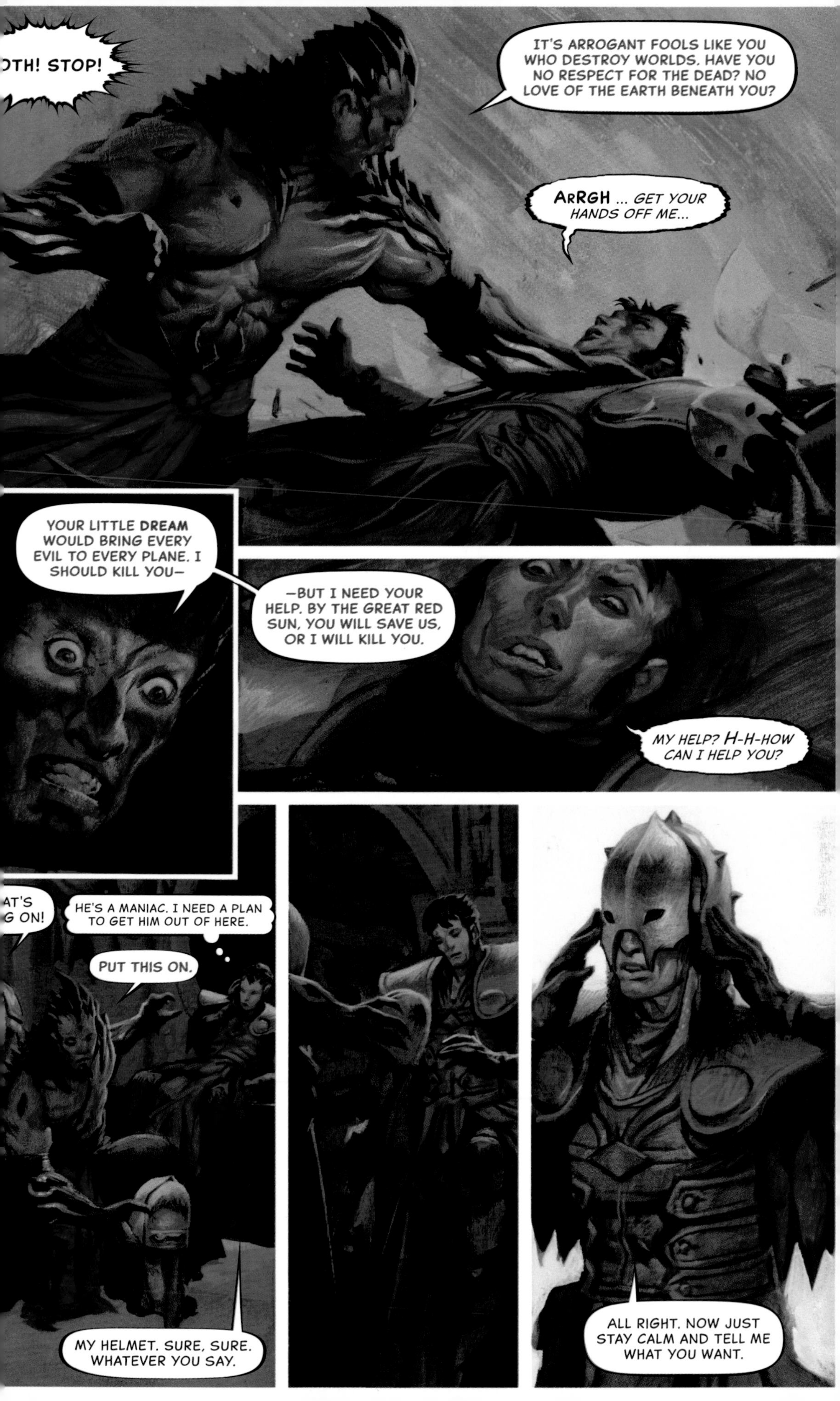

OTH! STOP!
IT'S ARROGANT FOOLS LIKE YOU WHO DESTROY WORLDS. HAVE YOU NO RESPECT FOR THE DEAD? NO LOVE OF THE EARTH BENEATH YOU?
ARRGH ... GET YOUR HANDS OFF ME...
YOUR LITTLE DREAM WOULD BRING EVERY EVIL TO EVERY PLANE. I SHOULD KILL YOU—
—BUT I NEED YOUR HELP. BY THE GREAT RED SUN, YOU WILL SAVE US, OR I WILL KILL YOU.
MY HELP? H-H-HOW CAN I HELP YOU?
AT'S G ON!
HE'S A MANIAC. I NEED A PLAN TO GET HIM OUT OF HERE.
PUT THIS ON.
MY HELMET. SURE, SURE. WHATEVER YOU SAY.
ALL RIGHT. NOW JUST STAY CALM AND TELL ME WHAT YOU WANT.

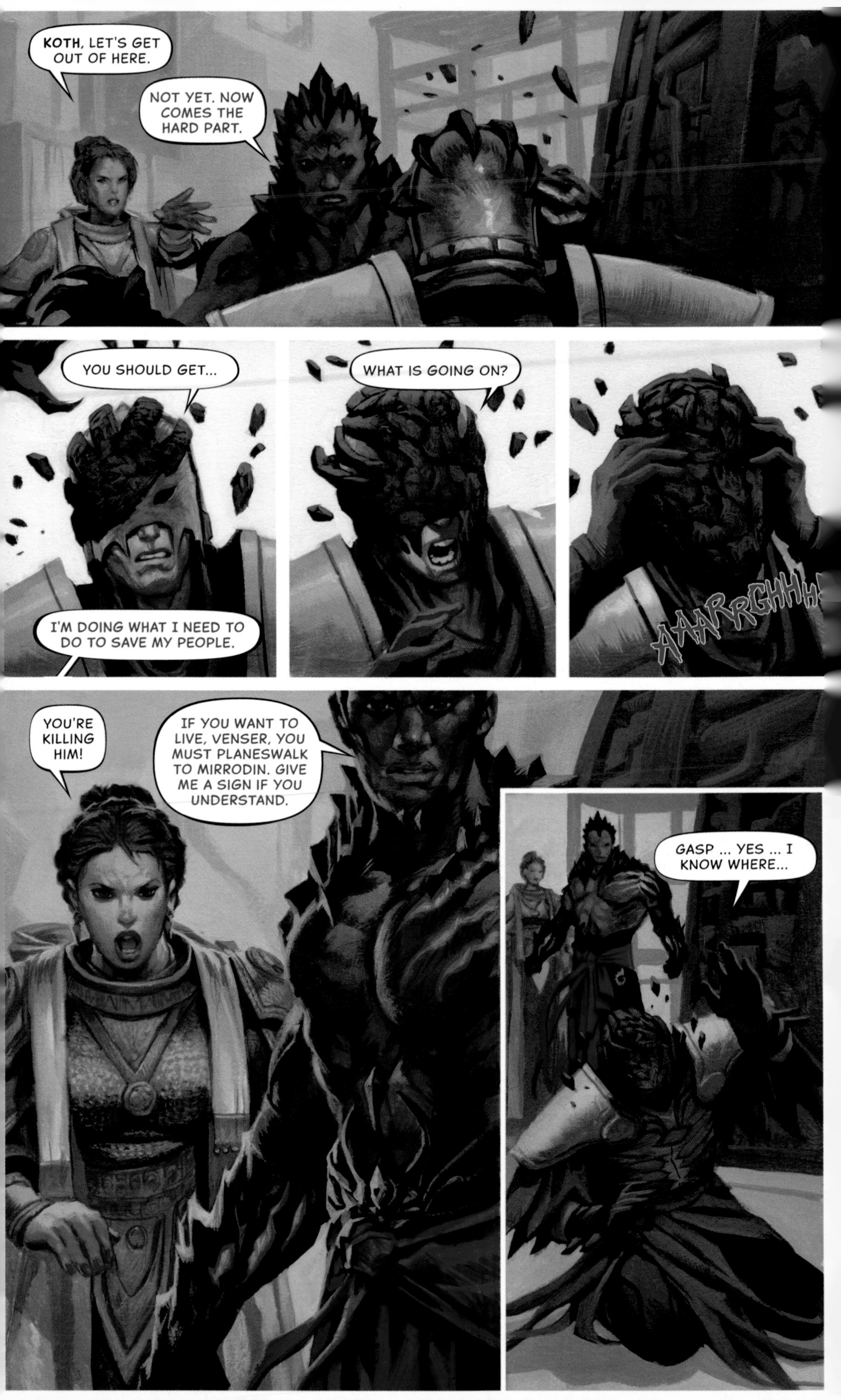
KOTH, LET'S GET OUT OF HERE.
NOT YET. NOW COMES THE HARD PART.
YOU SHOULD GET...
I'M DOING WHAT I NEED TO DO TO SAVE MY PEOPLE.
WHAT IS GOING ON?
AAARRGHHH!
YOU'RE KILLING HIM!
IF YOU WANT TO LIVE, VENSER, YOU MUST PLANESWALK TO MIRRODIN. GIVE ME A SIGN IF YOU UNDERSTAND.
GASP ... YES ... I KNOW WHERE...

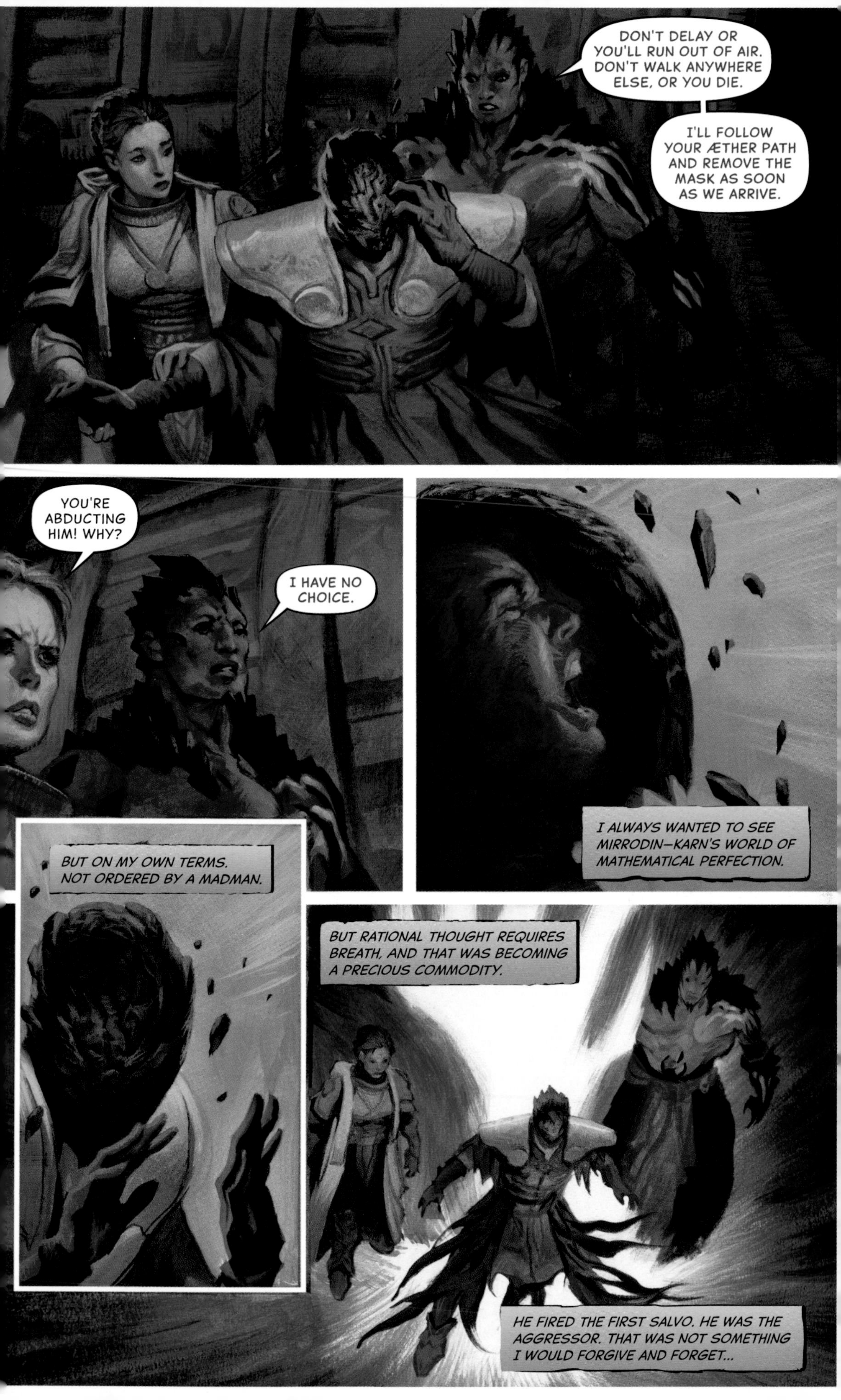

DON'T DELAY OR YOU'LL RUN OUT OF AIR. DON'T WALK ANYWHERE ELSE, OR YOU DIE.
I'LL FOLLOW YOUR ÆTHER PATH AND REMOVE THE MASK AS SOON AS WE ARRIVE.
YOU'RE ABDUCTING HIM! WHY?
I HAVE NO CHOICE.
I ALWAYS WANTED TO SEE MIRRODIN—KARN'S WORLD OF MATHEMATICAL PERFECTION.
BUT ON MY OWN TERMS. NOT ORDERED BY A MADMAN.
BUT RATIONAL THOUGHT REQUIRES BREATH, AND THAT WAS BECOMING A PRECIOUS COMMODITY.
HE FIRED THE FIRST SALVO. HE WAS THE AGGRESSOR. THAT WAS NOT SOMETHING I WOULD FORGIVE AND FORGET...

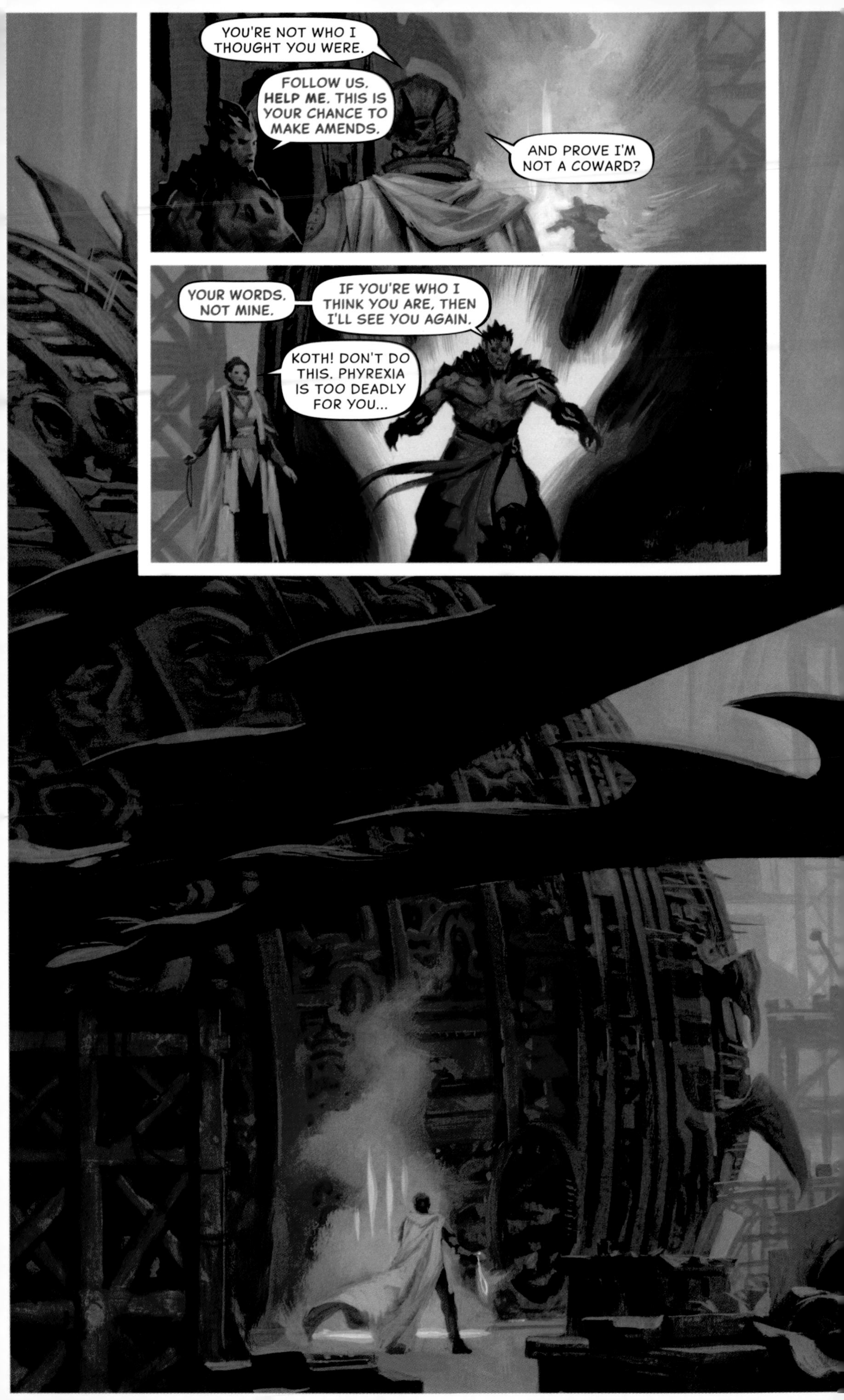

YOU'RE NOT WHO I THOUGHT YOU WERE.
FOLLOW US. HELP ME. THIS IS YOUR CHANCE TO MAKE AMENDS.
AND PROVE I'M NOT A COWARD?
YOUR WORDS. NOT MINE.
IF YOU'RE WHO I THINK YOU ARE, THEN I'LL SEE YOU AGAIN.
KOTH! DON'T DO THIS. PHYREXIA IS TOO DEADLY FOR YOU...

SCARRED

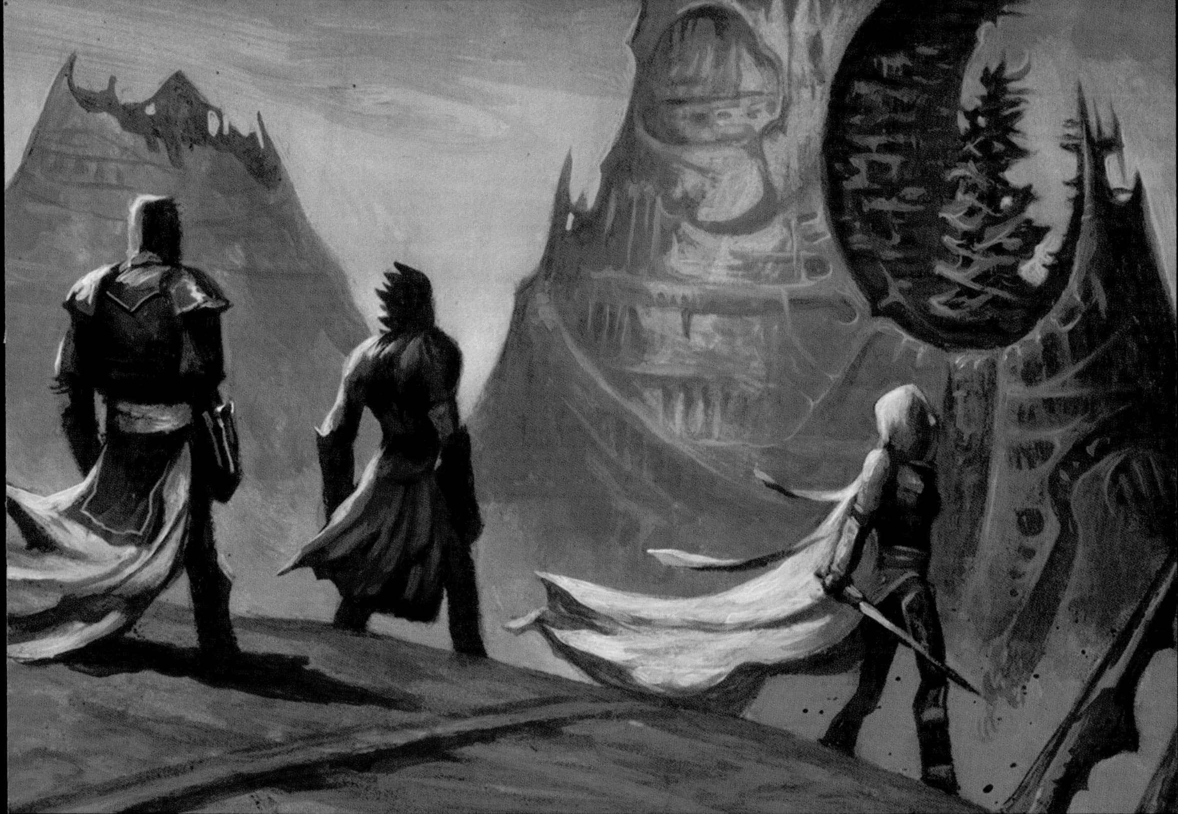

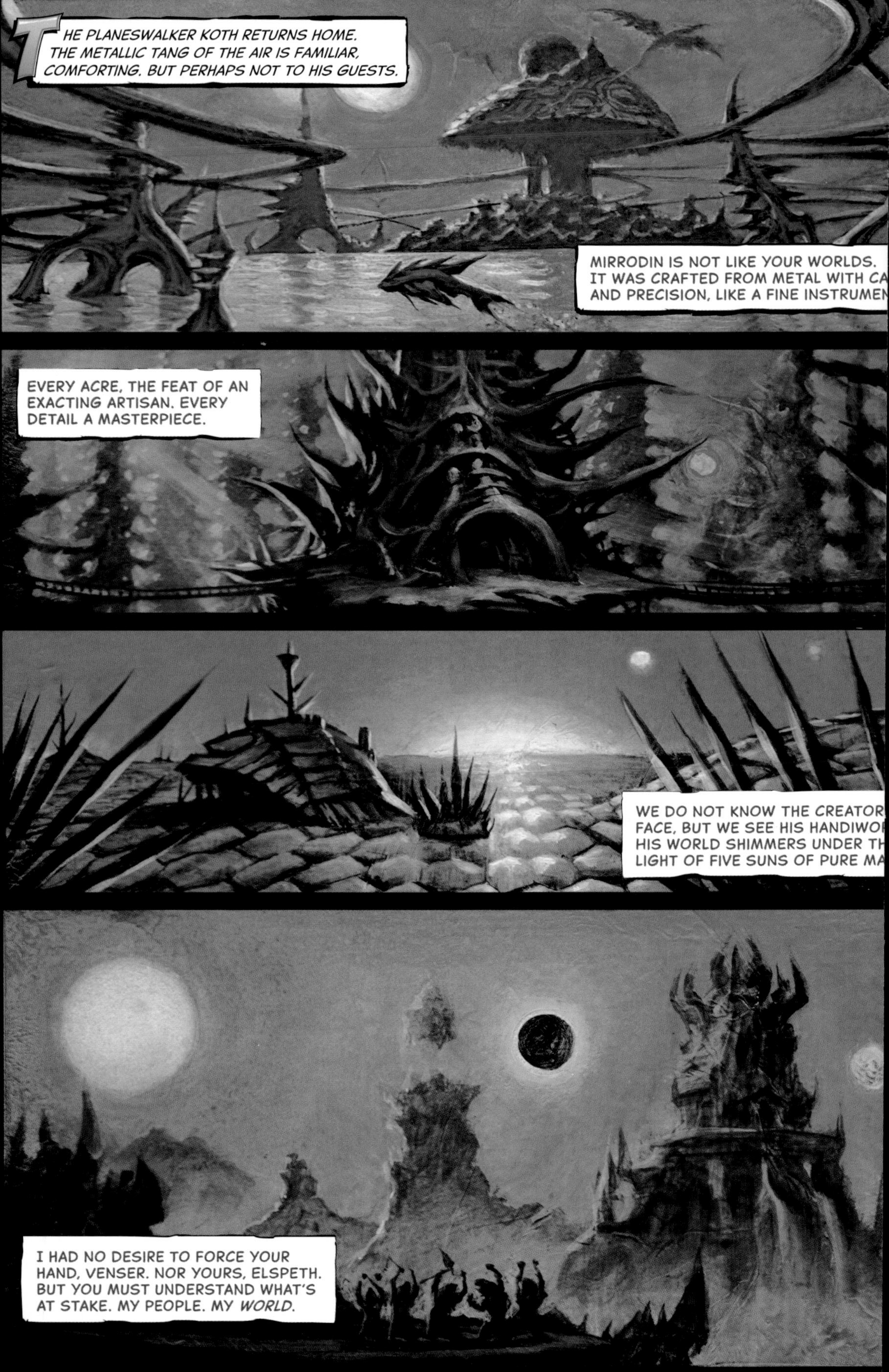
THE PLANESWALKER KOTH RETURNS HOME. THE METALLIC TANG OF THE AIR IS FAMILIAR, COMFORTING. BUT PERHAPS NOT TO HIS GUESTS.
MIRRODIN IS NOT LIKE YOUR WORLDS. IT WAS CRAFTED FROM METAL WITH CA AND PRECISION, LIKE A FINE INSTRUMEN
EVERY ACRE, THE FEAT OF AN EXACTING ARTISAN. EVERY DETAIL A MASTERPIECE.
WE DO NOT KNOW THE CREATOR FACE, BUT WE SEE HIS HANDIWO HIS WORLD SHIMMERS UNDER TH LIGHT OF FIVE SUNS OF PURE MA
I HAD NO DESIRE TO FORCE YOUR HAND, VENSER. NOR YOURS, ELSPETH. BUT YOU MUST UNDERSTAND WHAT'S AT STAKE. MY PEOPLE. MY *WORLD*.

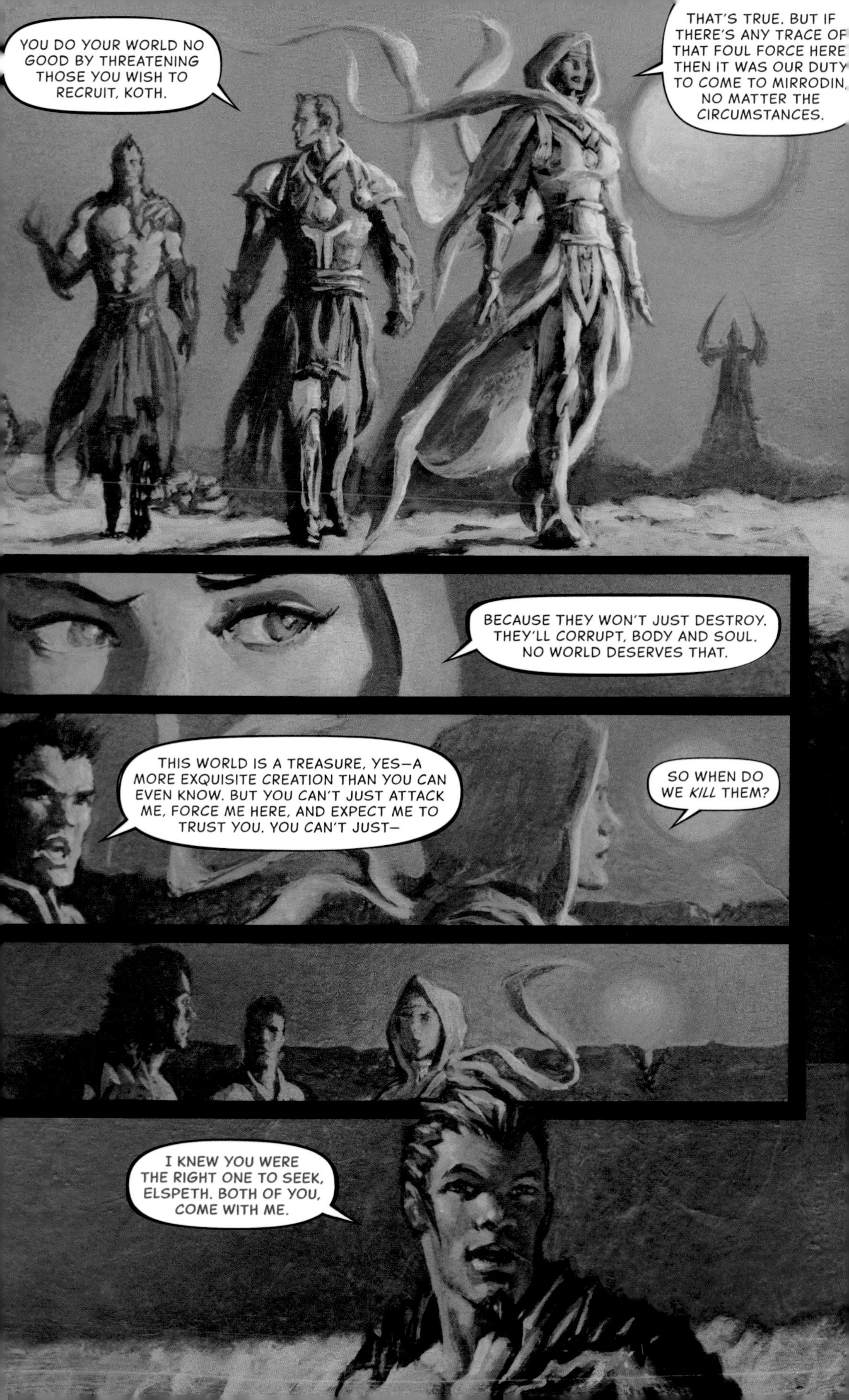
YOU DO YOUR WORLD NO GOOD BY THREATENING THOSE YOU WISH TO RECRUIT, KOTH.
THAT'S TRUE. BUT IF THERE'S ANY TRACE OF THAT FOUL FORCE HERE THEN IT WAS OUR DUTY TO COME TO MIRRODIN, NO MATTER THE CIRCUMSTANCES.
BECAUSE THEY WON'T JUST DESTROY. THEY'LL *CORRUPT*, BODY AND SOUL. NO WORLD DESERVES THAT.
THIS WORLD IS A TREASURE, YES—A MORE EXQUISITE CREATION THAN YOU CAN EVEN KNOW. BUT *YOU* CAN'T JUST ATTACK ME, FORCE ME HERE, AND EXPECT ME TO TRUST YOU. YOU CAN'T JUST—
SO WHEN DO WE *KILL* THEM?
I KNEW YOU WERE THE RIGHT ONE TO SEEK, ELSPETH. BOTH OF YOU, COME WITH ME.

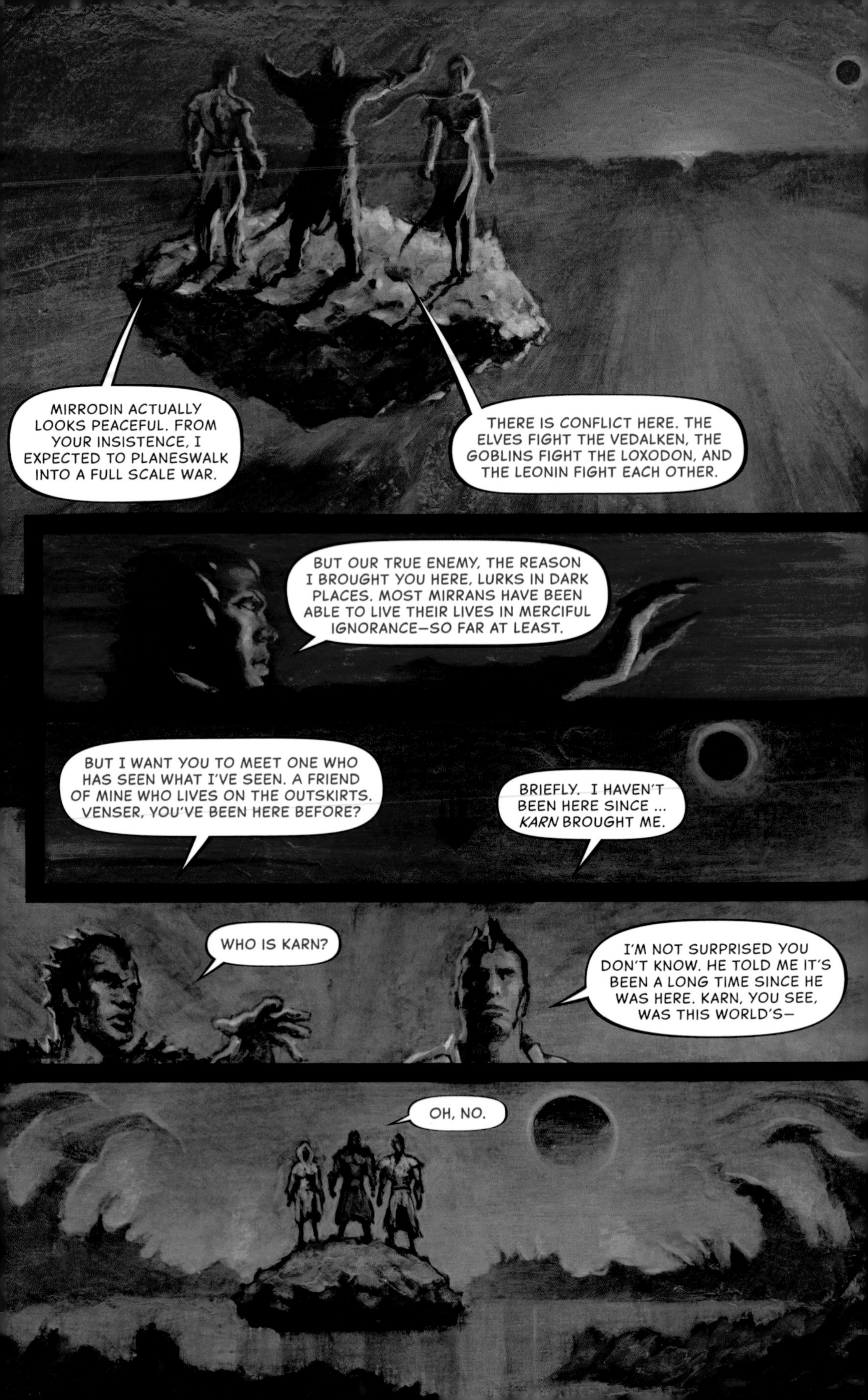
MIRRODIN ACTUALLY LOOKS PEACEFUL. FROM YOUR INSISTENCE, I EXPECTED TO PLANESWALK INTO A FULL SCALE WAR.
THERE IS CONFLICT HERE. THE ELVES FIGHT THE VEDALKEN, THE GOBLINS FIGHT THE LOXODON, AND THE LEONIN FIGHT EACH OTHER.
BUT OUR TRUE ENEMY, THE REASON I BROUGHT YOU HERE, LURKS IN DARK PLACES. MOST MIRRANS HAVE BEEN ABLE TO LIVE THEIR LIVES IN MERCIFUL IGNORANCE—SO FAR AT LEAST.
BUT I WANT YOU TO MEET ONE WHO HAS SEEN WHAT I'VE SEEN. A FRIEND OF MINE WHO LIVES ON THE OUTSKIRTS. VENSER, YOU'VE BEEN HERE BEFORE?
BRIEFLY. I HAVEN'T BEEN HERE SINCE ... *KARN* BROUGHT ME.
WHO IS KARN?
I'M NOT SURPRISED YOU DON'T KNOW. HE TOLD ME IT'S BEEN A LONG TIME SINCE HE WAS HERE. KARN, YOU SEE, WAS THIS WORLD'S—
OH, NO.

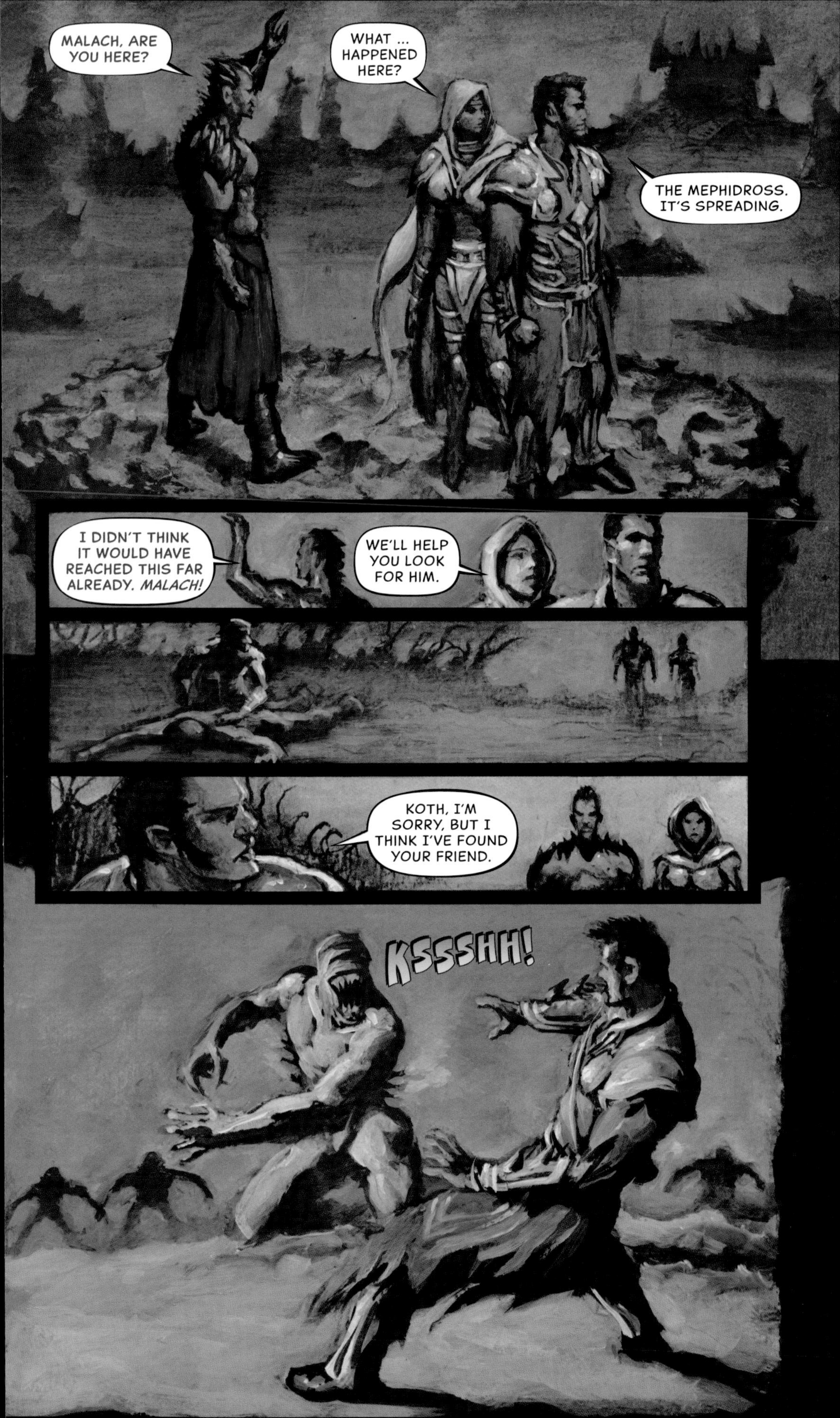
MALACH, ARE YOU HERE?
WHAT ... HAPPENED HERE?
THE MEPHIDROSS. IT'S SPREADING.
I DIDN'T THINK IT WOULD HAVE REACHED THIS FAR ALREADY. *MALACH!*
WE'LL HELP YOU LOOK FOR HIM.
KOTH, I'M SORRY, BUT I THINK I'VE FOUND YOUR FRIEND.
KSSSHH!

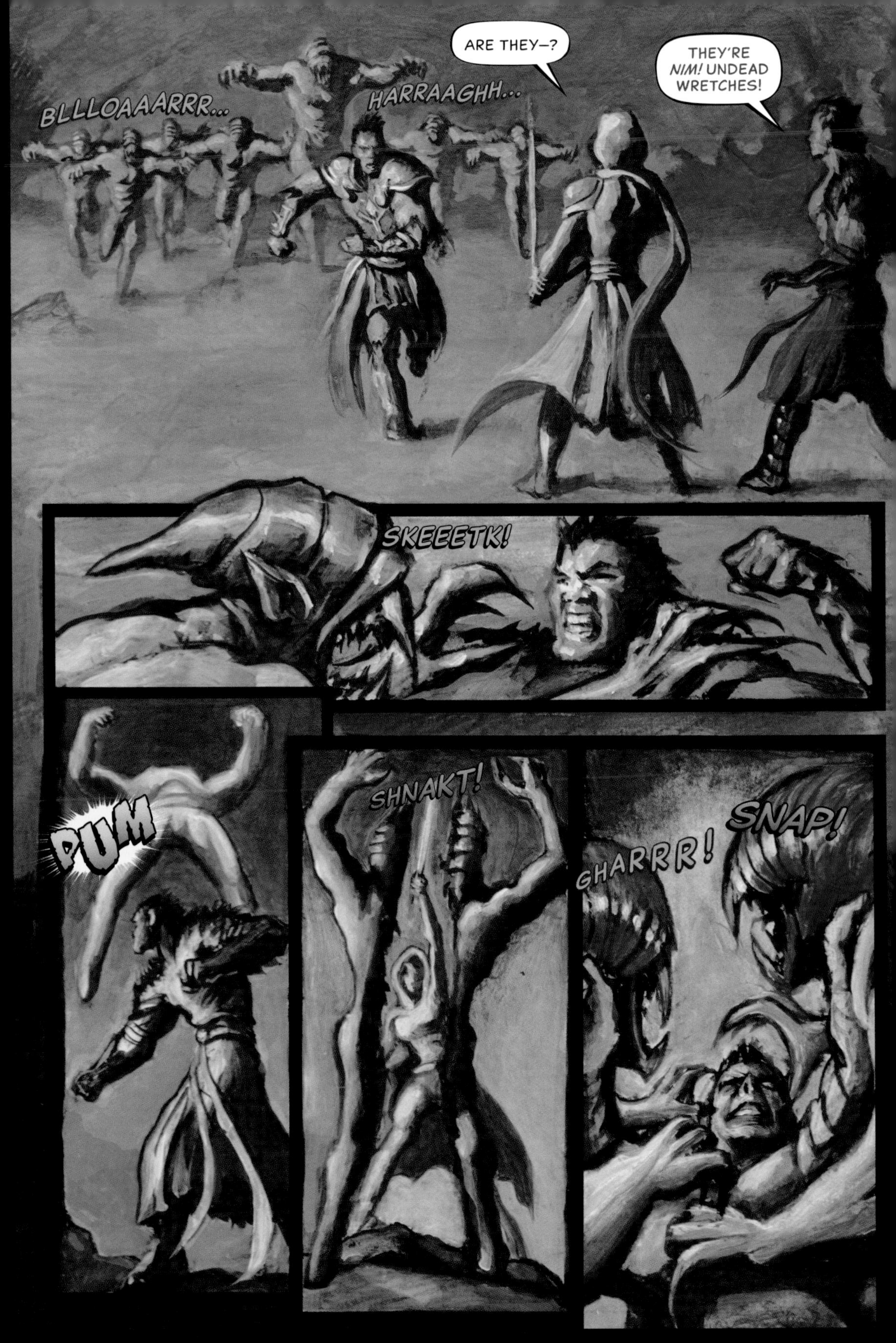
BLLLOAAARRR...
HARRAAGHH...
ARE THEY—?
THEY'RE *NIM!* UNDEAD WRETCHES!
SKEEEETK!
PUM
SHNAKT!
GHARRR!
SNAP!

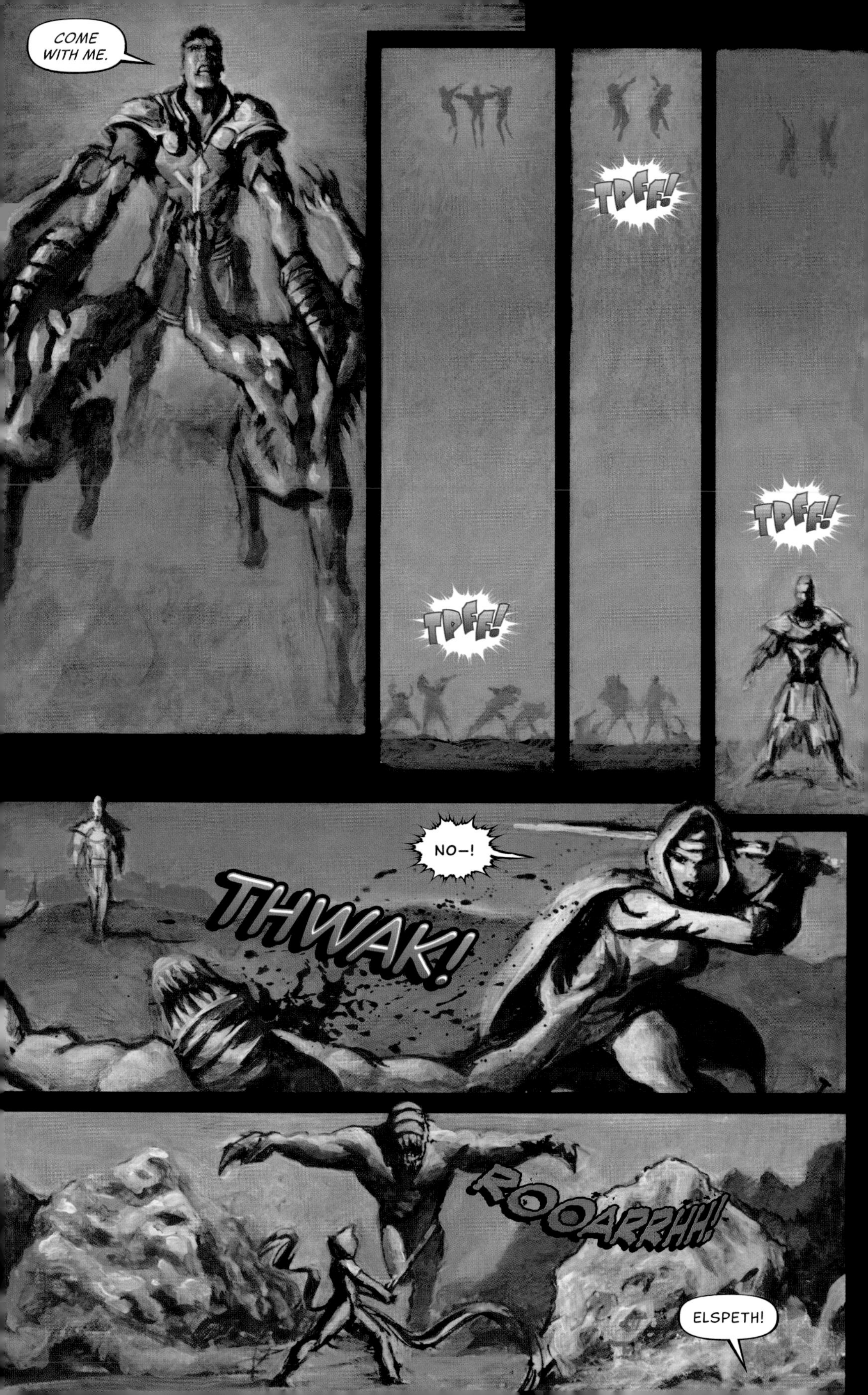
COME WITH ME.
TPFF!
TPFF!
TPFF!
NO—!
THWAK!
ROOARRHH!
ELSPETH!

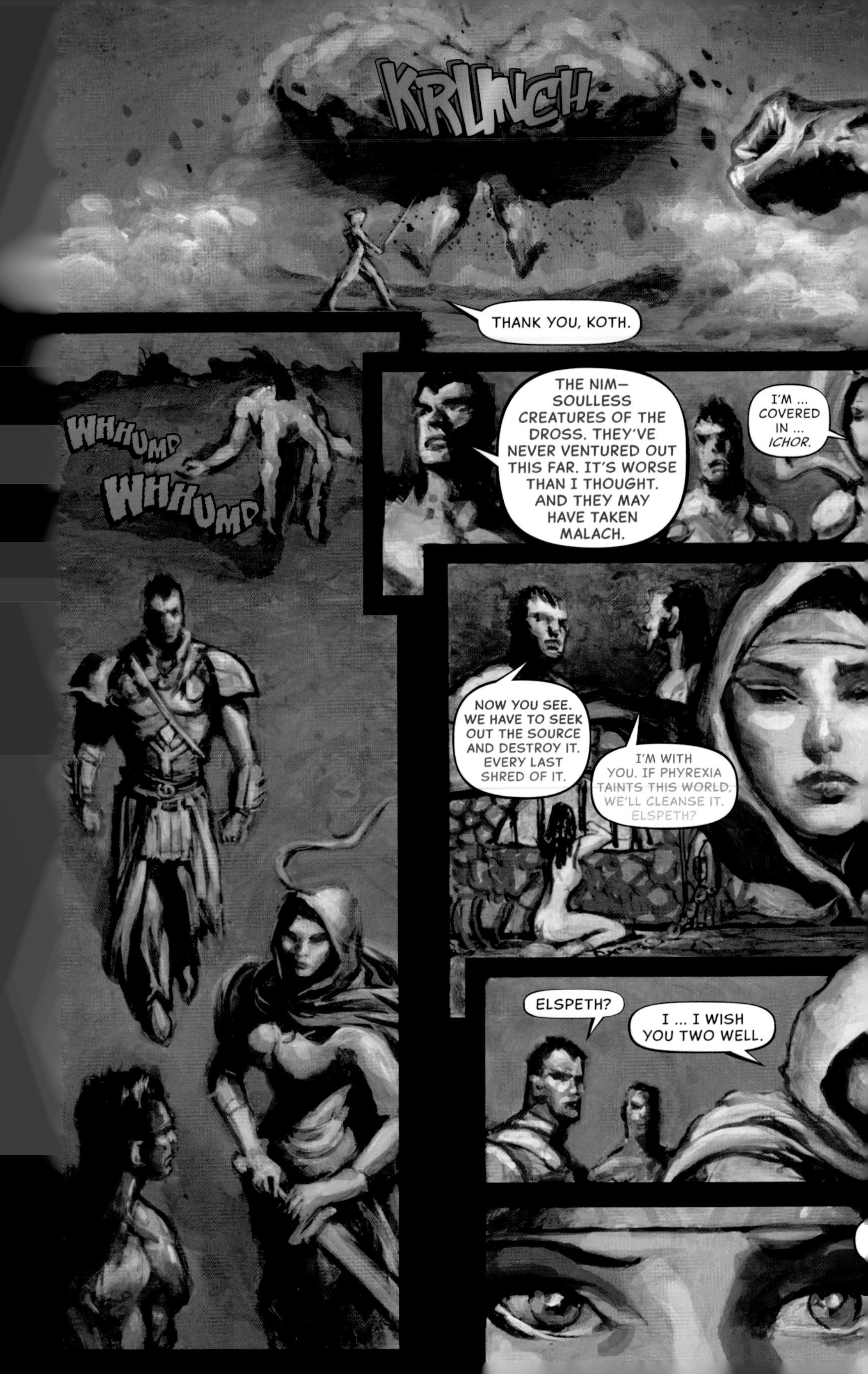
KRUNCH
THANK YOU, KOTH.
WHHUMP
WHHUMP
THE NIM— SOULLESS CREATURES OF THE DROSS. THEY'VE NEVER VENTURED OUT THIS FAR. IT'S WORSE THAN I THOUGHT. AND THEY MAY HAVE TAKEN MALACH.
I'M ... COVERED IN ... *ICHOR.*
NOW YOU SEE. WE HAVE TO SEEK OUT THE SOURCE AND DESTROY IT. EVERY LAST SHRED OF IT.
I'M WITH YOU. IF PHYREXIA TAINTS THIS WORLD, WE'LL CLEANSE IT. ELSPETH?
ELSPETH?
I ... I WISH YOU TWO WELL.

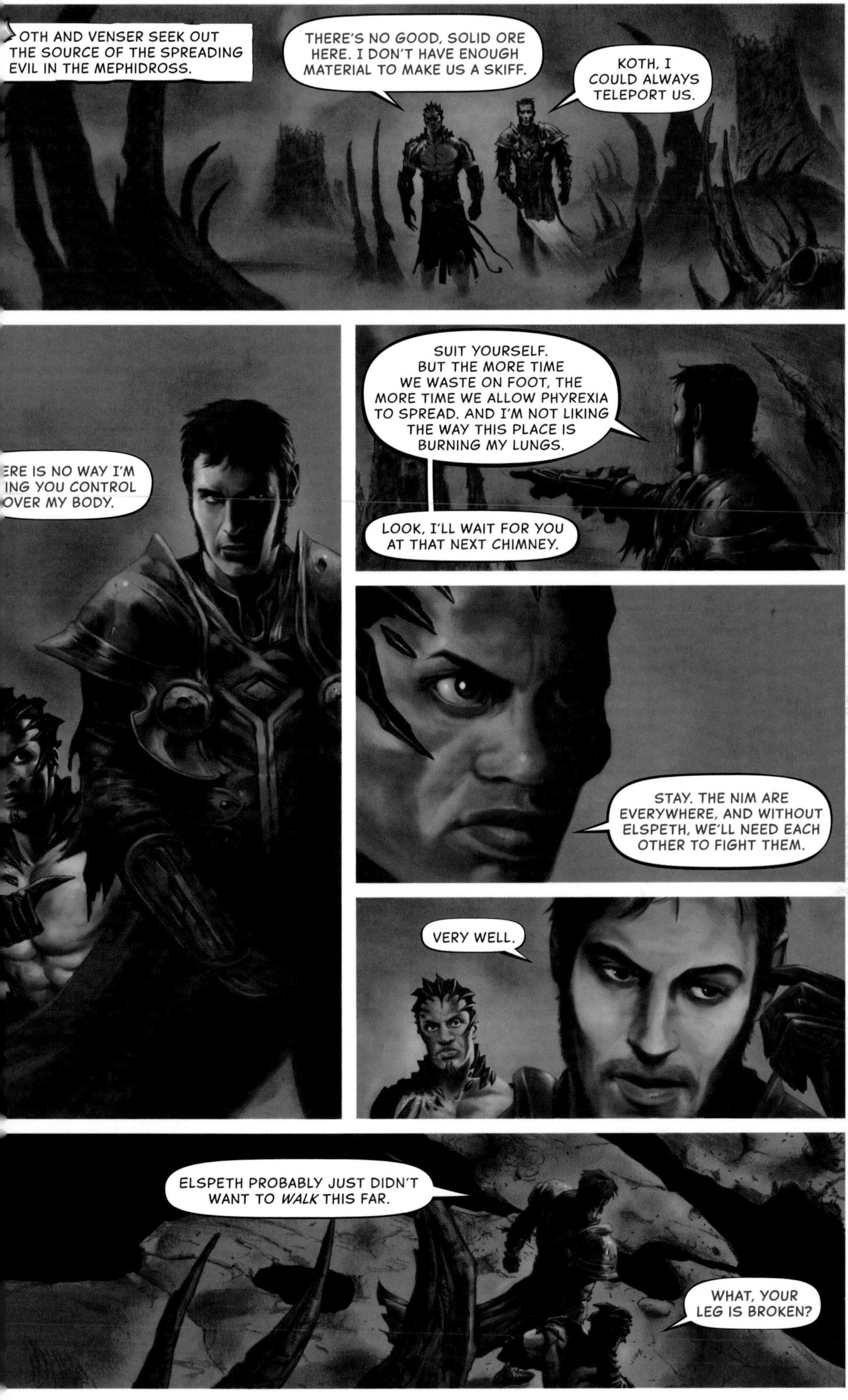
OTH AND VENSER SEEK OUT THE SOURCE OF THE SPREADING EVIL IN THE MEPHIDROSS.
THERE'S NO GOOD, SOLID ORE HERE. I DON'T HAVE ENOUGH MATERIAL TO MAKE US A SKIFF.
KOTH, I COULD ALWAYS TELEPORT US.
ERE IS NO WAY I'M ING YOU CONTROL OVER MY BODY.
SUIT YOURSELF. BUT THE MORE TIME WE WASTE ON FOOT, THE MORE TIME WE ALLOW PHYREXIA TO SPREAD. AND I'M NOT LIKING THE WAY THIS PLACE IS BURNING MY LUNGS.
LOOK, I'LL WAIT FOR YOU AT THAT NEXT CHIMNEY.
STAY. THE NIM ARE EVERYWHERE, AND WITHOUT ELSPETH, WE'LL NEED EACH OTHER TO FIGHT THEM.
VERY WELL.
ELSPETH PROBABLY JUST DIDN'T WANT TO *WALK* THIS FAR.
WHAT, YOUR LEG IS BROKEN?

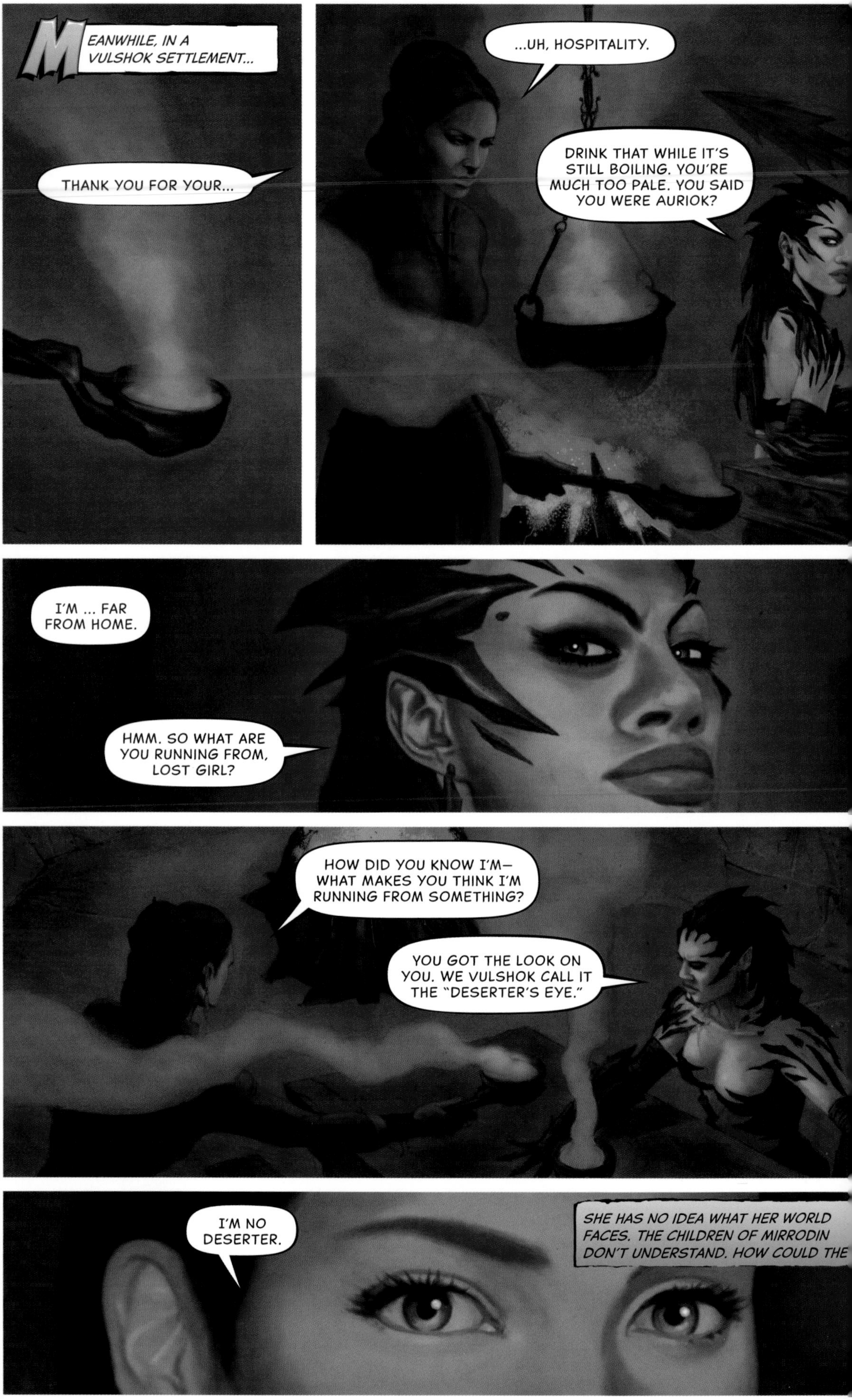
MEANWHILE, IN A VULSHOK SETTLEMENT...
THANK YOU FOR YOUR...
...UH, HOSPITALITY.
DRINK THAT WHILE IT'S STILL BOILING. YOU'RE MUCH TOO PALE. YOU SAID YOU WERE AURIOK?
I'M ... FAR FROM HOME.
HMM. SO WHAT ARE YOU RUNNING FROM, LOST GIRL?
HOW DID YOU KNOW I'M— WHAT MAKES YOU THINK I'M RUNNING FROM SOMETHING?
YOU GOT THE LOOK ON YOU. WE VULSHOK CALL IT THE "DESERTER'S EYE."
I'M NO DESERTER.
SHE HAS NO IDEA WHAT HER WORLD FACES. THE CHILDREN OF MIRRODIN DON'T UNDERSTAND. HOW COULD THE

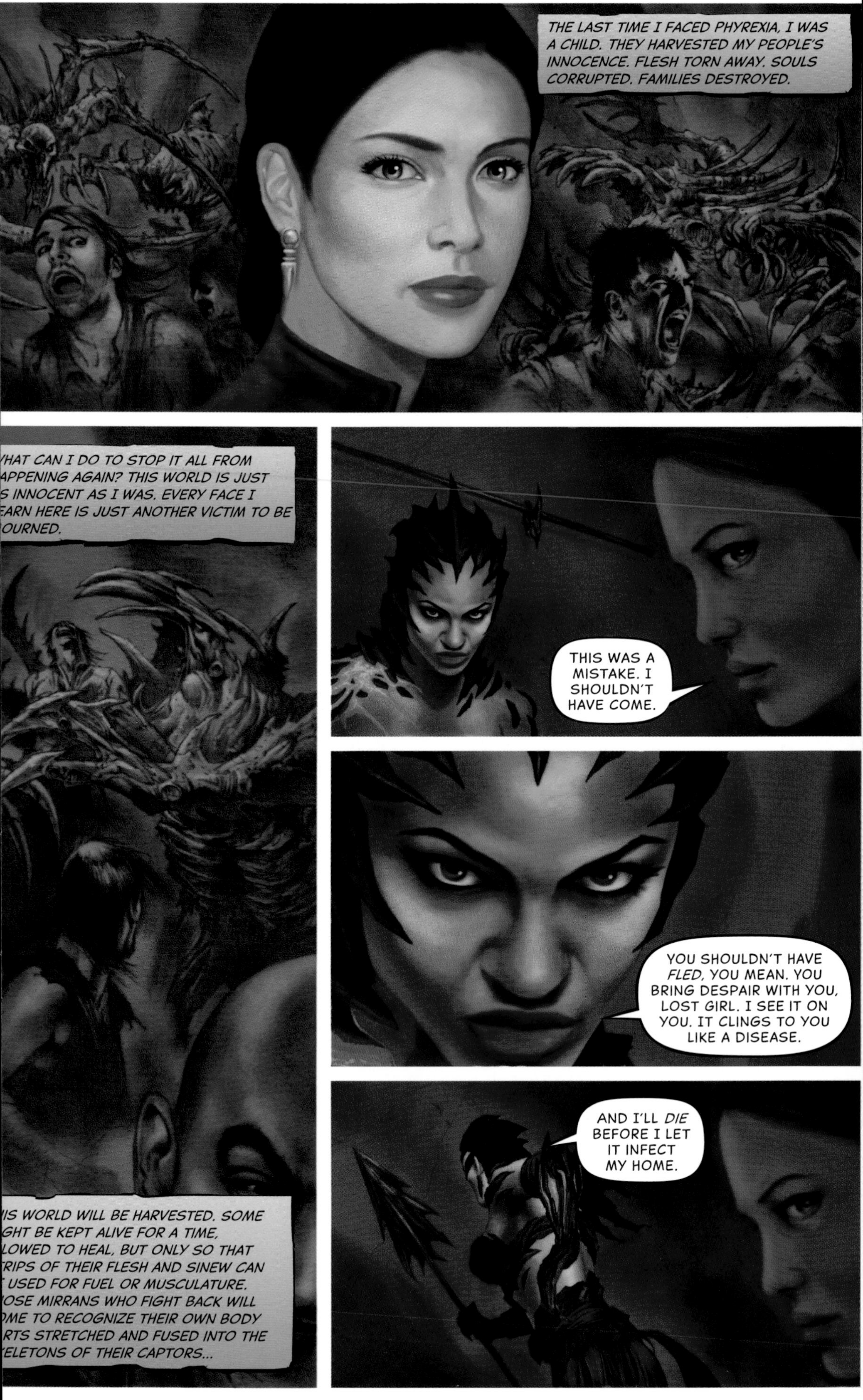
THE LAST TIME I FACED PHYREXIA, I WAS A CHILD. THEY HARVESTED MY PEOPLE'S INNOCENCE. FLESH TORN AWAY. SOULS CORRUPTED. FAMILIES DESTROYED.
HAT CAN I DO TO STOP IT ALL FROM APPENING AGAIN? THIS WORLD IS JUST S INNOCENT AS I WAS. EVERY FACE I EARN HERE IS JUST ANOTHER VICTIM TO BE OURNED.
IS WORLD WILL BE HARVESTED. SOME GHT BE KEPT ALIVE FOR A TIME, LOWED TO HEAL, BUT ONLY SO THAT RIPS OF THEIR FLESH AND SINEW CAN USED FOR FUEL OR MUSCULATURE. OSE MIRRANS WHO FIGHT BACK WILL OME TO RECOGNIZE THEIR OWN BODY RTS STRETCHED AND FUSED INTO THE ELETONS OF THEIR CAPTORS...
THIS WAS A MISTAKE. I SHOULDN'T HAVE COME.
YOU SHOULDN'T HAVE *FLED*, YOU MEAN. YOU BRING DESPAIR WITH YOU, LOST GIRL. I SEE IT ON YOU. IT CLINGS TO YOU LIKE A DISEASE.
AND I'LL *DIE* BEFORE I LET IT INFECT MY HOME.

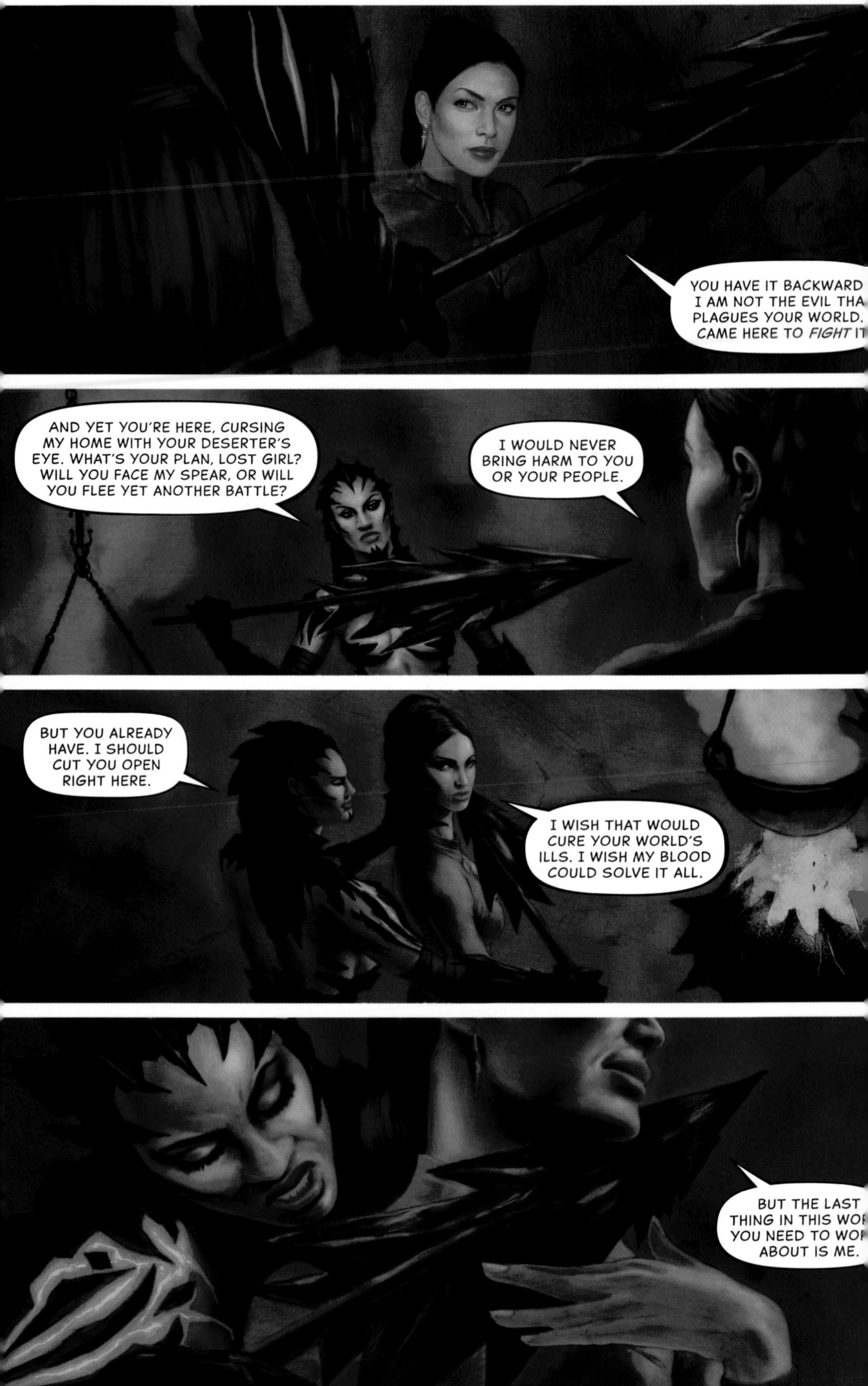
YOU HAVE IT BACKWARD I AM NOT THE EVIL THA PLAGUES YOUR WORLD. CAME HERE TO *FIGHT* IT
AND YET YOU'RE HERE, CURSING MY HOME WITH YOUR DESERTER'S EYE. WHAT'S YOUR PLAN, LOST GIRL? WILL YOU FACE MY SPEAR, OR WILL YOU FLEE YET ANOTHER BATTLE?
I WOULD NEVER BRING HARM TO YOU OR YOUR PEOPLE.
BUT YOU ALREADY HAVE. I SHOULD CUT YOU OPEN RIGHT HERE.
I WISH THAT WOULD CURE YOUR WORLD'S ILLS. I WISH MY BLOOD COULD SOLVE IT ALL.
BUT THE LAST THING IN THIS WO YOU NEED TO WO ABOUT IS ME.

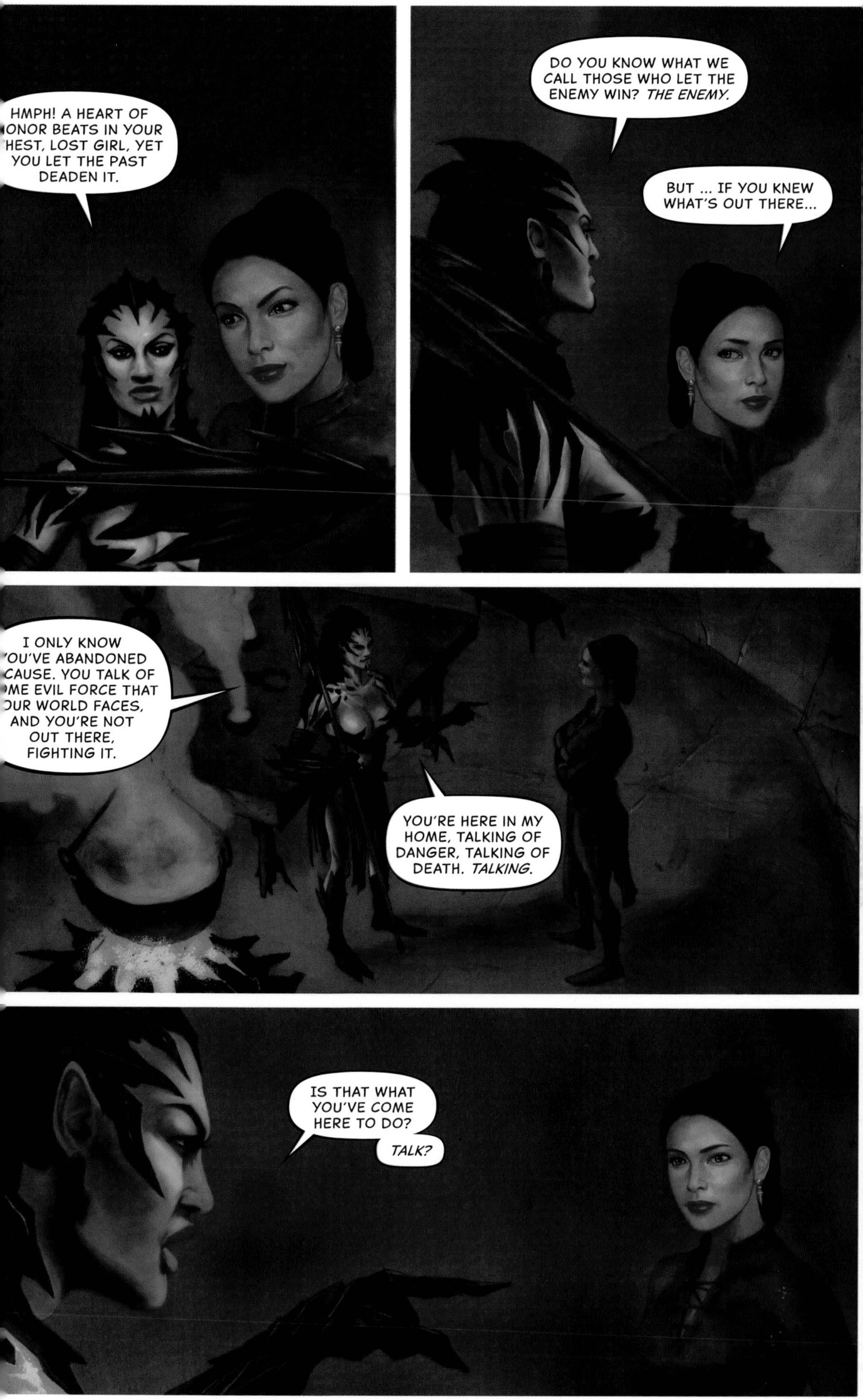
HMPH! A HEART OF ONOR BEATS IN YOUR HEST, LOST GIRL, YET YOU LET THE PAST DEADEN IT.
DO YOU KNOW WHAT WE CALL THOSE WHO LET THE ENEMY WIN? *THE ENEMY.*
BUT ... IF YOU KNEW WHAT'S OUT THERE...
I ONLY KNOW OU'VE ABANDONED CAUSE. YOU TALK OF ME EVIL FORCE THAT UR WORLD FACES, AND YOU'RE NOT OUT THERE, FIGHTING IT.
YOU'RE HERE IN MY HOME, TALKING OF DANGER, TALKING OF DEATH. *TALKING.*
IS THAT WHAT YOU'VE COME HERE TO DO?
TALK?

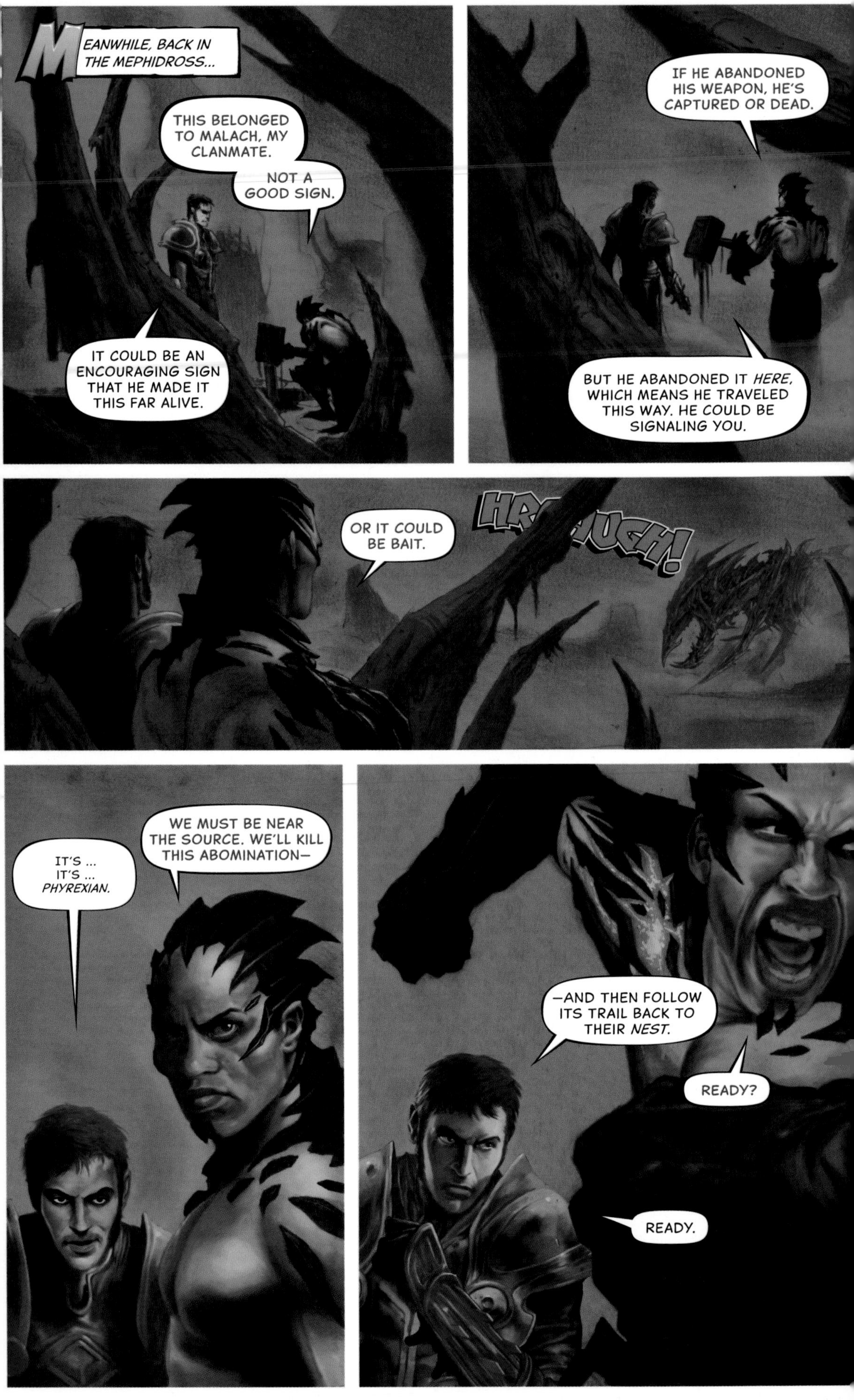
MEANWHILE, BACK IN THE MEPHIDROSS...
THIS BELONGED TO MALACH, MY CLANMATE.
NOT A GOOD SIGN.
IT COULD BE AN ENCOURAGING SIGN THAT HE MADE IT THIS FAR ALIVE.
IF HE ABANDONED HIS WEAPON, HE'S CAPTURED OR DEAD.
BUT HE ABANDONED IT *HERE*, WHICH MEANS HE TRAVELED THIS WAY. HE COULD BE SIGNALING YOU.
OR IT COULD BE BAIT.
IT'S ... IT'S ... *PHYREXIAN.*
WE MUST BE NEAR THE SOURCE. WE'LL KILL THIS ABOMINATION—
—AND THEN FOLLOW ITS TRAIL BACK TO THEIR *NEST*.
READY?
READY.

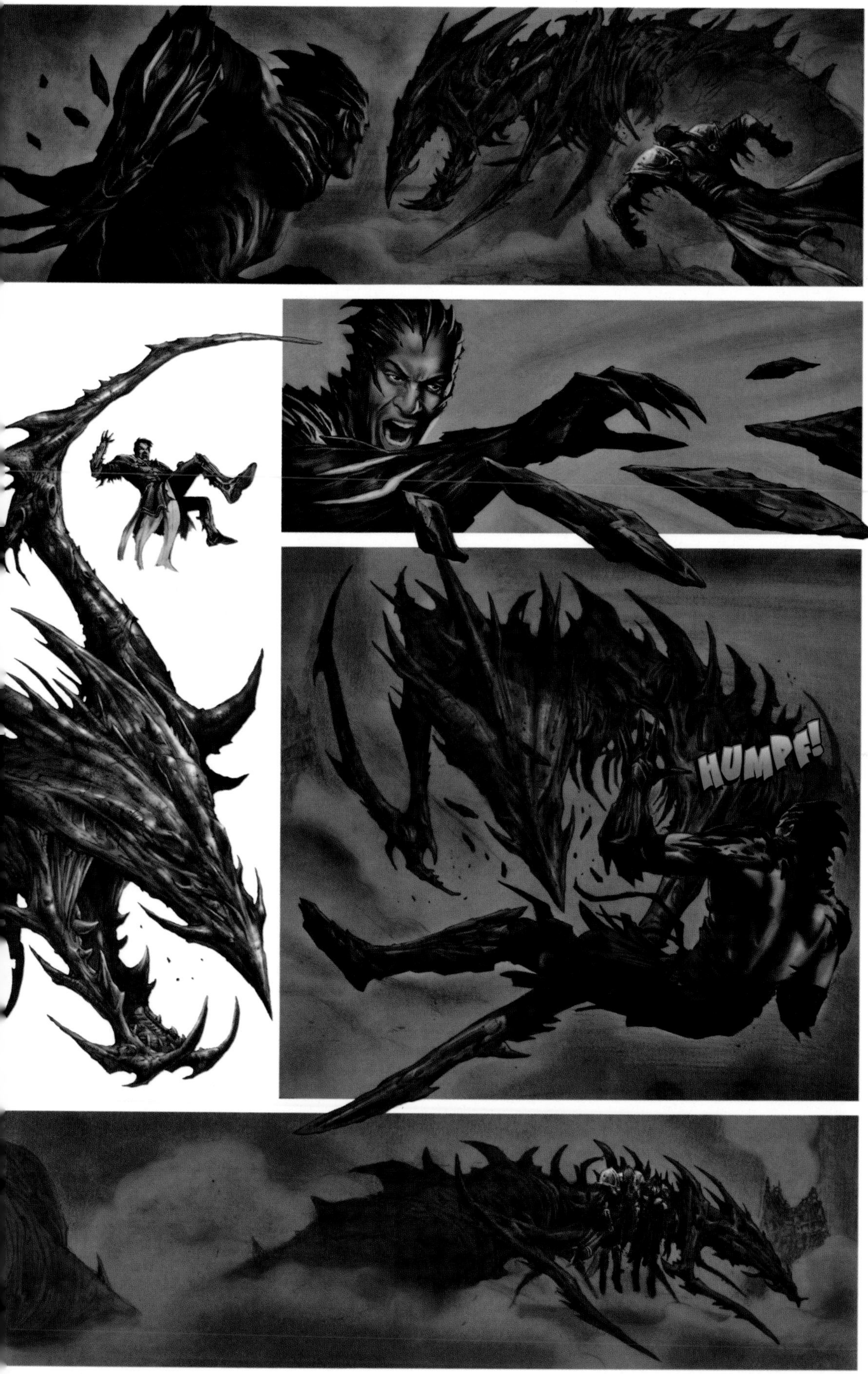
HUMPF!

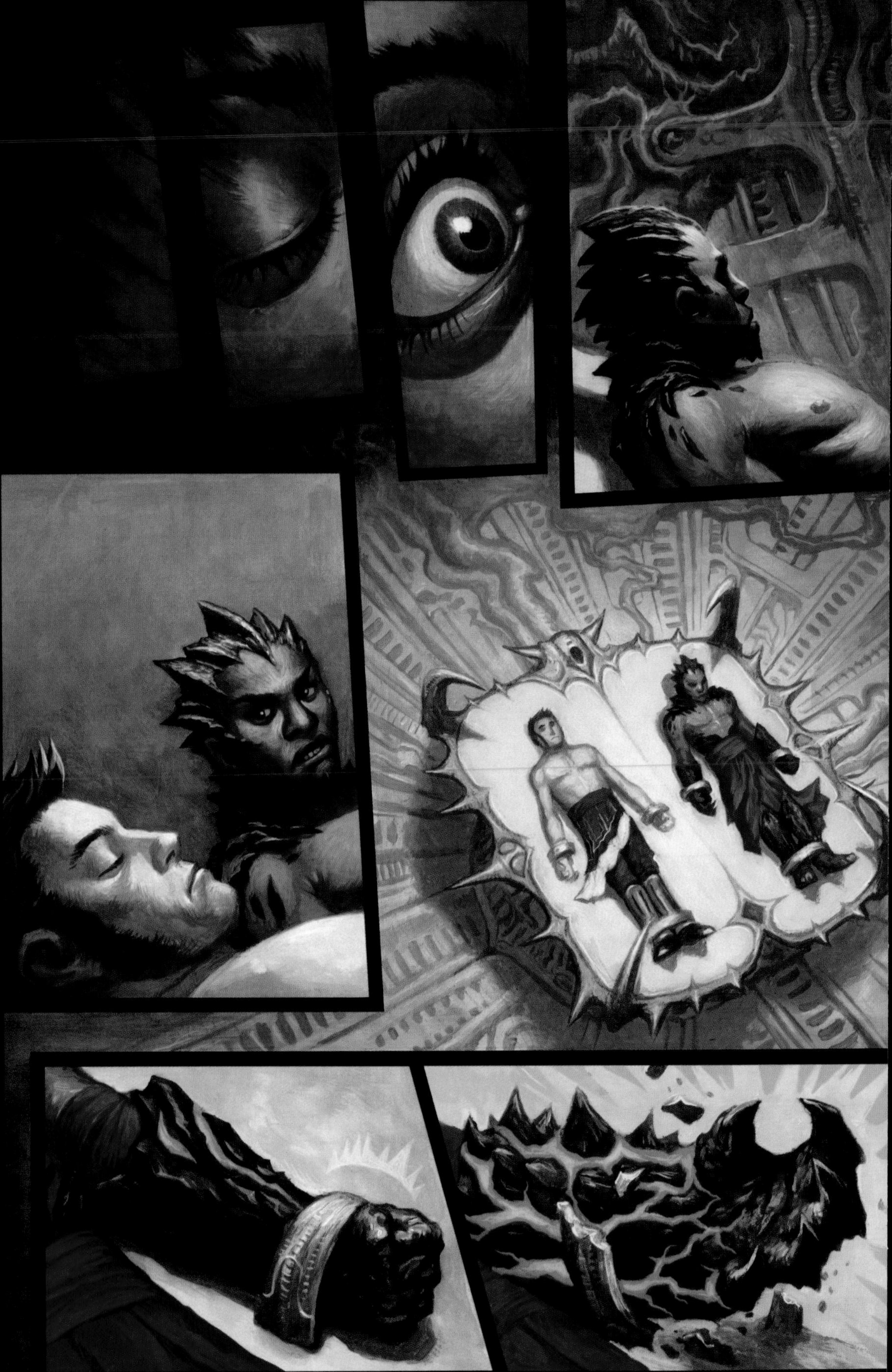

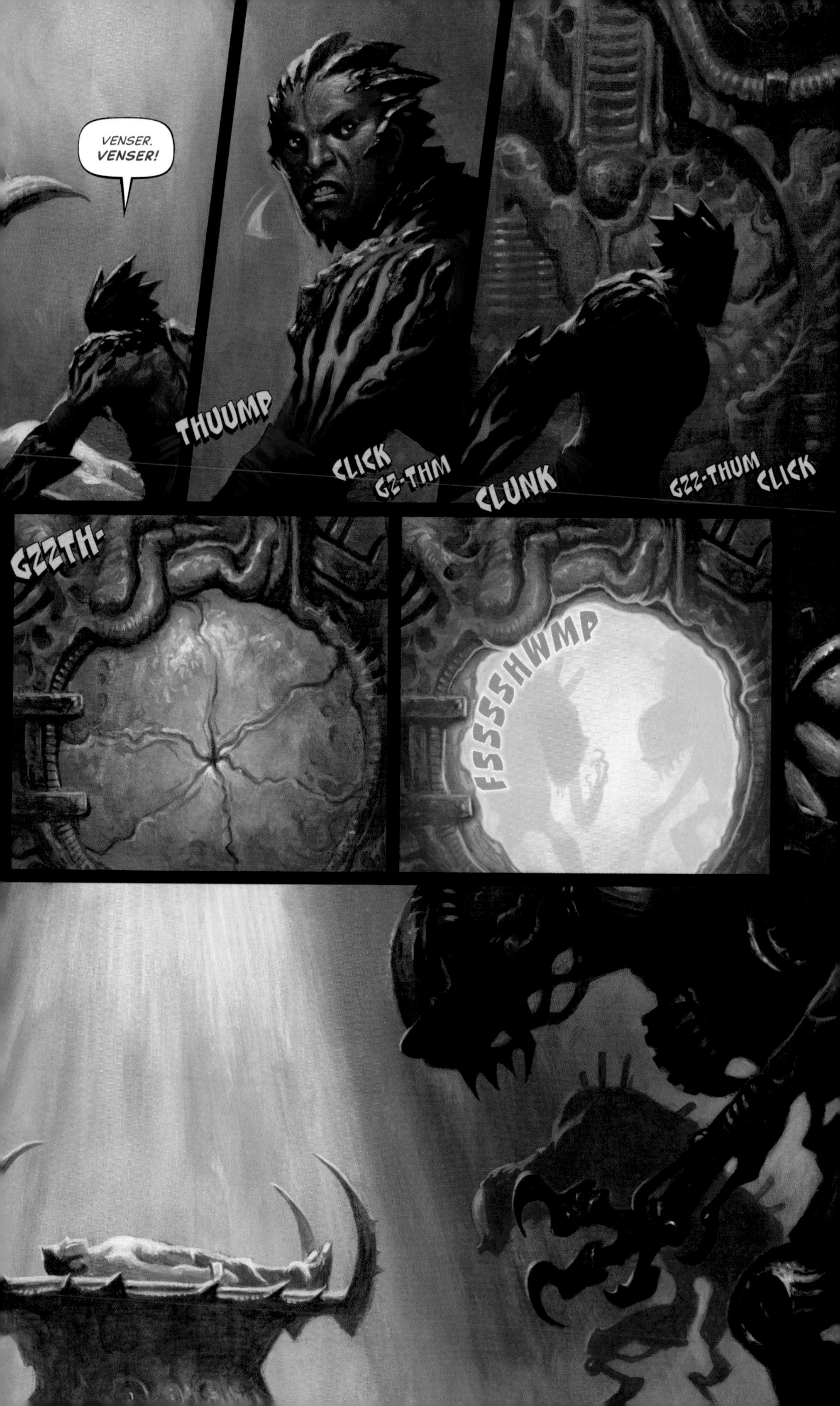

VENSER.
VENSER!
THUUMP
CLICK
GZ-THM
CLUNK
GZZ-THUM
CLICK
GZZTH-
FSSSSHWMP

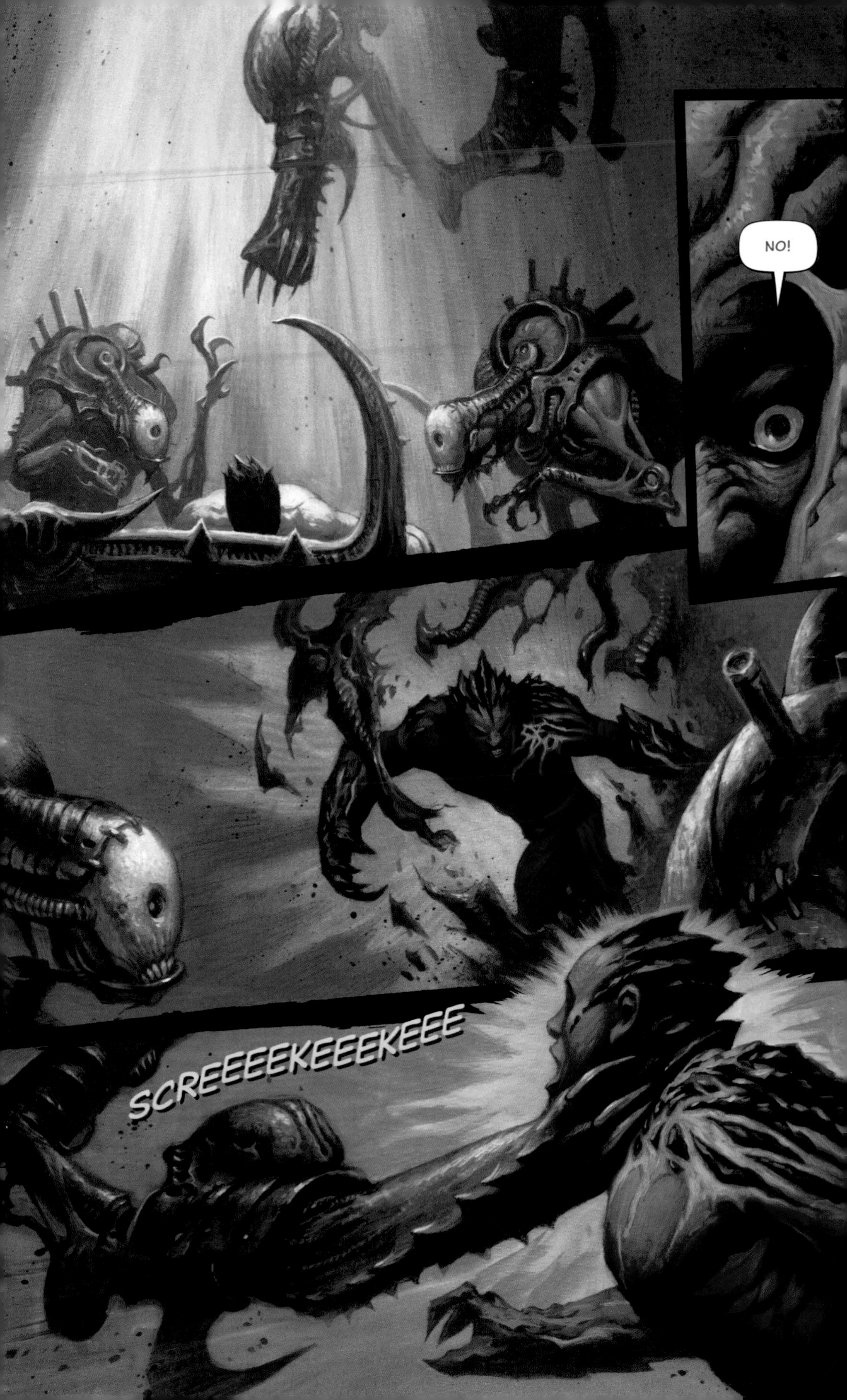
NO!
SCREEEEEKEEEEKEEE

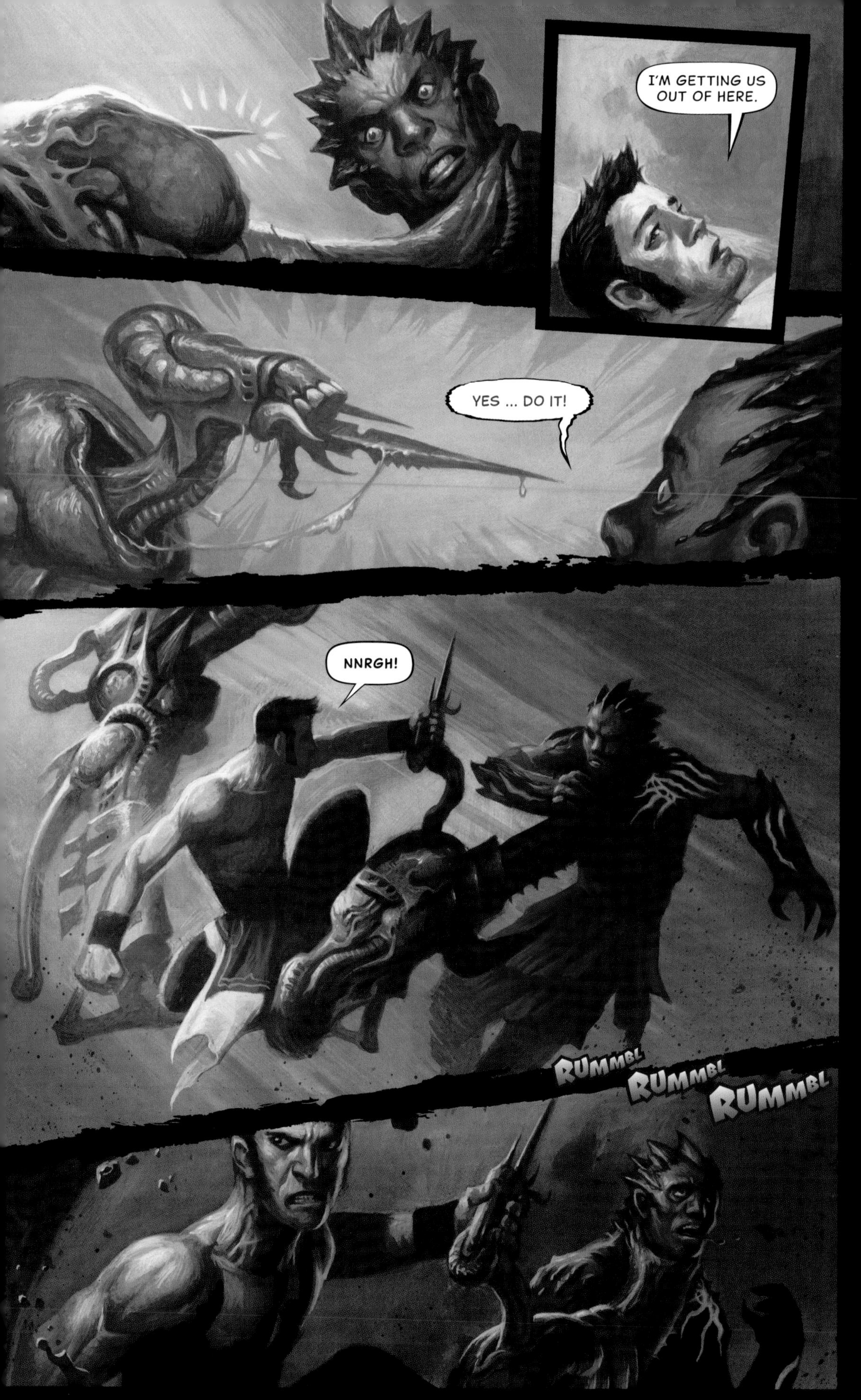
I'M GETTING US OUT OF HERE.
YES ... DO IT!
NNRGH!
RUMMBL
RUMMBL
RUMMBL

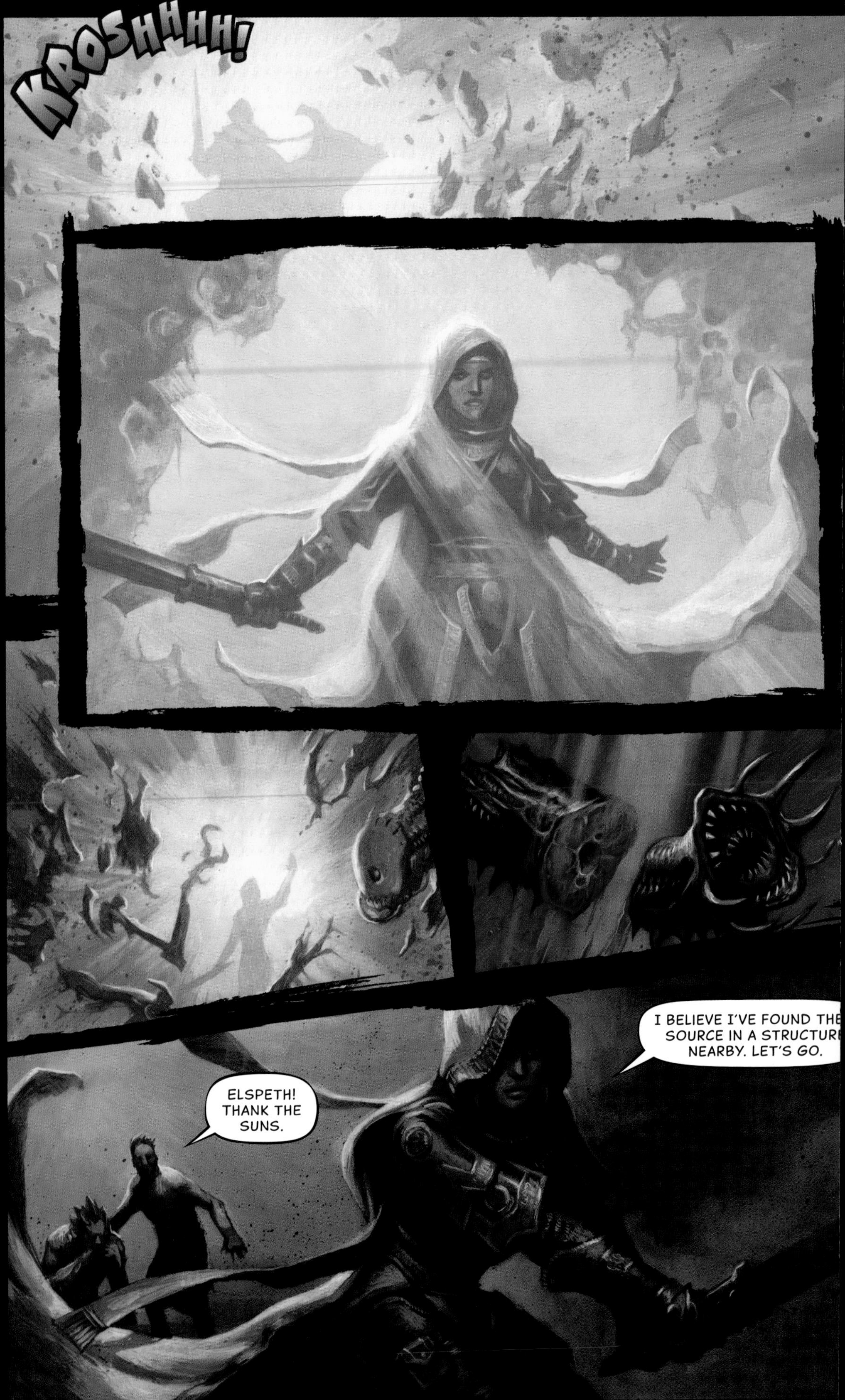
KROSHHHH!
ELSPETH! THANK THE SUNS.
I BELIEVE I'VE FOUND THE SOURCE IN A STRUCTURE NEARBY. LET'S GO.

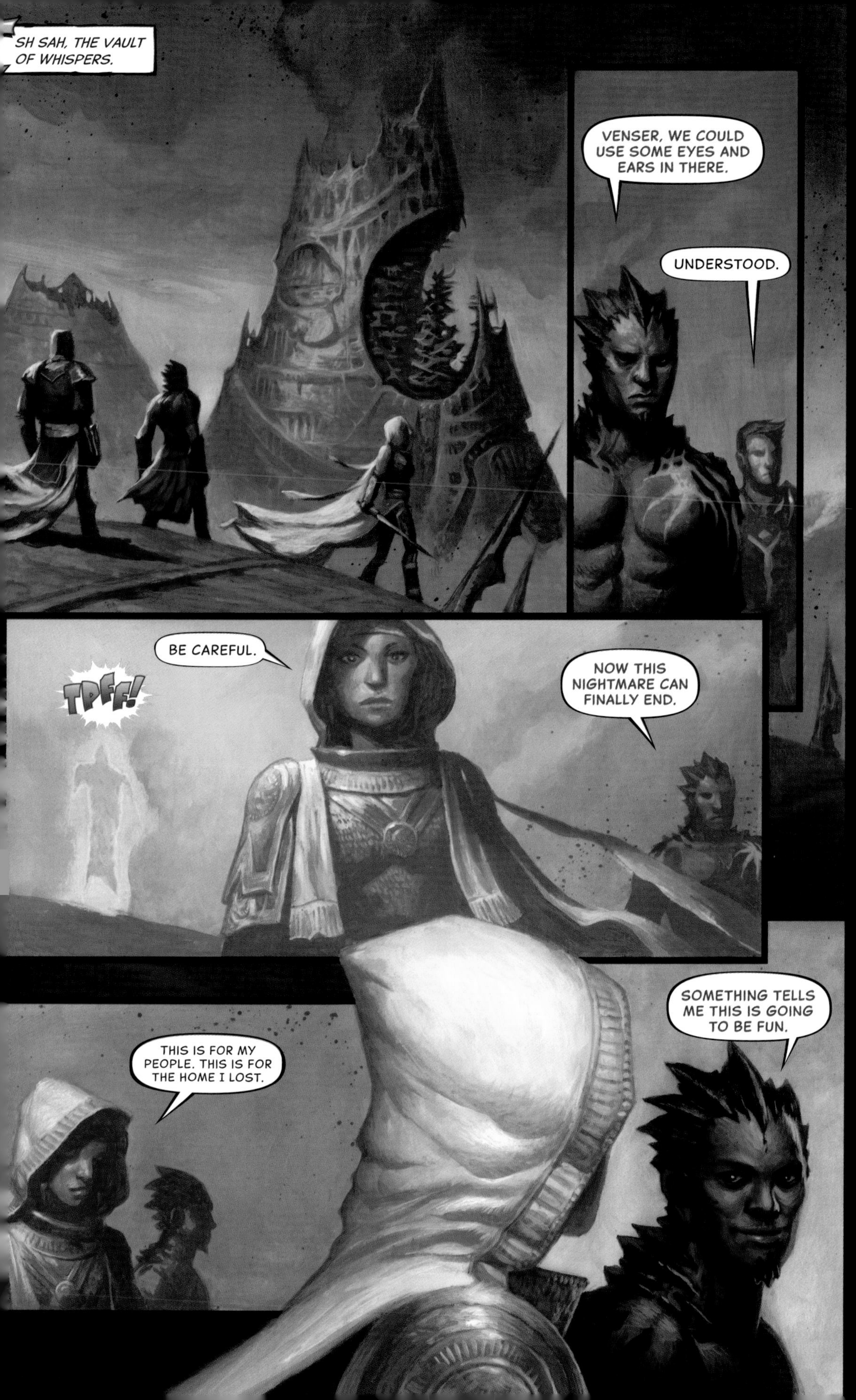
SH SAH, THE VAULT OF WHISPERS.
VENSER, WE COULD USE SOME EYES AND EARS IN THERE.
UNDERSTOOD.
BE CAREFUL.
TPFF!
NOW THIS NIGHTMARE CAN FINALLY END.
THIS IS FOR MY PEOPLE. THIS IS FOR THE HOME I LOST.
SOMETHING TELLS ME THIS IS GOING TO BE FUN.

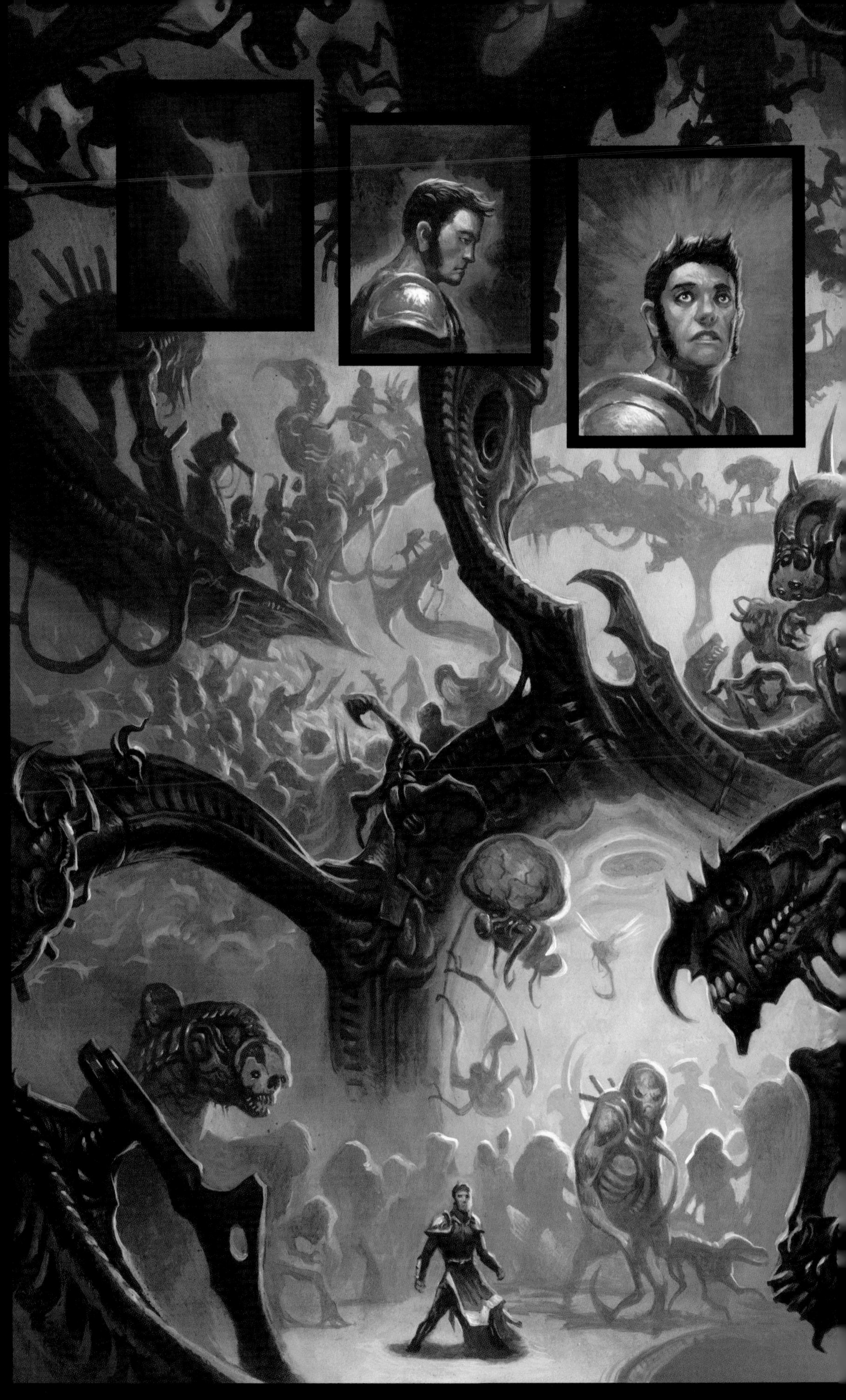

DARK DISCOVERIES

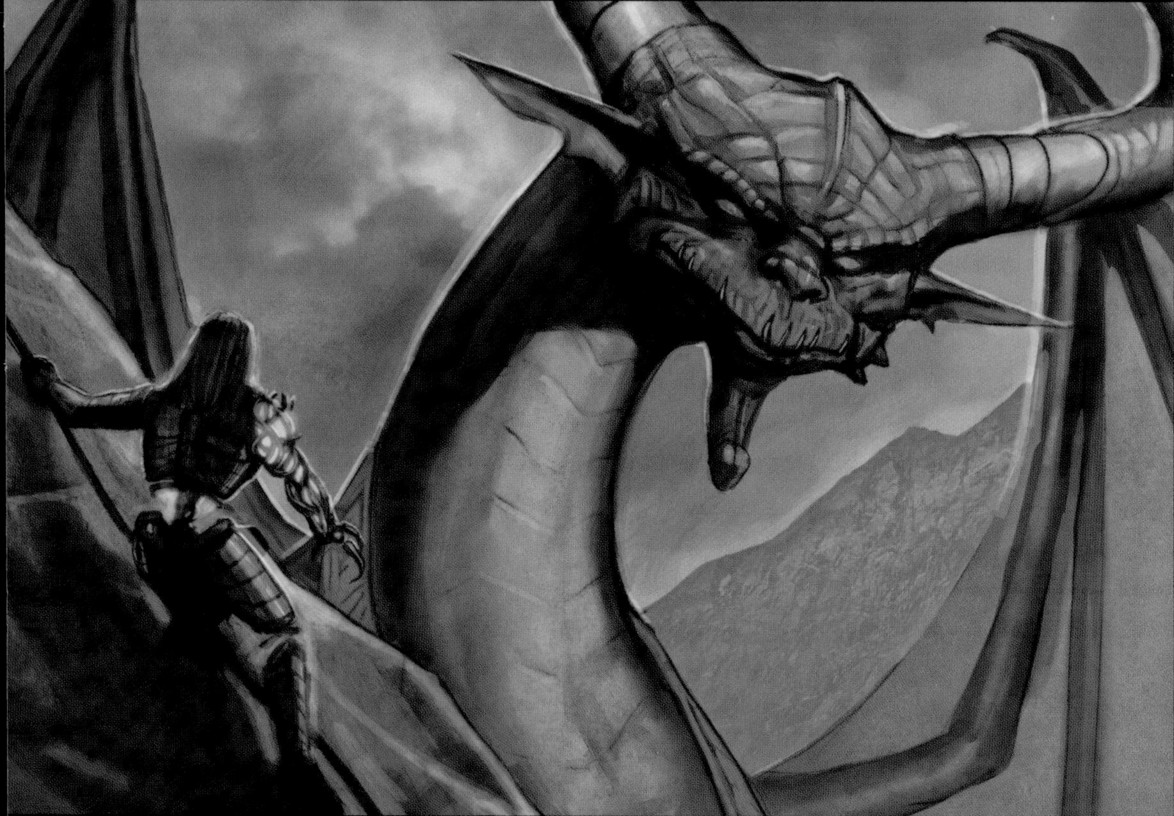

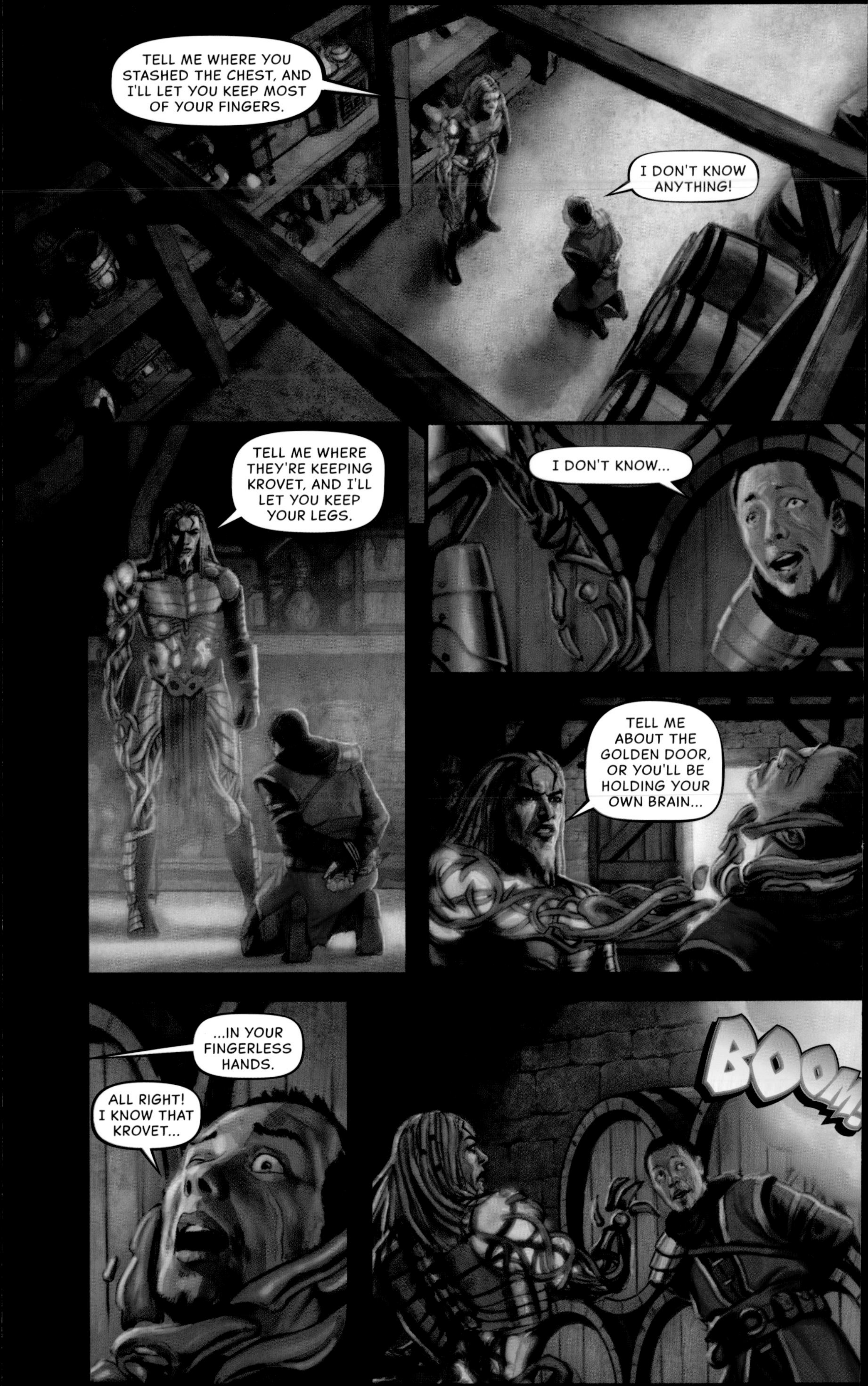
TELL ME WHERE YOU STASHED THE CHEST, AND I'LL LET YOU KEEP MOST OF YOUR FINGERS.
I DON'T KNOW ANYTHING!
TELL ME WHERE THEY'RE KEEPING KROVET, AND I'LL LET YOU KEEP YOUR LEGS.
I DON'T KNOW...
TELL ME ABOUT THE GOLDEN DOOR, OR YOU'LL BE HOLDING YOUR OWN BRAIN...
...IN YOUR FINGERLESS HANDS.
ALL RIGHT! I KNOW THAT KROVET...
BOOM!

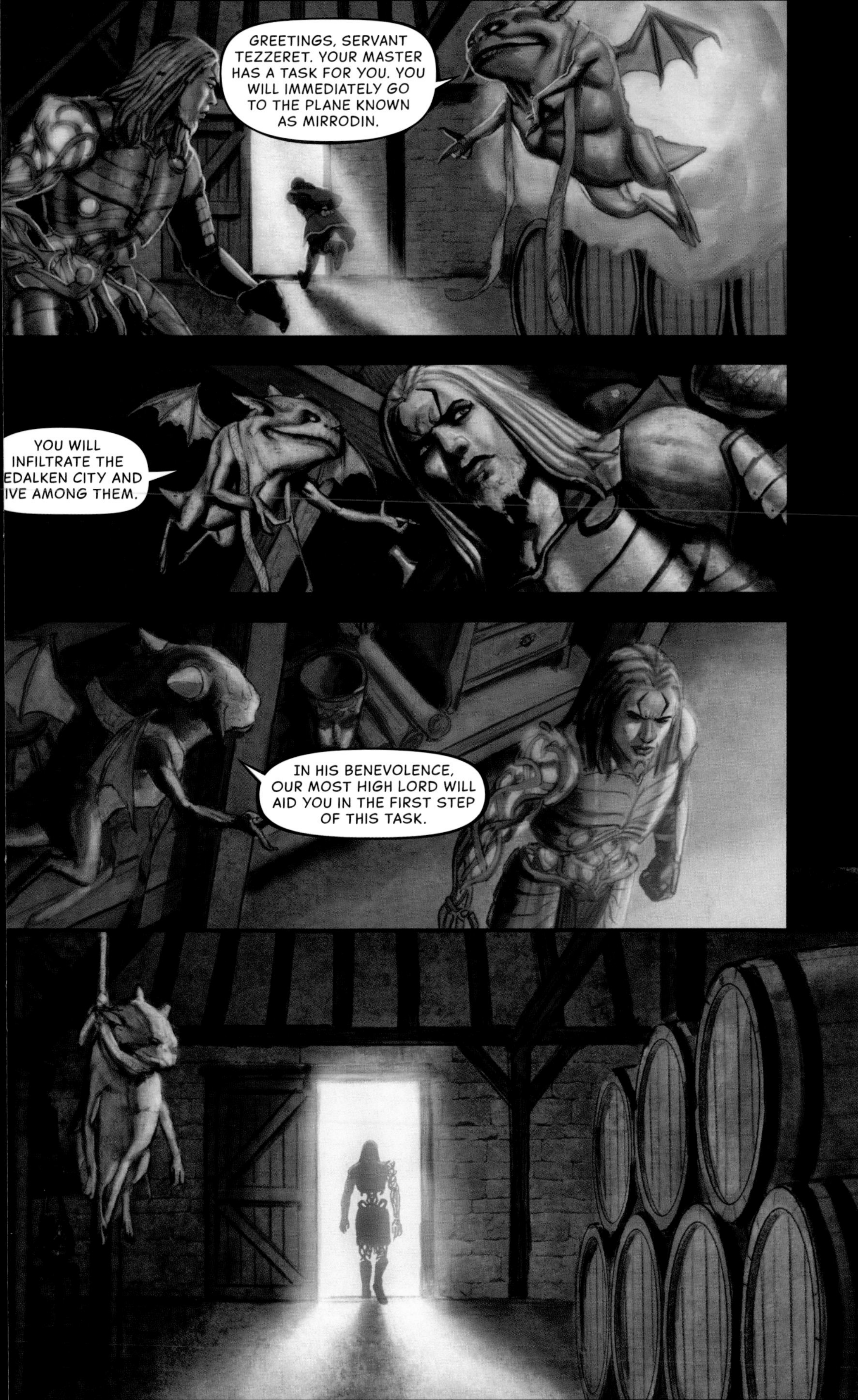
GREETINGS, SERVANT TEZZERET. YOUR MASTER HAS A TASK FOR YOU. YOU WILL IMMEDIATELY GO TO THE PLANE KNOWN AS MIRRODIN.
YOU WILL INFILTRATE THE EDALKEN CITY AND IVE AMONG THEM.
IN HIS BENEVOLENCE, OUR MOST HIGH LORD WILL AID YOU IN THE FIRST STEP OF THIS TASK.

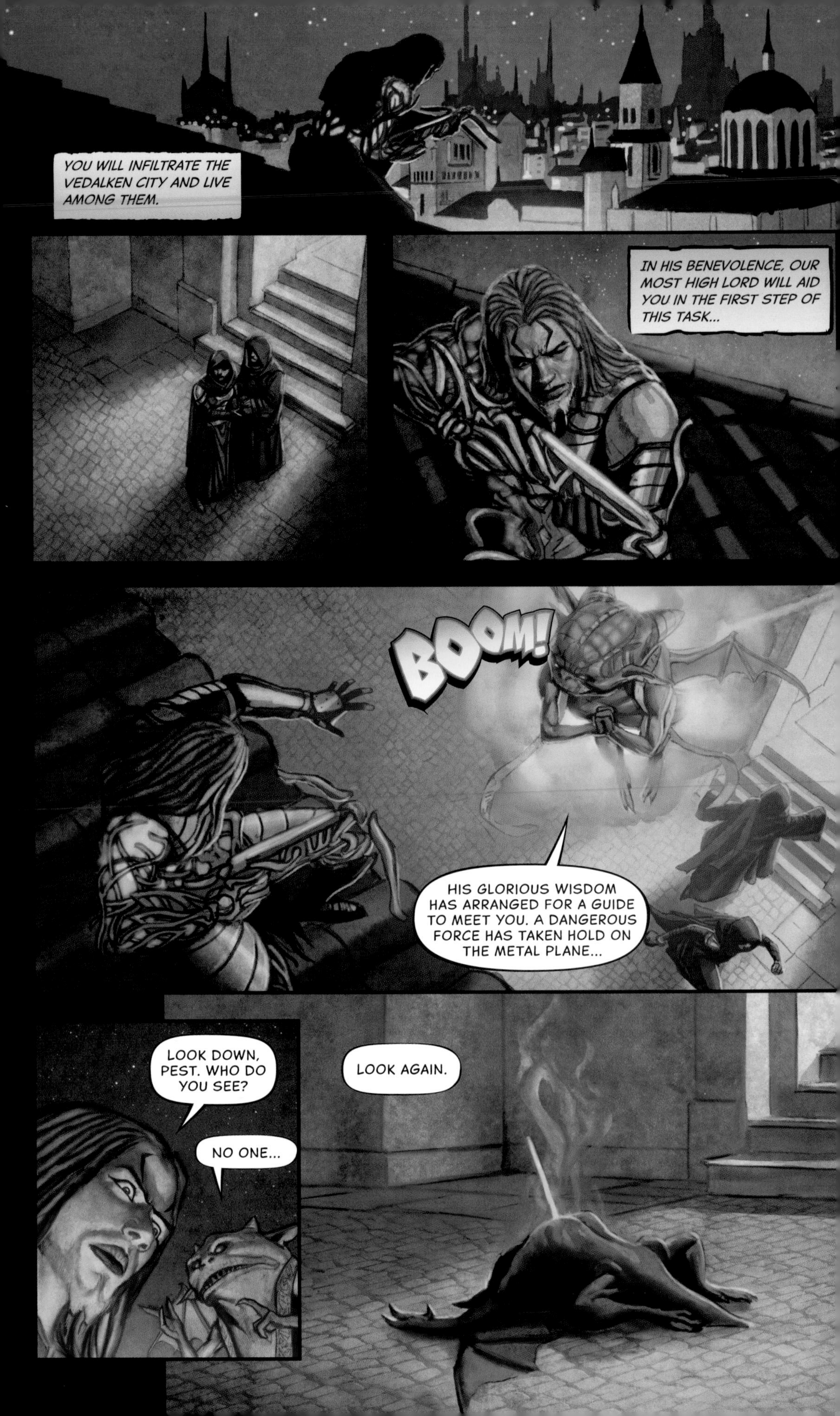
YOU WILL INFILTRATE THE VEDALKEN CITY AND LIVE AMONG THEM.
IN HIS BENEVOLENCE, OUR MOST HIGH LORD WILL AID YOU IN THE FIRST STEP OF THIS TASK...
BOOM!
HIS GLORIOUS WISDOM HAS ARRANGED FOR A GUIDE TO MEET YOU. A DANGEROUS FORCE HAS TAKEN HOLD ON THE METAL PLANE...
LOOK DOWN, PEST. WHO DO YOU SEE?
NO ONE...
LOOK AGAIN.

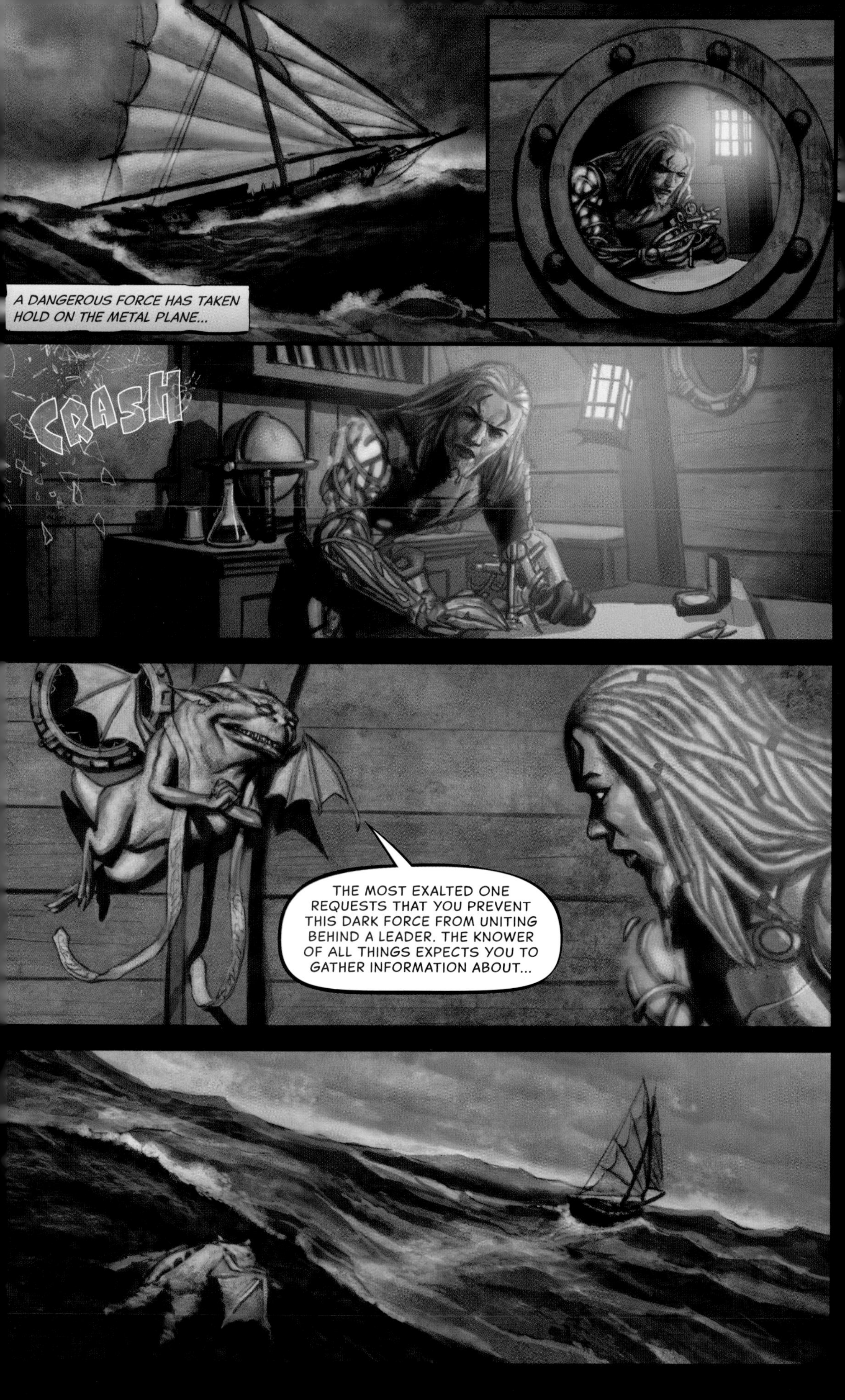
A DANGEROUS FORCE HAS TAKEN HOLD ON THE METAL PLANE...
CRASH
THE MOST EXALTED ONE REQUESTS THAT YOU PREVENT THIS DARK FORCE FROM UNITING BEHIND A LEADER. THE KNOWER OF ALL THINGS EXPECTS YOU TO GATHER INFORMATION ABOUT...

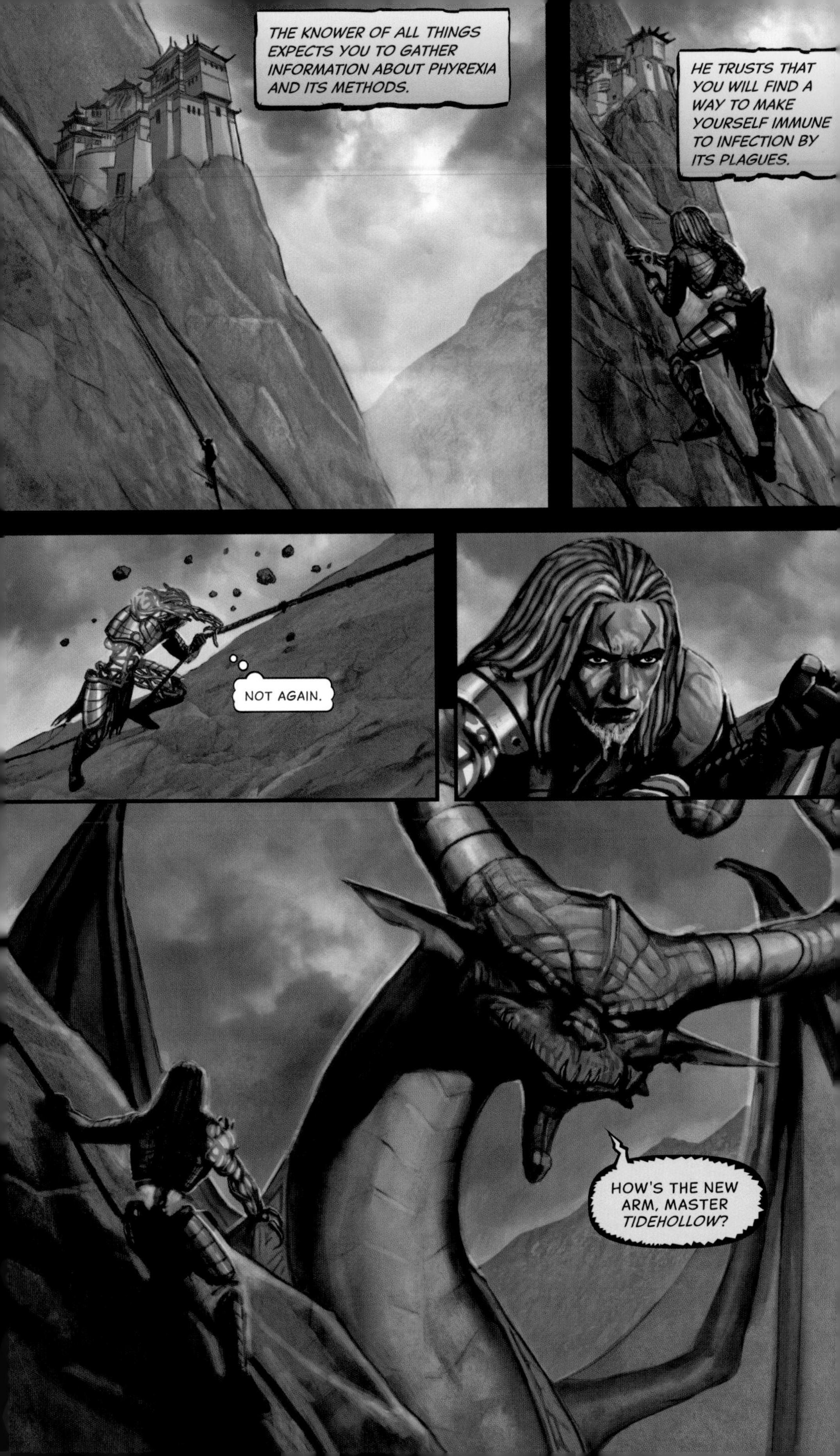
THE KNOWER OF ALL THINGS EXPECTS YOU TO GATHER INFORMATION ABOUT PHYREXIA AND ITS METHODS.
HE TRUSTS THAT YOU WILL FIND A WAY TO MAKE YOURSELF IMMUNE TO INFECTION BY ITS PLAGUES.
NOT AGAIN.
HOW'S THE NEW ARM, MASTER TIDEHOLLOW?

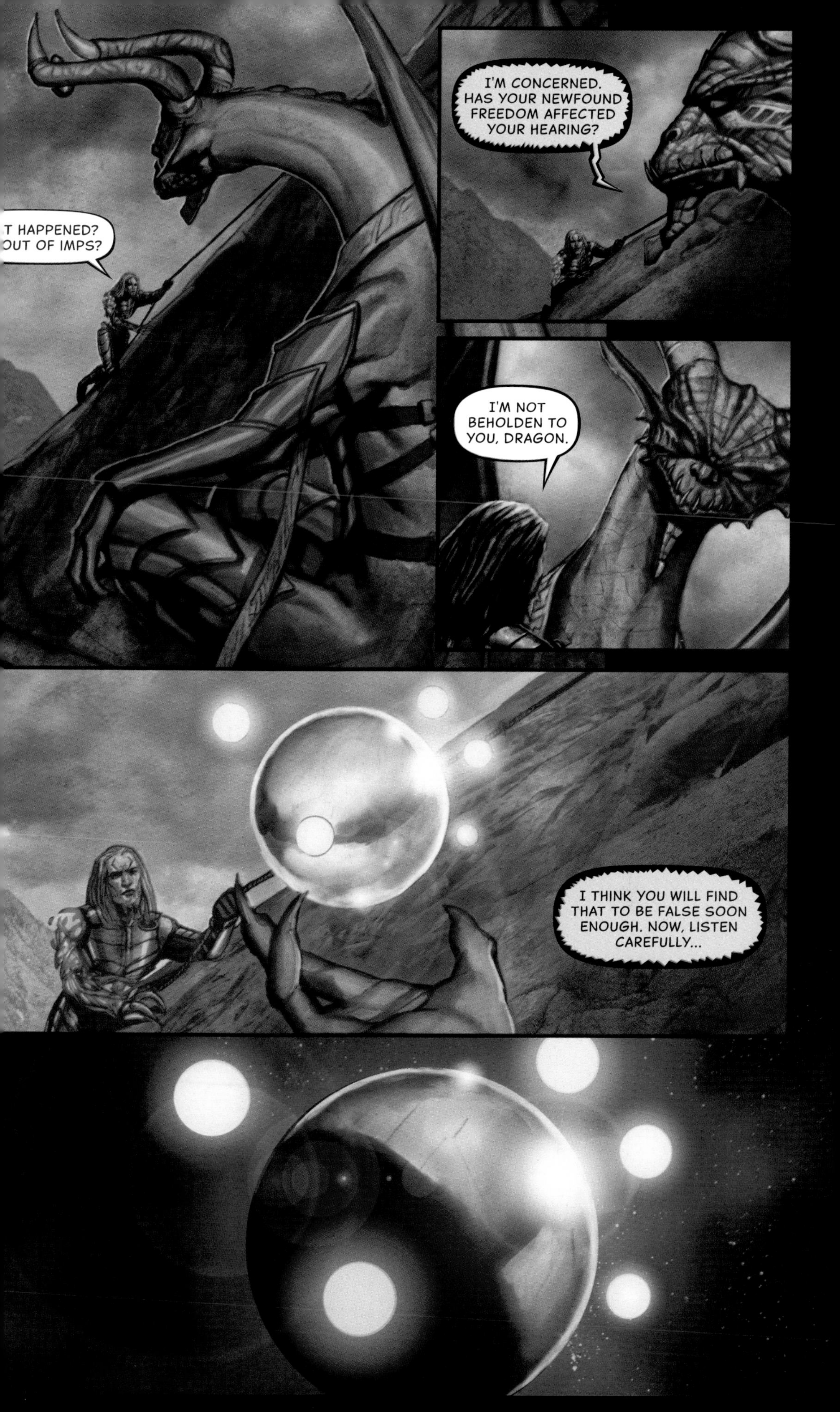
T HAPPENED?
OUT OF IMPS?
I'M CONCERNED. HAS YOUR NEWFOUND FREEDOM AFFECTED YOUR HEARING?
I'M NOT BEHOLDEN TO YOU, DRAGON.
I THINK YOU WILL FIND THAT TO BE FALSE SOON ENOUGH. NOW, LISTEN CAREFULLY...

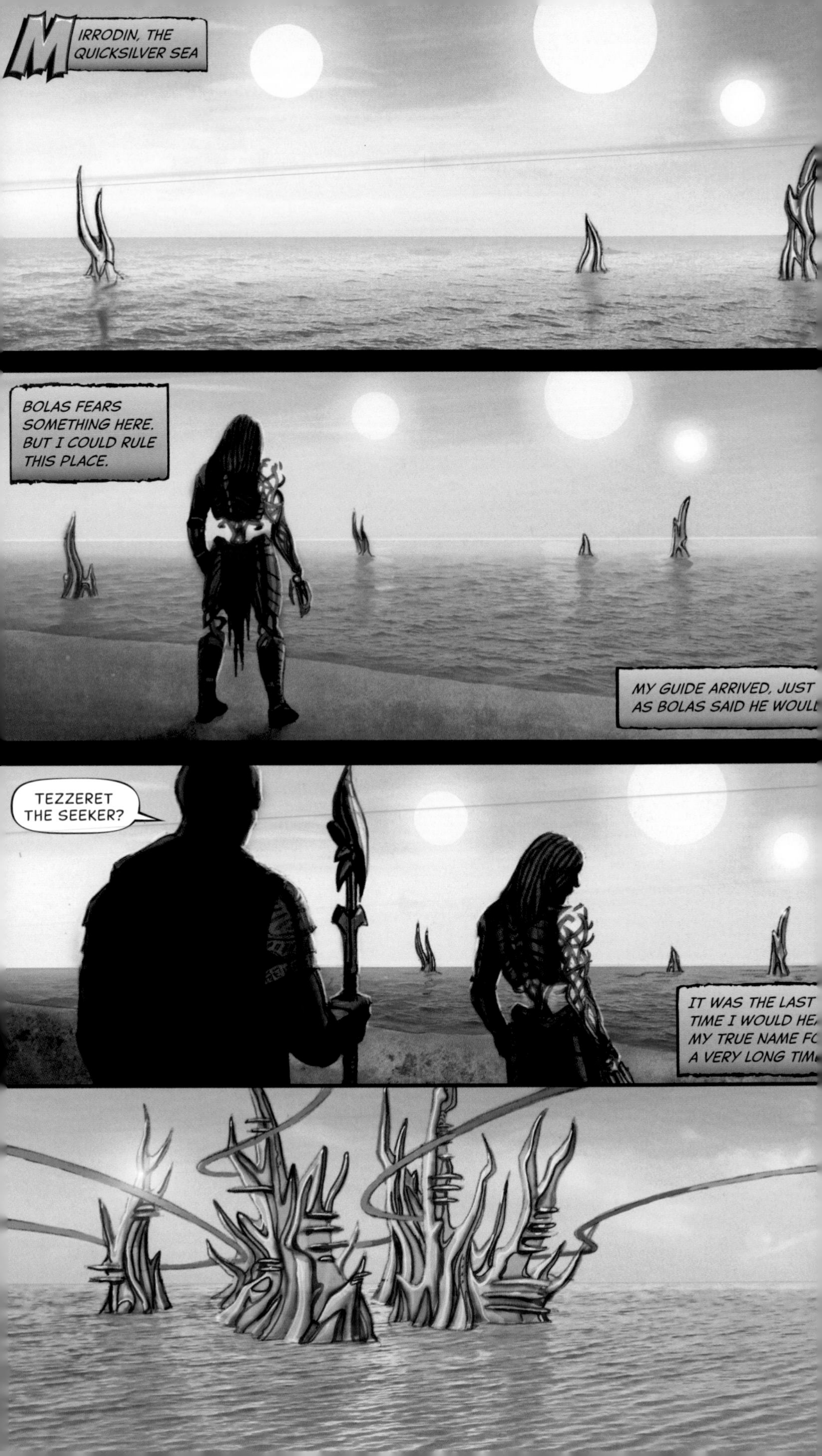
MIRRODIN, THE QUICKSILVER SEA
BOLAS FEARS SOMETHING HERE. BUT I COULD RULE THIS PLACE.
MY GUIDE ARRIVED, JUST AS BOLAS SAID HE WOUL
TEZZERET THE SEEKER?
IT WAS THE LAST TIME I WOULD HE MY TRUE NAME FO A VERY LONG TIM

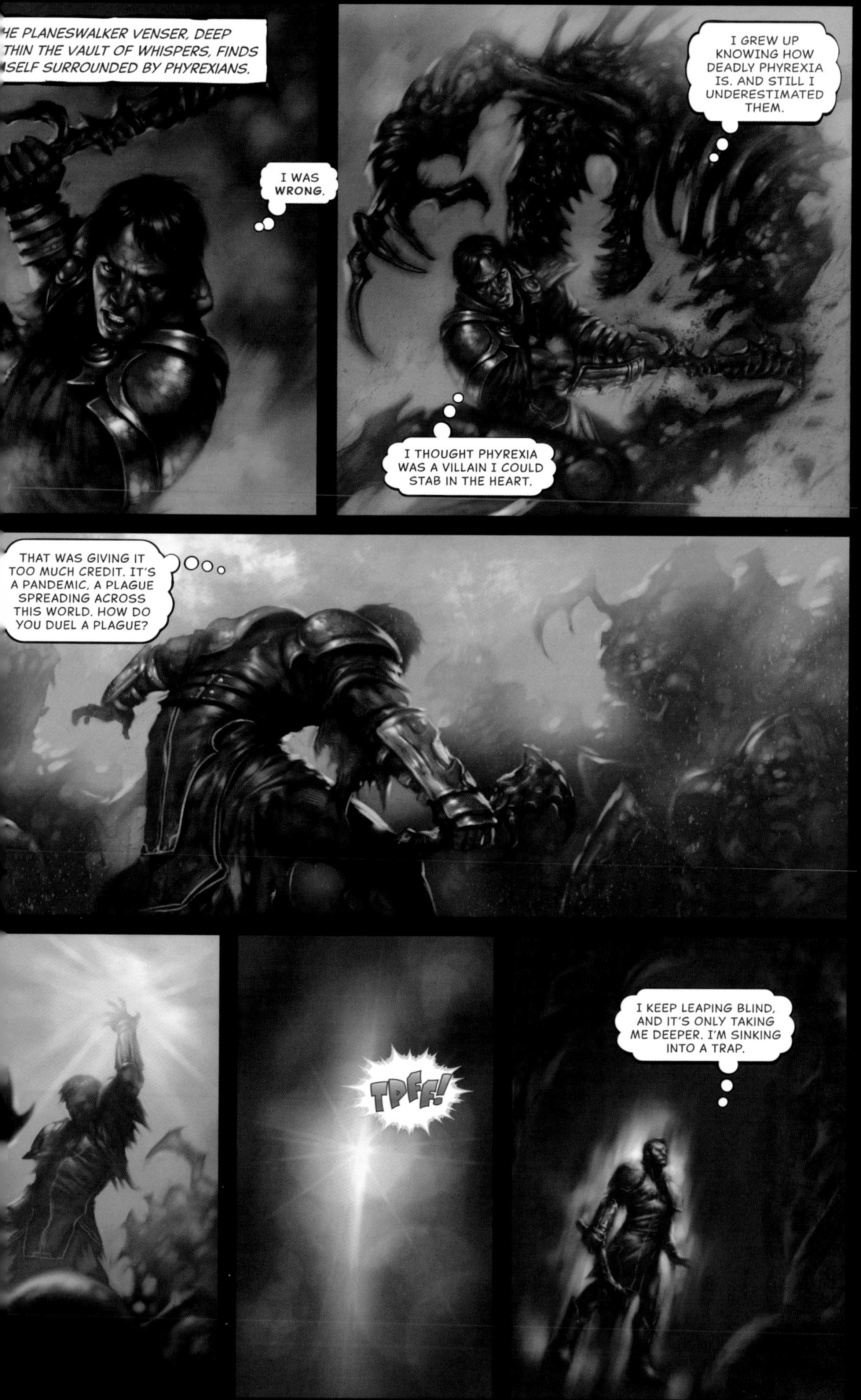
HE PLANESWALKER VENSER, DEEP THIN THE VAULT OF WHISPERS, FINDS SELF SURROUNDED BY PHYREXIANS.
I WAS WRONG.
I GREW UP KNOWING HOW DEADLY PHYREXIA IS. AND STILL I UNDERESTIMATED THEM.
I THOUGHT PHYREXIA WAS A VILLAIN I COULD STAB IN THE HEART.
THAT WAS GIVING IT TOO MUCH CREDIT. IT'S A PANDEMIC, A PLAGUE SPREADING ACROSS THIS WORLD. HOW DO YOU DUEL A PLAGUE?
TPFF!
I KEEP LEAPING BLIND, AND IT'S ONLY TAKING ME DEEPER. I'M SINKING INTO A TRAP.

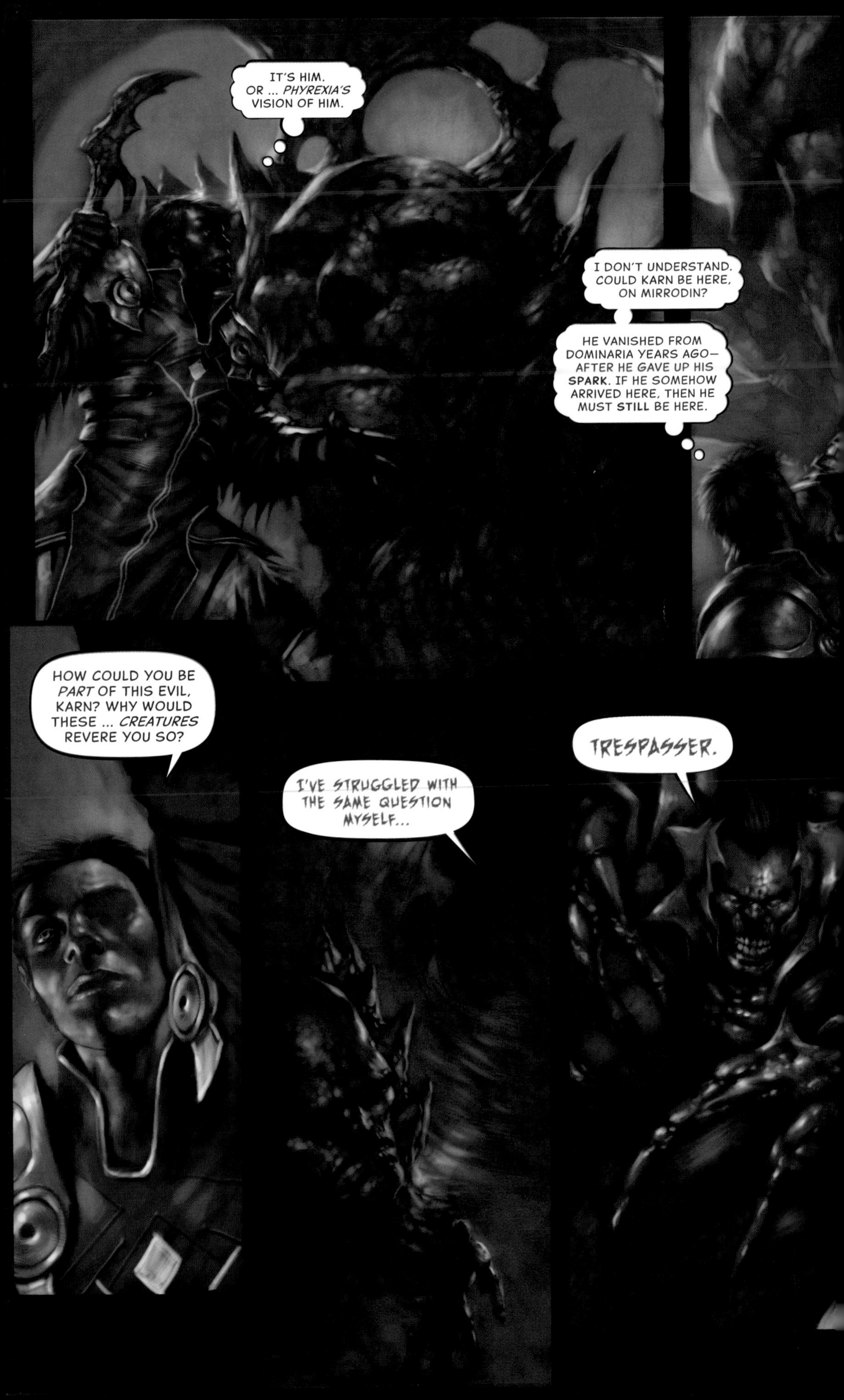
IT'S HIM. OR ... *PHYREXIA'S* VISION OF HIM.
I DON'T UNDERSTAND. COULD KARN BE HERE, ON MIRRODIN?
HE VANISHED FROM DOMINARIA YEARS AGO— AFTER HE GAVE UP HIS **SPARK**. IF HE SOMEHOW ARRIVED HERE, THEN HE MUST **STILL** BE HERE.
HOW COULD YOU BE *PART* OF THIS EVIL, KARN? WHY WOULD THESE ... *CREATURES* REVERE YOU SO?
I'VE STRUGGLED WITH THE SAME QUESTION MYSELF...
TRESPASSER.

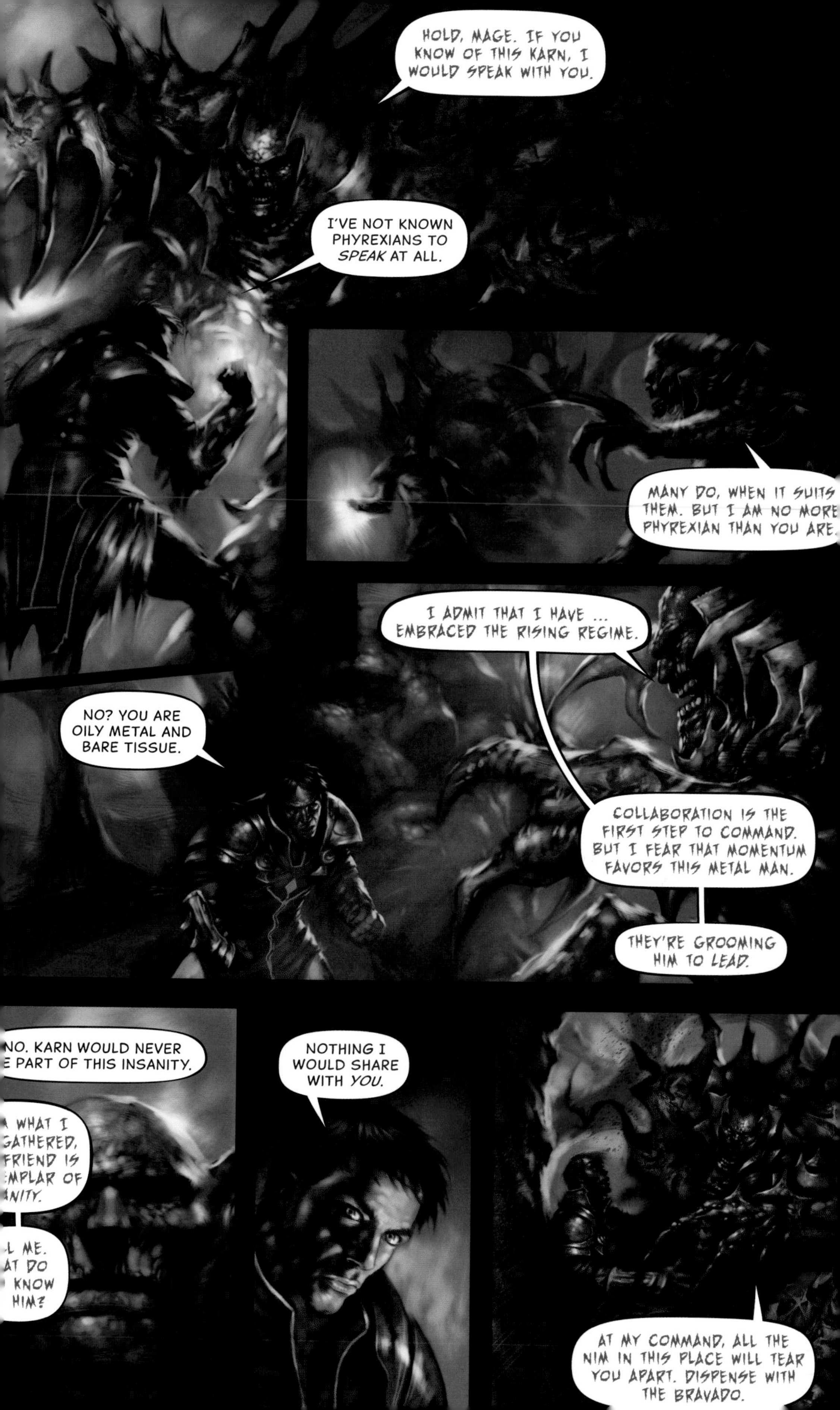
HOLD, MAGE. IF YOU KNOW OF THIS KARN, I WOULD SPEAK WITH YOU.
I'VE NOT KNOWN PHYREXIANS TO SPEAK AT ALL.
MANY DO, WHEN IT SUITS THEM. BUT I AM NO MORE PHYREXIAN THAN YOU ARE.
NO? YOU ARE OILY METAL AND BARE TISSUE.
I ADMIT THAT I HAVE ... EMBRACED THE RISING REGIME.
COLLABORATION IS THE FIRST STEP TO COMMAND. BUT I FEAR THAT MOMENTUM FAVORS THIS METAL MAN.
THEY'RE GROOMING HIM TO LEAD.
NO. KARN WOULD NEVER
PART OF THIS INSANITY.
WHAT I
GATHERED,
FRIEND IS
EMPLAR OF
ANITY.
L ME.
AT DO
KNOW
HIM?
NOTHING I WOULD SHARE WITH YOU.
AT MY COMMAND, ALL THE NIM IN THIS PLACE WILL TEAR YOU APART. DISPENSE WITH THE BRAVADO.

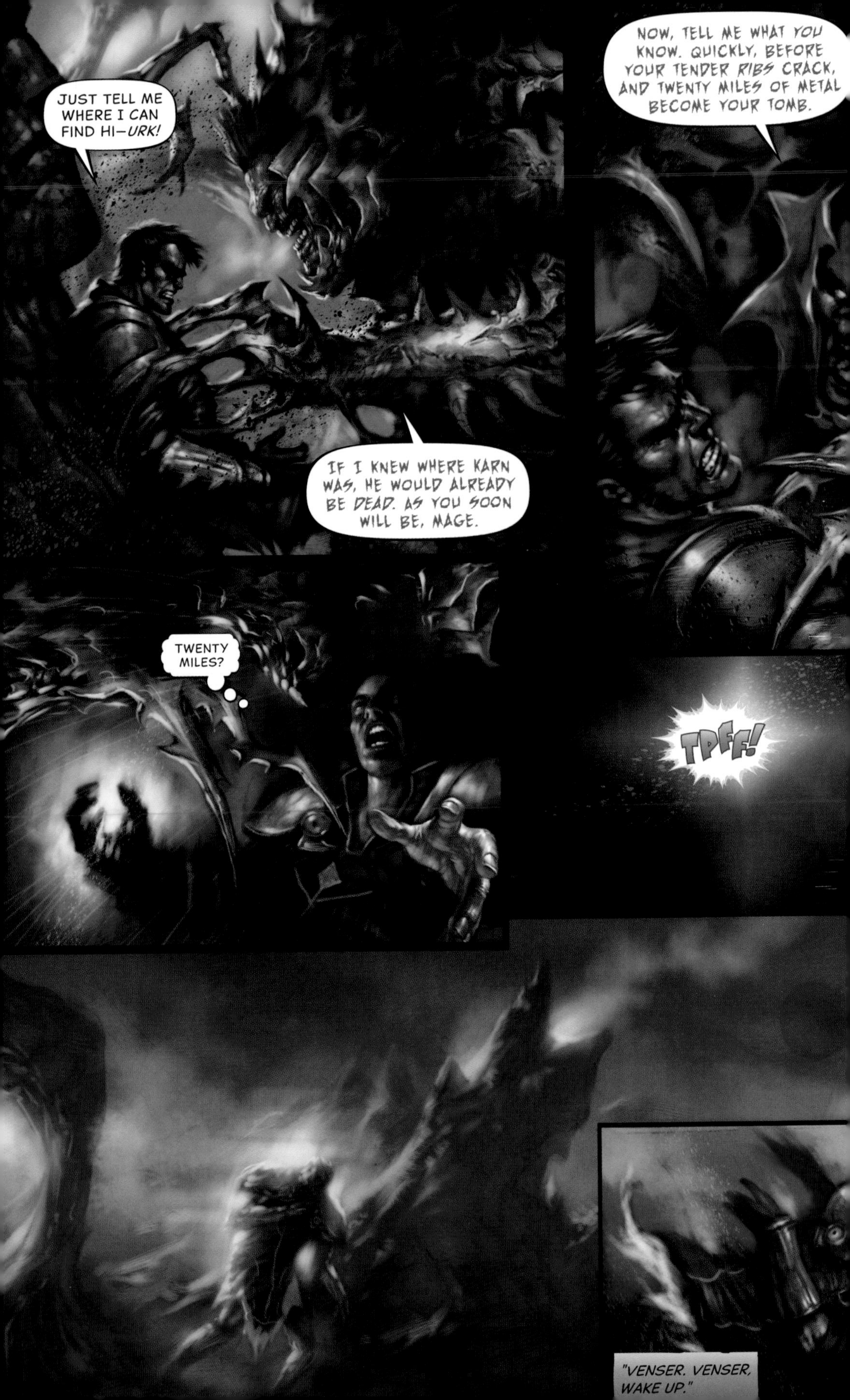
JUST TELL ME WHERE I CAN FIND HI—*URK!*
IF I KNEW WHERE KARN WAS, HE WOULD ALREADY BE *DEAD*. AS YOU SOON WILL BE, MAGE.
NOW, TELL ME WHAT *YOU* KNOW. QUICKLY, BEFORE YOUR TENDER *RIBS* CRACK, AND TWENTY MILES OF METAL BECOME YOUR TOMB.
TWENTY MILES?
TPFF!
"VENSER. VENSER, WAKE UP."

I'M GLAD WE FOUND YOU. CAN YOU WALK? WE HAVE TO GO, NOW.

NO.

WHAT DO YOU MEAN, NO? WE HAVE TO *REGROUP*, AND FIND A WAY TO DESTROY PHYREXIA.

KARN, MY FORMER MENTOR, IS HERE. ON MIRRODIN. AND WE HAVE TO FIND HIM.

DON'T BACK OUT ON US NOW. I SOUGHT YOU TO HELP US FIGHT.

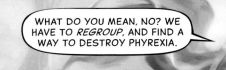

PHYREXIA CAN'T BE *FOUGHT*. WE HAVE TO GET TO KARN. HE IS TO BE THEIR NEW *LEADER*.

THE VAULT OF WHISPERS IS INFESTED. THIS WHOLE PLANE IS *INFESTED*.

THERE'S NO WAY TO *STOP* WHAT WE CAME HERE TO STOP. NOT WITHOUT HIM.

NOW YOU'RE MAKING SENSE. WE KILL THIS KARN, WE STOP PHYREXIA.

YOU DON'T UNDERSTAND. WE MUST *SAVE* HIM.

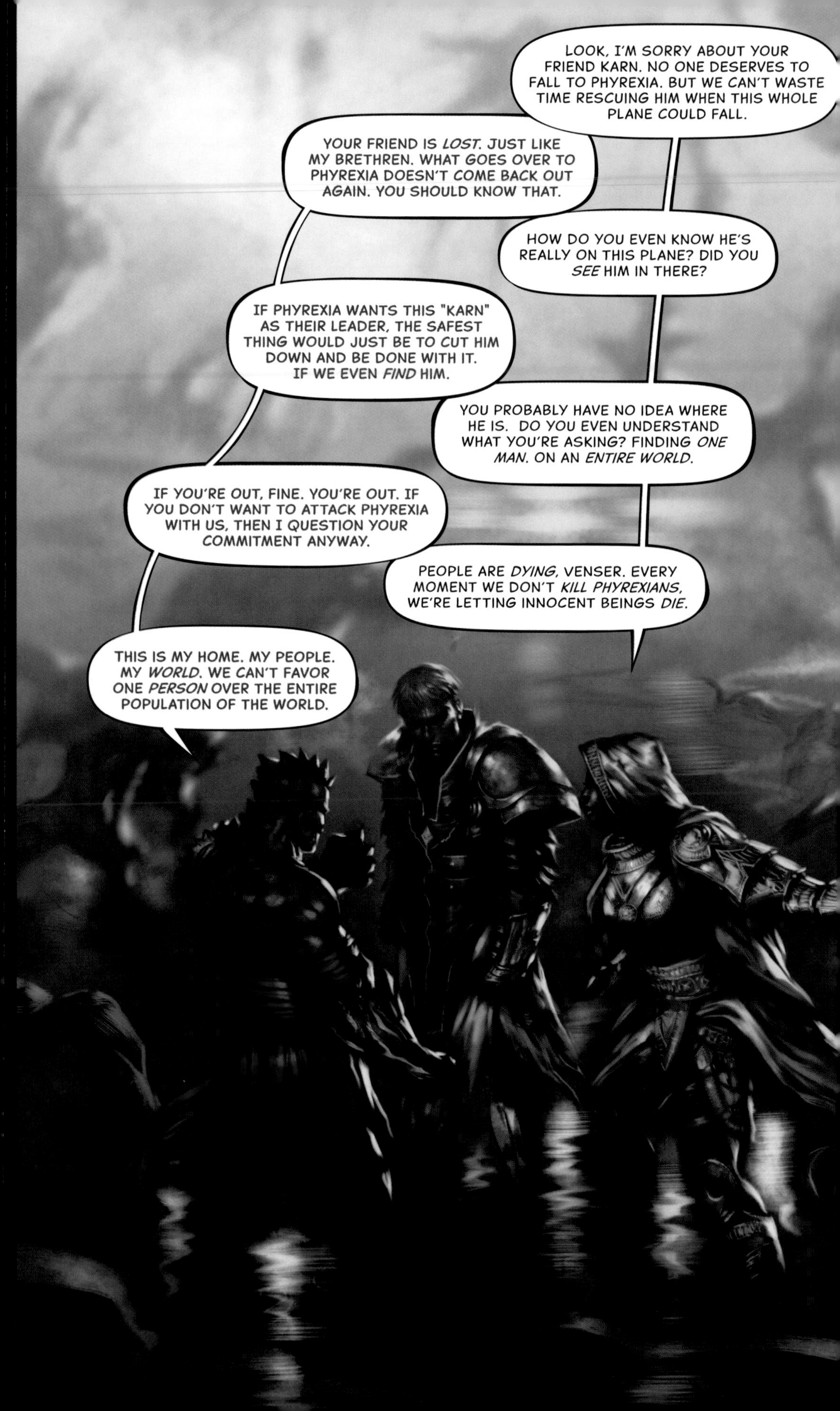

LOOK, I'M SORRY ABOUT YOUR FRIEND KARN. NO ONE DESERVES TO FALL TO PHYREXIA. BUT WE CAN'T WASTE TIME RESCUING HIM WHEN THIS WHOLE PLANE COULD FALL.
YOUR FRIEND IS *LOST*. JUST LIKE MY BRETHREN. WHAT GOES OVER TO PHYREXIA DOESN'T COME BACK OUT AGAIN. YOU SHOULD KNOW THAT.
HOW DO YOU EVEN KNOW HE'S REALLY ON THIS PLANE? DID YOU *SEE* HIM IN THERE?
IF PHYREXIA WANTS THIS "KARN" AS THEIR LEADER, THE SAFEST THING WOULD JUST BE TO CUT HIM DOWN AND BE DONE WITH IT. IF WE EVEN *FIND* HIM.
YOU PROBABLY HAVE NO IDEA WHERE HE IS. DO YOU EVEN UNDERSTAND WHAT YOU'RE ASKING? FINDING *ONE MAN*. ON AN *ENTIRE WORLD*.
IF YOU'RE OUT, FINE. YOU'RE OUT. IF YOU DON'T WANT TO ATTACK PHYREXIA WITH US, THEN I QUESTION YOUR COMMITMENT ANYWAY.
PEOPLE ARE *DYING*, VENSER. EVERY MOMENT WE DON'T *KILL PHYREXIANS*, WE'RE LETTING INNOCENT BEINGS *DIE*.
THIS IS MY HOME. MY PEOPLE. MY *WORLD*. WE CAN'T FAVOR ONE *PERSON* OVER THE ENTIRE POPULATION OF THE WORLD.

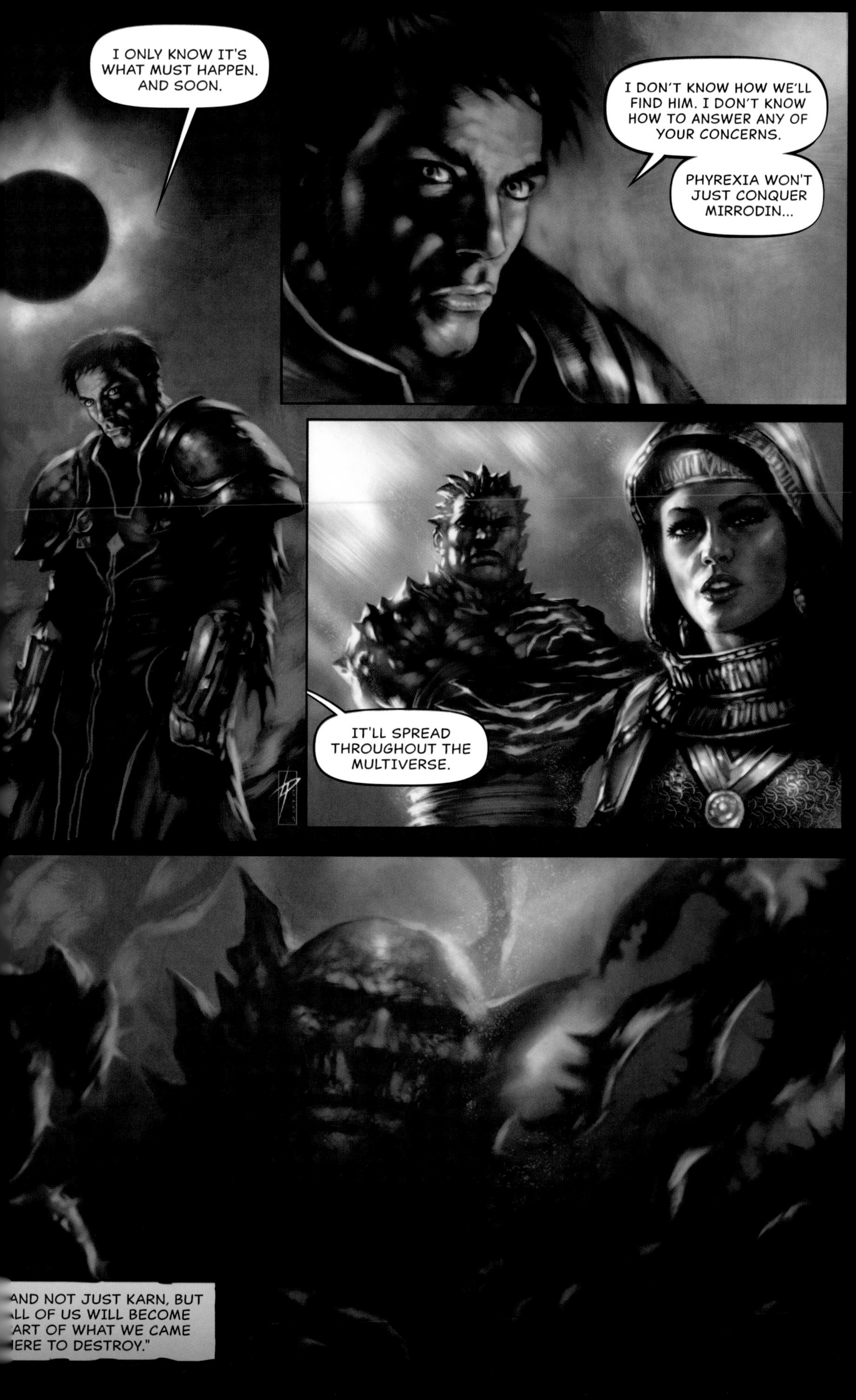
I ONLY KNOW IT'S WHAT MUST HAPPEN. AND SOON.
I DON'T KNOW HOW WE'LL FIND HIM. I DON'T KNOW HOW TO ANSWER ANY OF YOUR CONCERNS.
PHYREXIA WON'T JUST CONQUER MIRRODIN...
IT'LL SPREAD THROUGHOUT THE MULTIVERSE.
AND NOT JUST KARN, BUT LL OF US WILL BECOME ART OF WHAT WE CAME ERE TO DESTROY."

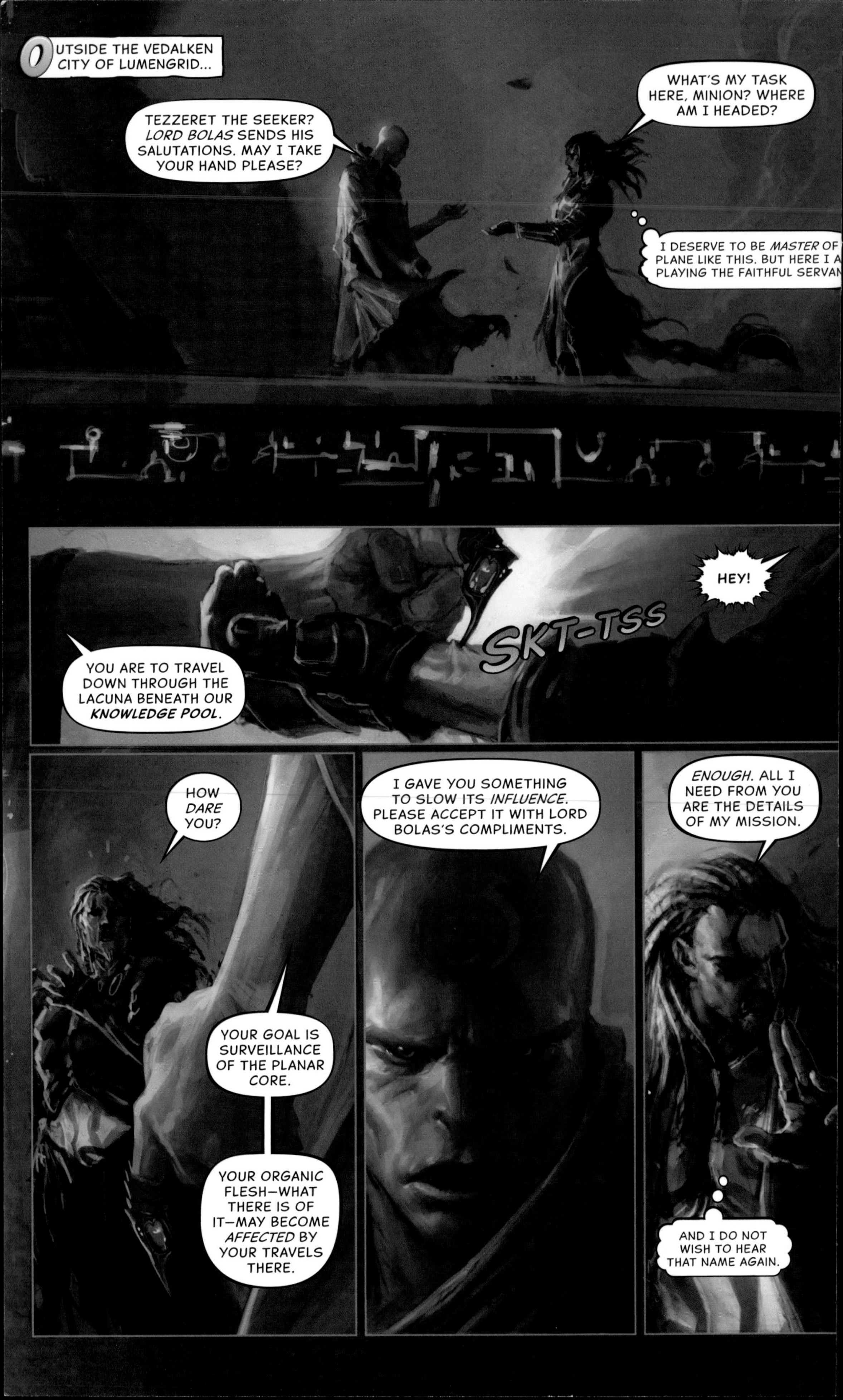
OUTSIDE THE VEDALKEN CITY OF LUMENGRID...
TEZZERET THE SEEKER? LORD BOLAS SENDS HIS SALUTATIONS. MAY I TAKE YOUR HAND PLEASE?
WHAT'S MY TASK HERE, MINION? WHERE AM I HEADED?
I DESERVE TO BE MASTER OF PLANE LIKE THIS. BUT HERE I A PLAYING THE FAITHFUL SERVAN
HEY!
SKT-TSS
YOU ARE TO TRAVEL DOWN THROUGH THE LACUNA BENEATH OUR KNOWLEDGE POOL.
HOW DARE YOU?
YOUR GOAL IS SURVEILLANCE OF THE PLANAR CORE.
YOUR ORGANIC FLESH—WHAT THERE IS OF IT—MAY BECOME AFFECTED BY YOUR TRAVELS THERE.
I GAVE YOU SOMETHING TO SLOW ITS INFLUENCE. PLEASE ACCEPT IT WITH LORD BOLAS'S COMPLIMENTS.
ENOUGH. ALL I NEED FROM YOU ARE THE DETAILS OF MY MISSION.
AND I DO NOT WISH TO HEAR THAT NAME AGAIN.

I'M TREATED THIS WAY BY A VEDALKEN *PEON*, OR BY ONE OF BOLAS'S MIRAGES.
THIS IS THE PRICE I PAY FOR BEING SPARED.
I VOWED NEVER TO BECOME A SCRAPPER LIKE MY FATHER.
I VOWED NEVER TO *SERVE*. YET HERE I AM, VING THROUGH THIS METAL ORLD AT THE PLEASURE OF AN ELDERLY DRAGON.
WHAT BARGAIN HAVE I STRUCK?

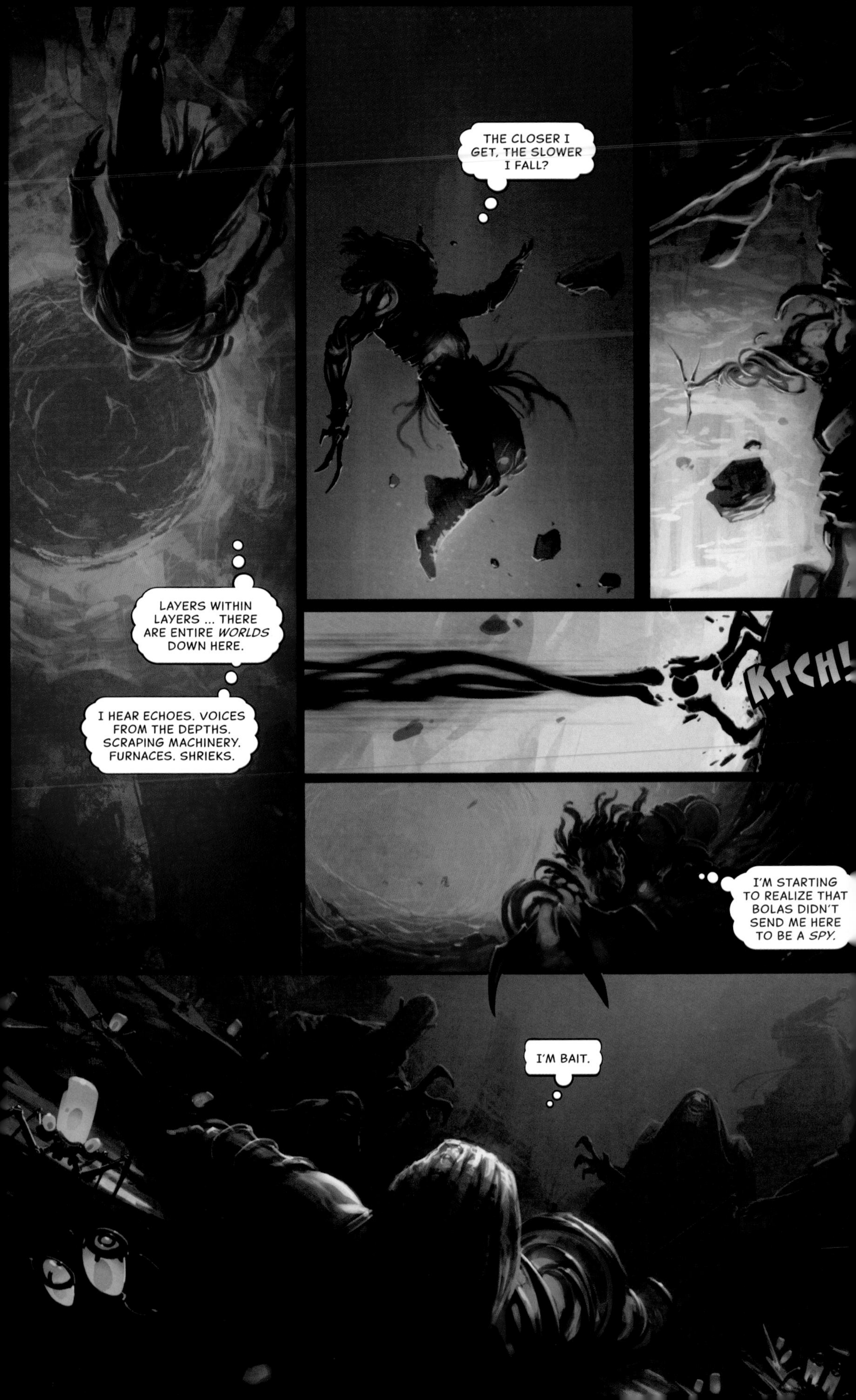
THE CLOSER I GET, THE SLOWER I FALL?
LAYERS WITHIN LAYERS ... THERE ARE ENTIRE *WORLDS* DOWN HERE.
I HEAR ECHOES. VOICES FROM THE DEPTHS. SCRAPING MACHINERY. FURNACES. SHRIEKS.
KTCH!
I'M STARTING TO REALIZE THAT BOLAS DIDN'T SEND ME HERE TO BE A *SPY*.
I'M BAIT.

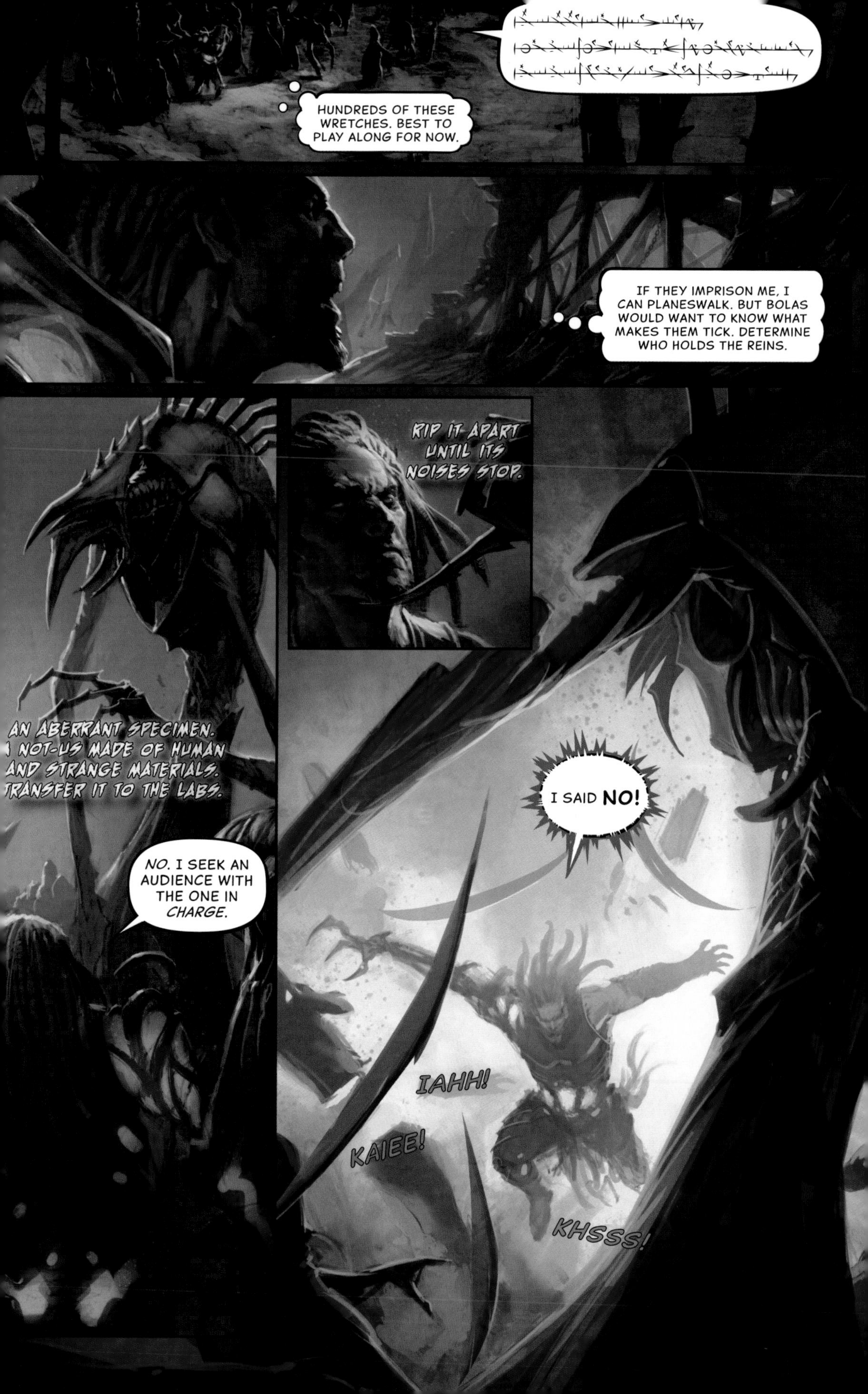
HUNDREDS OF THESE WRETCHES. BEST TO PLAY ALONG FOR NOW.
IF THEY IMPRISON ME, I CAN PLANESWALK. BUT BOLAS WOULD WANT TO KNOW WHAT MAKES THEM TICK. DETERMINE WHO HOLDS THE REINS.
AN ABERRANT SPECIMEN. A NOT-US MADE OF HUMAN AND STRANGE MATERIALS. TRANSFER IT TO THE LABS.
NO. I SEEK AN AUDIENCE WITH THE ONE IN *CHARGE*.
RIP IT APART UNTIL ITS NOISES STOP.
I SAID **NO!**
IAHH!
KAIEE!
KHSSS!

IF I AM NOT HARMED, I WILL HARM NO OTHER. JUST ... LET ME *SPEAK*.

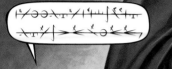

THE NOT-US MUST COME WITH US. THE FATHER OF MACHINES WILL SEE IT.

THANK YOU.

IF IT CHANNELS MANA AGAIN, I SHALL VIVISECT IT PERSONALLY AND FEED ITS TISSUES TO MY LARVAE.

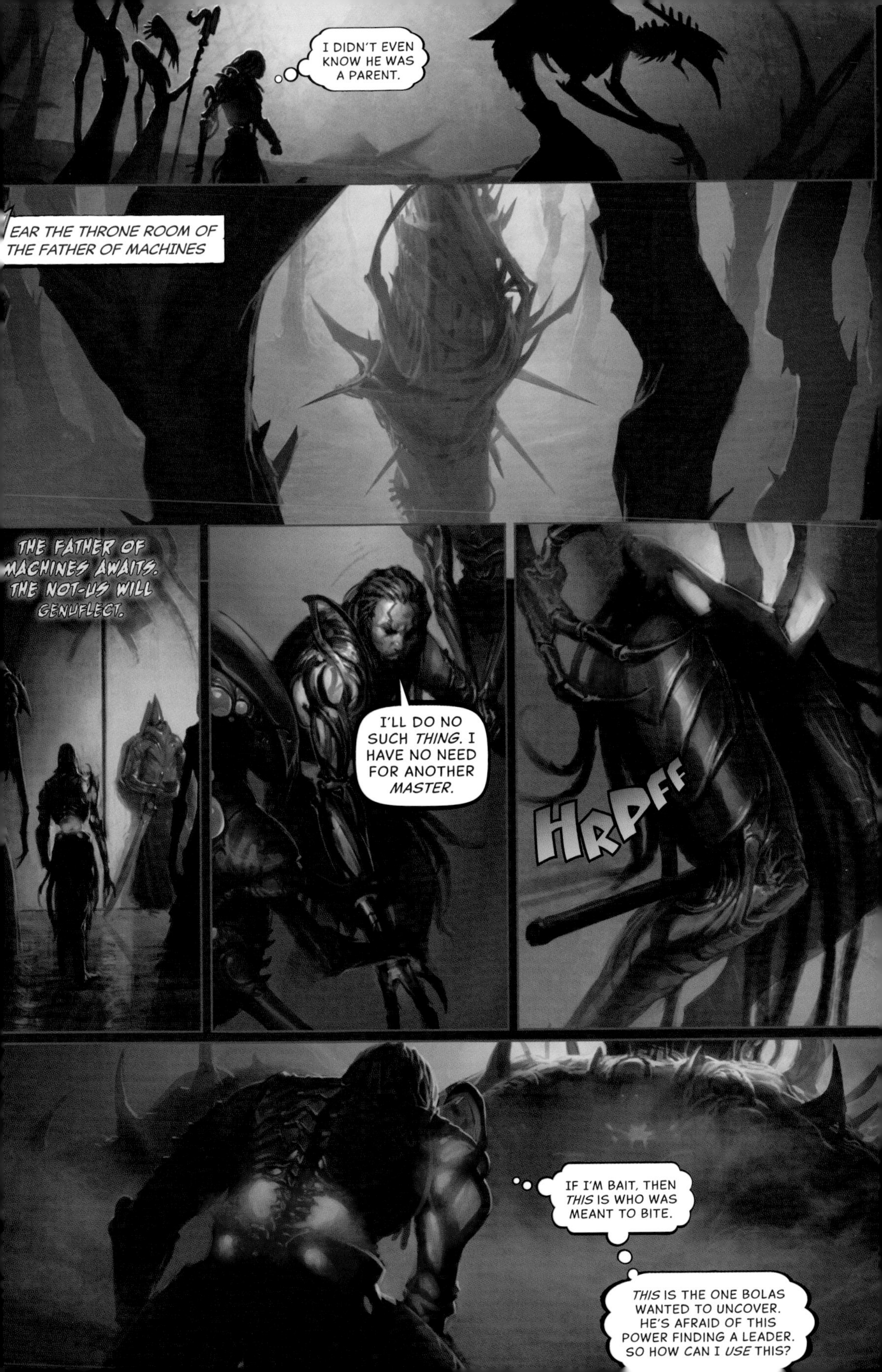
I DIDN'T EVEN KNOW HE WAS A PARENT.
EAR THE THRONE ROOM OF THE FATHER OF MACHINES
THE FATHER OF MACHINES AWAITS. THE NOT-US WILL GENUFLECT.
I'LL DO NO SUCH *THING*. I HAVE NO NEED FOR ANOTHER *MASTER*.
HRPFF
IF I'M BAIT, THEN *THIS* IS WHO WAS MEANT TO BITE.
THIS IS THE ONE BOLAS WANTED TO UNCOVER. HE'S AFRAID OF THIS POWER FINDING A LEADER. SO HOW CAN I *USE* THIS?

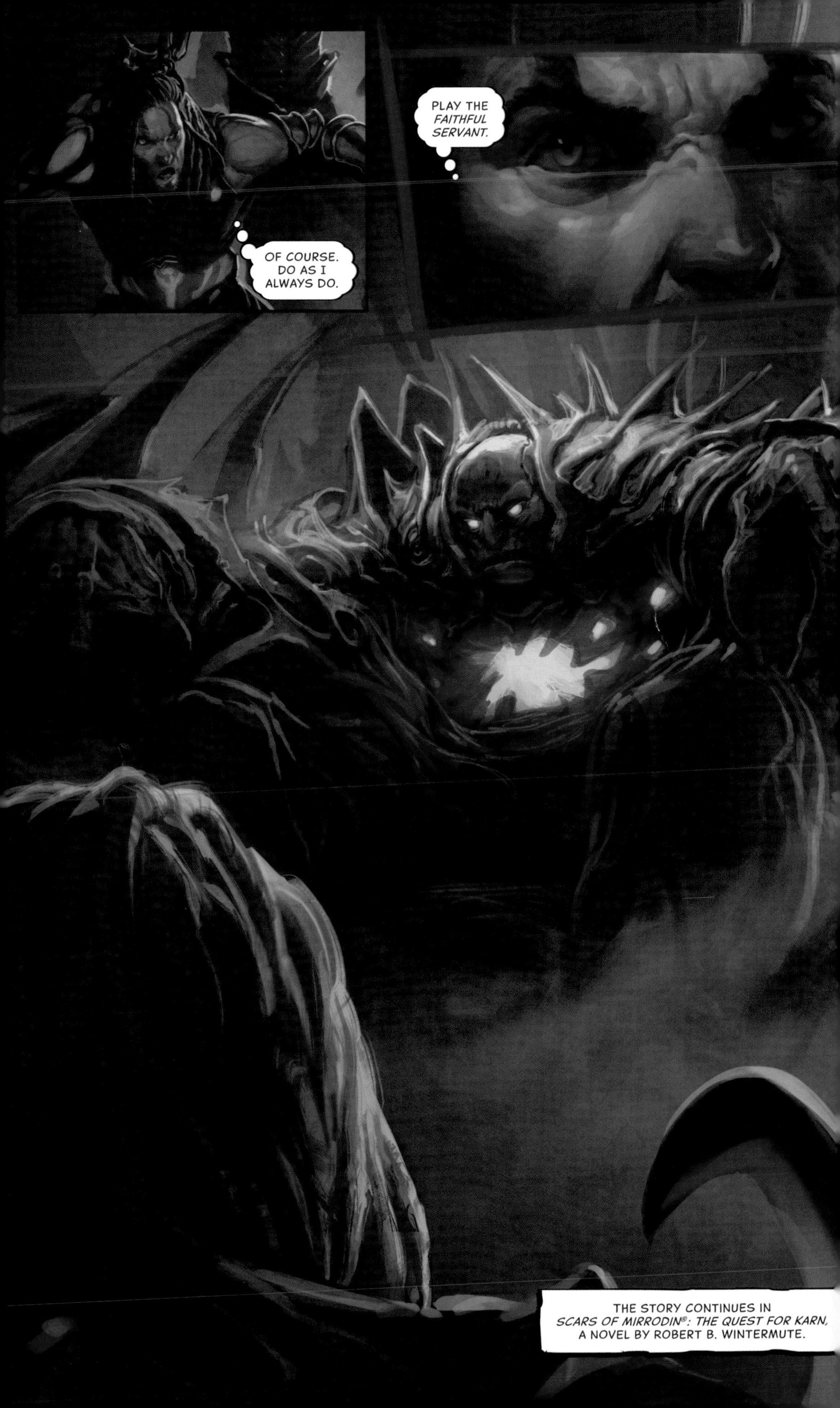
PLAY THE *FAITHFUL* *SERVANT.*
OF COURSE. DO AS I ALWAYS DO.
THE STORY CONTINUES IN *SCARS OF MIRRODIN®: THE QUEST FOR KARN,* A NOVEL BY ROBERT B. WINTERMUTE.

About the Authors

Doug Beyer started as a MAGIC: THE GATHERING® fan, became web developer for magicthegathering.com, moved on to prolific flavor text writer, and eventually became a MAGIC creative designer. His background is in philosophy, computer programming, and cognitive science. He is the author of *Alara Unbroken* and *A Planeswalker's Guide to Alara* (with Jenna Helland). He resides in Seattle.

Jenna Helland is a creative designer and writer for Wizards of the Coast. Her short story, "The Cloudbreaker", appeared in the MAGIC: THE GATHERING anthology *Shadowmoor*. Her books include *The Planeswalker's Guide to Alara* (with Doug Beyer), *Path of the Planeswalker* (with Doug Beyer and Brady Dommermuth), and *The Fanged Crown*.

Brady Dommermuth is the MAGIC: THE GATHERING creative director and world-building lead. He has worked on Magic for over fourteen of its eighteen years, during which his training in literature, theater, and drama criticism has actually been relevant! He started reading comics and playing DUNGEONS & DRAGONS® in 1982. It was a very good year.

Dan Brereton is an award-winning illustrator and writer who has worked in the comics industry for over twenty-three years. Widely known for his unique painted storytelling style, he has worked on various titles including JLA, Vampirella, Buffy the Vampire Slayer, Thor, Punisher, Immortal Iron Fist, Red Sonja, Batman and Bart Simpson's Treehouse of Horror. Other clients include Disney Worldwide Publishing, Disney TV Animation, Hasbro Toys, and NBC. Comics properties he has created include Nocturnals, Giantkiller, and The Psycho. He lives in Northern California with his family. Visit www.nocturnals.com for more information.

Paul Davidson's first comic book work appeared in the UK publication Warhammer Monthly, where he created the ongoing series Dwarflords in the 1990s. After spending nearly ten years as a concept artist in the video games industry, Paul has returned to comics full time, working on titles such as New Mutants and X-Men: Legacy for Marvel.

Dave Dorman is an Eisner Award-winning illustrator who has done artwork for The Batman for DC Comics and the Indiana Jones and Star Wars series for Dark Horse Comics. In addition he has done covers for the Aliens paperback series and the Lone Wolf series among many others. His work is also showcased in the Bram Stoker nominated, illustrated novel Dead Heat from MoJo Press, and a book collection of his art, Star Wars: The Art of Dave Dorman. Aliens: Tribes, an award-winning illustrated novel featuring twenty-four of his full paintings is available in hardcover and has been released as a trade paperback. His many continuing projects include the ongoing Young Jedi Knights and Han Solo series of paperbacks, and toy design for the Aliens 4: Resurrection movie.

Brian Haberlin is known as a Witchblade co-creator, for his work on titles such as Aria and Hellcop, and for his recent run on Spawn with David Hine. Readers can learn more about his original 00 graphic novel at his site, digitalarttutorials.com.

Alex Horley-Orlandelli was born in the outskirts of Milan, Italy. He spent his early career working for DC Comics (Lobo), Dark Horse, Image, and *Heavy Metal*. In recent years his main focus has been producing artwork for Magic: The Gathering and World of Warcraft trading card games.

Izzy is a senior concept artist in the video game industry. His art has contributed to such games as Gun, the Tony Hawk series, God of War III, and many more. Find out more at www.cannibalcandy.com and www.mercilessdesign.blogspot.com.

Dave Kendall was corrupted by his grandma at age five when she introduced him to Marvel's Zombie, Simon Garth. That early education has led to many illustrations for Magic: The Gathering and Blizzard, and finishing the first of three graphic novels for French publisher, Soleil.

Nic Klein has worked for Marvel, Radical Comics, Panini Comics, and on such titles as New Warriors, Man-Thing, and Star-Lord. His new, creator-owned series Viking with Ivan Brandon is published by Image Comics. His work can also be found in Spectrum 13, 14, and 15. Visit his website at www.nic-klein.com.

Karl Kopinski's career began as co-creator of Kal Jerico for Warhammer Monthly. He went on to spend seven years as an in-house artist for Games Workshop until leaving to go freelance in 2004.

Paul Lee is a freelance illustrator. His projects include Conan, Buffy the Vampire Slayer, Batman, Green Arrow, and Star Wars. In his free time, Paul is a competitive Lego builder.

Christopher Moeller has been writing and painting graphic novels from his studio in Pittsburgh since 1991. His two creator-owned Iron Empires graphic novels are published Dark Horse Comics. Moeller was the cover artist for the monthly comic *Lucifer* from Vertigo, and *Batman: Shadow of the Bat* from DC Comics. An avid war gamer, Moeller has provided illustrations for a variety of game publishers, including Magic: The Gathering, OSC, White Wolf, FASA, Wiz Kids and Columbia Games

Lucio Parrillo, Lucio Parrillo, an Italian artist who works in Europe and the U.S.A., has worked for Marvel, including covers for Iron Man and Doctor Strange as well as illustration for Siege, The Hulk, World War Hulk, What if, and Thor. He has illustrated covers for Dynamite's Red Sonja, Vampirella, the Expendables, Project Super Powers, and Army of Darkness. Lucio has also illustrated cards for the World of Warcraft TCG, plus many covers of video games and roleplaying games in Europe.

Steve Prescott jumped into the gaming industry doing work for White Wolf and Shadowrun. He has since spread his personal brand of bacteria into Dungeons & Dragons, World of Warcraft, and Magic: The Gathering to name just a few. In his free time, Steve enjoys complaining about not having any free time.

Doug Sirois was born and raised in Massachusetts. He graduated from the Art Institute of Boston in 2001 with a BFA in illustration. His MFA in illustration is from California State University, Fullerton, where he teaches part time. He currently resides in Claremont, California with his wife Jenn, son Micah, dog Miles, and cat Willow. He has since illustrated and designed everything from comic books, children's book covers, and CD covers to clothing and apparel.

Dan Scott has been illustrating for Magic: The Gathering since the Champions of Kamigawa™ expansion and playing Magic since the Fallen Empires expansion. He also has done art for the World of Warcraft TCG, DC Comics, Marvel Comics, Dark Horse comics, Easton Press, Penguin Books, Electronic Arts, Big Huge Games, and many other fine companies.

Arthur Suydam is the award-winning artist of Marvel Zombies. Combining classical painting with comic book art, he helped to create a movement that made comics more accessible to a more mature audience.

Fine art illustrator **Mark Texeira** is known for his work on Ghost Rider, Moon Knight, Black Panther, and his creator-owned series Pscythe. His work can be seen in Wolverine: Origins, as well as a five-issue Punisher mini-series. Current books out on Mark include "Tex: The Art of Mark Texeira," and "Mark Texeira: Nightmares and Daydreams." For more information on Mark and his work, visit www.evainkartistgroup.com and www.marktexeira.com.

Kev Walker spent several years illustrating Judge Dredd and ABC Warriors (among others) for British comic 2000 AD as well as illustrating many Games Workshop products. Illustrations for comics, the Magic: The Gathering trading card game, and several computer game projects followed. Kev's comic clients includes 2000 AD, DC Comics, Dark Horse, and Marvel, for whom his most recent projects, Marvel Zombies 3 & 4, Imperial Guard, and an ongoing residency as the regular artist/ penciller on Thunderbolts, have actually attracted some attention. He has also illustrated book covers for Young Bond, Artemis Fowl, Changeling, and Vampirates and has created a full graphic novel adaptation of the first Young Bond novel, *Silverfin*. He is currently working mostly for Marvel Comics from his home in Yorkshire, England, struggling with his first novel and failing to delay the onset of middle age and baldness.

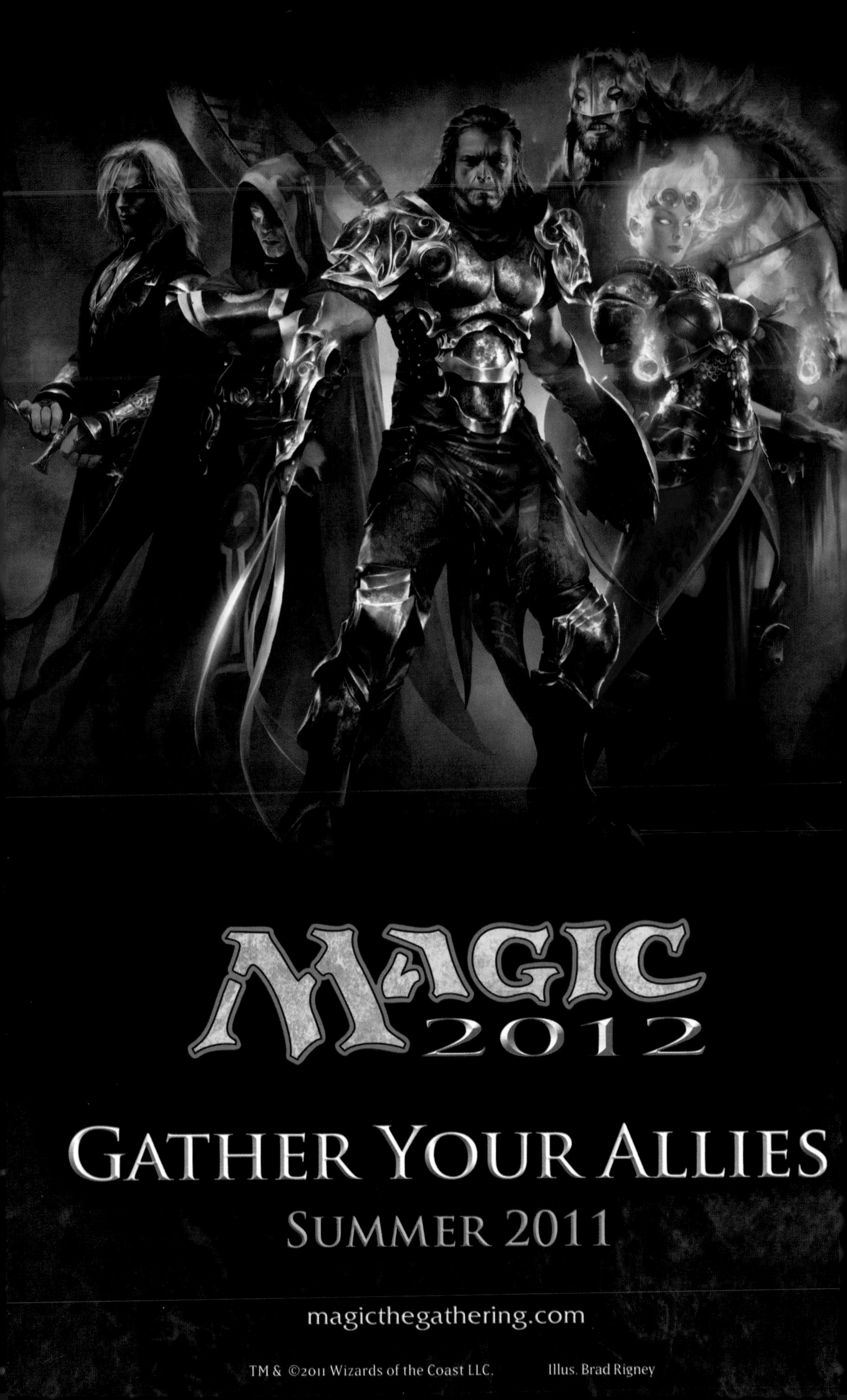
MAGIC 2012
GATHER YOUR ALLIES
SUMMER 2011
magicthegathering.com
TM & ©2011 Wizards of the Coast LLC.
Illus. Brad Rigney

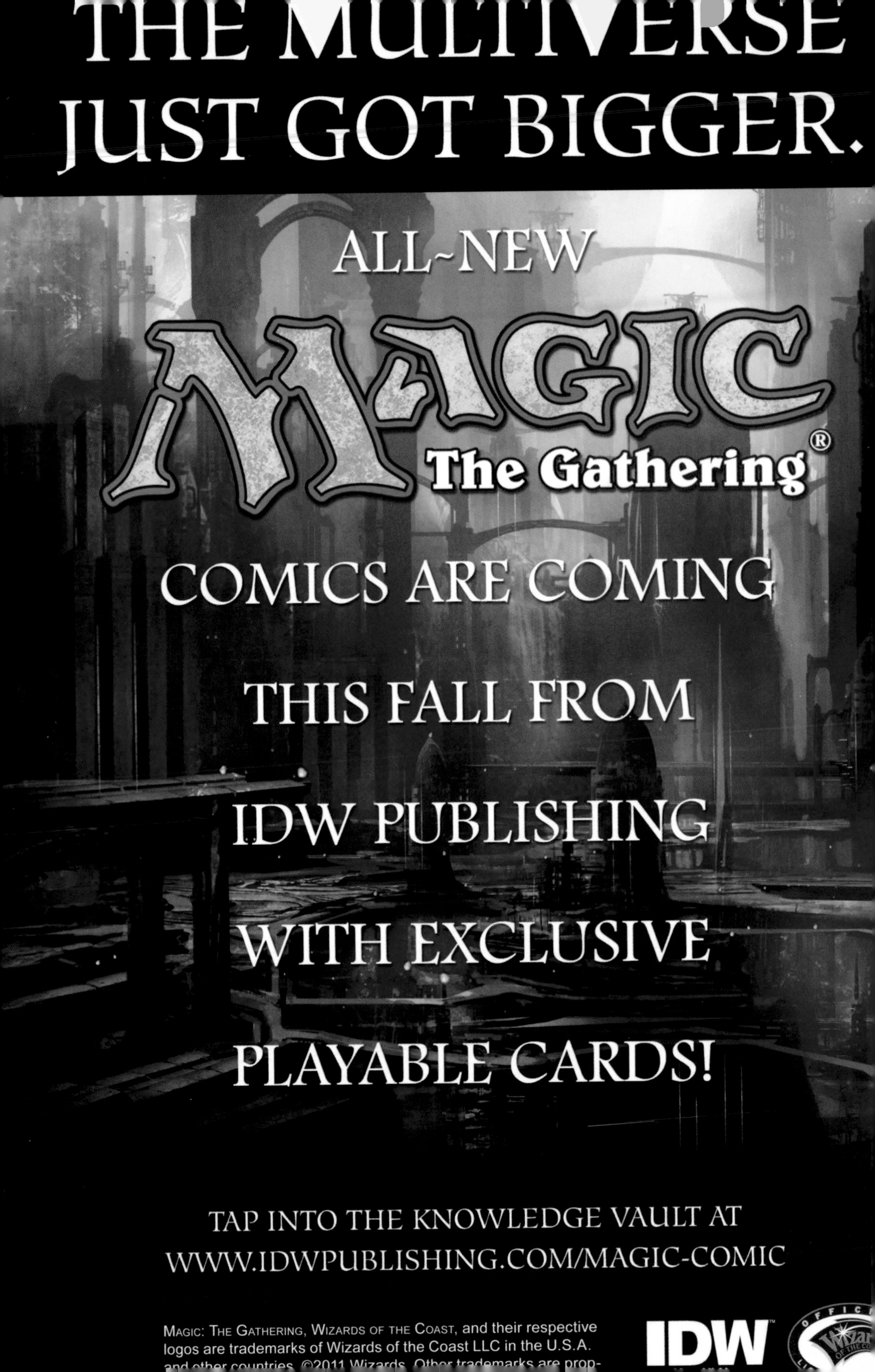

THE MULTIVERSE
JUST GOT BIGGER.
ALL~NEW
MAGIC
The Gathering®
COMICS ARE COMING
THIS FALL FROM
IDW PUBLISHING
WITH EXCLUSIVE
PLAYABLE CARDS!
TAP INTO THE KNOWLEDGE VAULT AT
WWW.IDWPUBLISHING.COM/MAGIC-COMIC
MAGIC: THE GATHERING, WIZARDS OF THE COAST, and their respective logos are trademarks of Wizards of the Coast LLC in the U.S.A. and other countries. ©2011 Wizards. Other trademarks are prop-
IDW™